Lecture Notes in Computer Science   7602

Commenced Publication in 1973
Founding and Former Series Editors:
Gerhard Goos, Juris Hartmanis, and Jan van Leeuwen

Alberto Abelló   Ladjel Bellatreche
Boualem Benatallah (Eds.)

Model and Data Engineering

2nd International Conference, MEDI 2012
Poitiers, France, October 3-5, 2012
Proceedings

 Springer

Volume Editors

Alberto Abelló
Universitat Politecnica de Catalunya
Departament d´Enginyeria de Serveis i Sistemes d'Informació
C/Jordi Girona Salgado 1-3
08034 Barcelona, Spain
E-mail: aabello@essi.upc.edu

Ladjel Bellatreche
LIAS/ISAE-ENSMA
1 avenue Clément Ader
86961 Futuroscope cedex, France
E-mail: ladjel.bellatreche@ensma.fr

Boualem Benatallah
The University of New South Wales
School of Computer Science and Engineering
Sydney, NSW 2052, Australia
E-mail: boualem@cse.unsw.edu.au

ISSN 0302-9743   e-ISSN 1611-3349
ISBN 978-3-642-33608-9   e-ISBN 978-3-642-33609-6
DOI 10.1007/978-3-642-33609-6
Springer Heidelberg Dordrecht London New York

Library of Congress Control Number: 2012947325

CR Subject Classification (1998): D.2.1-3, D.2.11, D.3.1-2, D.3.4, K.6.3, I.6.3-5, I.2.4, H.2.7, F.3.2

LNCS Sublibrary: SL 2 – Programming and Software Engineering

Typesetting: Camera-ready by author, data conversion by Scientific Publishing Services, Chennai, India

Printed on acid-free paper

Springer is part of Springer Science+Business Media (www.springer.com)

Preface

This volume contains the papers presented at MEDI 2012, the International Conference on Model & Data Engineering, held on October 3–5, 2012 at the Futuroscope, Poitiers, France. MEDI 2012 was an initiative of researchers from Euro-Mediterranean countries. Its aim was to promote the creation of north-south scientific networks, projects, and faculty/student exchanges, to provide a forum for the dissemination of research accomplishments, and to encourage the interaction and collaboration between the modeling and data management research communities. The first MEDI conference was held in Obidos, Portugal, in September 2011.

The conference focused on model engineering and data engineering. The scope of the papers covered the most recent and relevant topics in the areas of model driven engineering, ontology engineering, formal modeling, security, and data mining.

This year's MEDI received 35 submissions from over 12 countries. Each was reviewed by at least 2, and on average 2.6, program committee members. The committee decided to accept 12 long papers and 5 short papers. We are thankful to all the researchers that helped in the review process and made this possible. The conference program included two invited talks, namely, "Cloud Blueprint: A Model-Driven Approach to Configuring Federated Clouds" by Professor Mike Papazoglou, Tilburg University, Netherlands and "Model-Based Autocoding of Embedded Control Software with Full Semantics" by Eric Féron, Georgia Institute of Technology, USA.

Also profound thanks go to those institutions that actively supported the conference. These were:

- ISAE-ENSMA
- Région Poitou Charentes
- LIAS
- CRITT Informatique, Poitiers

We would also like to mention that EasyChair (www.easychair.org) made the life of these editors much easier by helping in the management of the review process, as well as in the generation of these proceedings.

October 2012

Alberto Abelló
Ladjel Bellatreche
Boualem Benatallah

Organization

General Chairman

Ladjel Bellatreche   ENSMA

Program Committee Chairmen

Alberto Abelló   Universitat Politècnica de Catalunya
Boualem Benatallah   University of New South Wales (UNSW)

Program Committee

El Hassan Abdelwahed   Cadi Ayyad University - Morocco
Alberto Abello   Universitat Politècnica de Catalunya
Yamine Ait Ameur   LISI/ENSMA
Jose F. Aldana Montes   University of Malaga
Marie-Aude Aufaure   Ecole Centrale Paris
Franck Barbier   LIUPPA
Ladjel Bellatreche   ENSMA
Boualem Benatallah   University of New South Wales (UNSW)
Salima Benbernou   Université Paris Descartes
Rafael Berlanga   Universitat Jaume I
Sandro Bimonte   cemagref
Alexander Borusan   TU Berlin / Fraunhofer FIRST
Azedine Boulmakoul   FST Mohammedia
Omar Boussaid   ERIC Laboratory
Coral Calero   Universidad de Castilla-La Mancha
Malu Castellanos   HP labs
Damianos Chatziantoniou   Athens University of Economics and Business
Mandy Chessell   IBM
Florian Daniel   University of Trento
Jerome Darmont   University of Lyon (ERIC Lyon 2)
Habiba Drias   USTHB University
Marlon Dumas   University of Tartu
Todd Eavis   Concordia University
Johann Eder   University of Klagenfurt
Mostafa Ezziyyani   Université Abdelmalek Essaâde
Marie-Christine Fauvet   Joseph Fourier University of Grenoble
Jamel Feki   Université de Sfax

Juan Trujillo	University of Alicante
Toni Urpí	Universitat Politècnica de Catalunya
Panos Vassiliadis	University of Ioannina
Pere Pau Vazquez	Universitat Politècnica de Catalunya
Boris Vrdoljak	FER-University of Zagreb
Virginie Wiels	ONERA / DTIM
Leandro Krug Wives	UFRGS
Robert Wrembel	Poznan Unviersity of Technology
Esteban Zimanyi	Université Libre de Bruxelles
Marta Zorrilla	University of Cantabria

Additional Reviewers

Adamek, Jochen
Bentounsi, Mehdi
Boden, Christoph
Chatatlic, Philippe
Imache, Rabah
Jovanovic, Petar
Kamel, Nadjet
Llorens, Hector
Soussi, Rania

Table of Contents

Session 3: Ontology Based Modelling, Role of Ontologies in Modelling Activities

Session 4: Miscelanea

Short Papers

Cloud Blueprint: A Model-Driven Approach to Configuring Federated Clouds

Mike P. Papazoglou

Tilburg University, The Netherlands

Current cloud solutions are fraught with problems. They introduce a monolithic cloud stack that imposes vendor lock-in and donot permit developers to mix and match services freely from diverse cloud service tiers and configure them dynamically to address application needs.

Cloud blueprinting is a novel model-driven approach that allows developers syndicate, configure, and deploy virtual service-based application payloads on virtual machine and resource pools in the cloud. Cloud blueprinting helps developers automatically provision services, effectively manage workload segmentation and portability (i.e., the seamless movement of workloads across many platforms and clouds), and manage virtual service instances, all while taking into account the availability of cloud resources and accelerating the deployment of new composed cloud services. Cloud blueprinting equips developers with a unified approach that allows them configure cloud applications by pooling appropriate resources at any layer of the cloud stack - irrespectively whether these are provided from multiple cloud providers.

A. Abelló, L. Bellatreche, and B. Benatallah (Eds.): MEDI 2012, LNCS 7602, p. 1, 2012.

Model-Based Auto Coding of Embedded Control Software with Full Semantics

Eric Féron

Georgia Institute of Technology, Atlanta, Georgia

Control software is one of the most important elements of safety-critical systems, whether it is used in aerospace, automotive, naval or medical engineering. Control software is used, for example, to regulate the altitude of an aircraft, the speed of an automobile, the heading of a ship or the intensity of an ion beam.

The design of modern embedded software requires that its functional and non functional semantics, including those of the entire system, be expressed clearly within the software to support its correctness at all levels of its implementation. Such semantics must be expressed in languages adapted to the different levels of software implementation and the systems they interact with. Therefore, block diagrams used by control theorists must also be able to support semantic properties, such as stability and performance, and their proofs. Software implementations of these block diagrams must be, correspondingly, fully documented with the same properties and their proofs, in such a way that they can be automatically parsed and verified.

An international team of researchers from ENSEEIHT, Georgia Tech, NASA, the National Institute of Aerospace, ONERA, Rockwell-Collins, SRI, and the University of Coruna, has engaged in designing the proof-of-concept for an autocoding environment for control software, where the strengths of control theory are combined with advanced specification languages. As input, the autocoder takes the block diagram of a control systems and its semantics. As output, the autocoder produces a C code, together with the controller semantics expressed in ACSL (ANSI C Specification Language). The ACSL comments, together with the C code, can be verified independently, as demonstrated by a prototype back-end also designed by the research team.

Current experiments and demonstrations include the autocoding of increasingly complex control laws for a three degree-of-freedom educational device that mimics a helicopter. Other experiments include autocoding of control laws for a model F-18 jet fighter.

Although significant work has been done already, many issues need addressing to transform the prototype into a fully functional tool, including properly addressing real/float mismatch issues.

A. Abelló, L. Bellatreche, and B. Benatallah (Eds.): MEDI 2012, LNCS 7602, p. 2, 2012.
© Springer-Verlag Berlin Heidelberg 2012

Modeling End-Users as Contributors in Human Computation Applications

Roula Karam, Piero Fraternali, Alessandro Bozzon, and Luca Galli

Dipartimento di Elettronica e Informazione Politecnico di Milano
{karam,fraterna,bozzon,lgalli}@elet.polimi.it

Abstract. User models have been defined since the '80s, mainly for the purpose of building context-based, user-adaptive applications. However, the advent of social networked media, serious games, and crowdsourcing platforms calls for a more pervasive notion of user model, capable of representing the multiple facets of a social user, including his social ties, capabilities, activity history, and topical affinities. In this paper, we overview several user models proposed recently to address the platform-independent representation of users embedded in a social context, and discuss the features of the *CUbRIK user model*, which is designed to support multi-platform human computation applications where users are called as collaborators in the resolution of complex tasks found in the multimedia information retrieval field.

Keywords: Human Computation, Multimedia, User Modeling, Social Networks.

1 Introduction

Research in user modeling has been crucial for the definition of adaptive and context-aware applications [8]. A user model is a knowledge source that describes the aspects of the user that may be relevant for the behavior of a system. Traditional ingredients of a user model include the *Identification and Authorization Model*, which is used to grant or restrict access to the application features based on the user's identity and role; the *Profile and Personalization Model*, which contains attributes of the user that can be exploited to adapt the user interface to his preferences, and the *Context Model*, which captures the different situations in which a user can access the application, most notably in the case of multi-channel solutions that can be exploited with different devices, with mobile or fixed connectivity, and in different locations and times of the day. These traditional user models are characterized by a focus *on the individual and his personal characteristics*: profile data, history, preferences, and context of usage. The advent of social applications, however, has brought to the foreground a novel class of users, *social users* embedded in a rich context of relations and networked media applications. These modern users spend their digital life in multiple social networks, generate, comment and tag content in several media formats and with

A. Abelló, L. Bellatreche, and B. Benatallah (Eds.): MEDI 2012, LNCS 7602, pp. 3–15, 2012.
© Springer-Verlag Berlin Heidelberg 2012

various applications, including gaming applications, maintain multiple friendship networks, and communicate and relate with each other with a variety of instruments. The social user is the protagonist of an emerging trend in problem solving and application development, which pushes the user-adaptation beyond mere access control, context-awareness, and personalization: *Human Computation*. A Human Computation application is defined as an approach to problem solving that integrates the computation power of machines with the perceptual, rational or social contribution of humans [16,20]. An area where human computation has been successfully employed is multimedia content processing for search applications. In this domain, the goal is to automatically classify non-textual assets, audio, images, video, to enable information retrieval and similarity search, for example, finding occurrences of an image within a video. Within the human computation domain, a special place is occupied by Crowdsourcing and Games With a Purpose.

Crowdsourcing addresses the distributed assignment of work to an open community of executors [13]. The users of a crowdsourcing application can submit to the system the specification of a piece of work to be solved or perform already proposed tasks. Examples of Crowdsourcing solutions are Amazon Mechanical Turk and Microtask.com.

Games with a Purpose (GWAPs), like the ESP Game, leverage the time spent online playing computer games by embedding complex problems that require human intelligence to be solved by the players [19,14]. Human computation applications motivate the need of a novel generation of user models, capable of expressing all the articulations of the digital life of the user, as content producer and consumer, social network member, volunteer or paid worker in a crowdsourcing scenario, or player in a game-based application. The focus of this paper is to introduce a comprehensive user model that caters for all the relevant characteristics of a social user, with the goal of enabling the development of human computation applications that could exploit user data coming from multiple knowledge sources, including social networks, gaming platforms and communities, and crowdsourcing markets.

The main contributions of the paper in this direction are: 1) the identification of the relevant components (sub-models) of a social user model that could cover all the aspects required by applications involving human computation; 2) the design of a metamodel that encodes the features of each of the identified sub-models; 3) a review of the state-of-the-art in social user modeling, to better position the proposal of a new model; 4) an overview of the architecture, currently in advanced status of implementation in the CUbRIK Project (www.cubrikproject.eu/), where the proposed social user model is used to structure the data tier common to a variety of human computation applications for multimedia information retrieval. The paper is organized as follows: Section 2 establishes the background of the user model definition effort, by briefly illustrating the architecture of the human computation framework. Section 3 presents the proposed user model, organized in different packages: the user and social model; the content model; the action model; the gaming model; and the

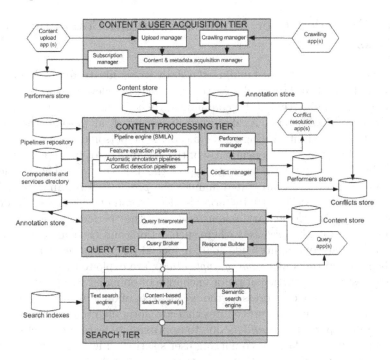

Fig. 1. The architecture of the Human Computation Framework

uncertainty and conflict model. Section 4 overviews related work on social user modeling and compares the proposed approach to the most relevant emerging social models. Section 5 briefly mentions the status of the implementation and reports on the first experiments in human computation with the proposed model. Section 6 draws the conclusions and outlines the future work.

2   Human Computation Framework Architecture

The new user model proposed in this paper is motivated by the need of gathering, storing and managing user information in a human computation framework for multimedia content processing called CUbRIK. Figure 1 shows the architecture of the system, which is centered around a set of *data warehouses* built through data extraction or data referencing from social networks, information explicitly provided by users, and pre-existing data sources such as content and entity repositories. The core element of the architecture is the *Conflict Manager*, which is an application for receiving conflict descriptions arising from multimedia content processing pipelines (e.g., low-confidence or contradictory image classifications) and turning them into tasks that can be addressed by social users. To do so, the Conflict Manager needs a rich description of the available users, their topical affinities, social context, and work history. More details about the different components can be found in [11].

3   An Extended User Model for Human Computation Tasks

One of the key challenges of building the data stores illustrated in Figure 1 is the design of a unified data model for representing the relevant aspects of users, their social ties and activity, the communities where they are active, and the actions they can contribute. As discussed in Section 4, at present, there is no universal data model integrating all the facets of the personal, social, and online contribution life of users, independently of the specificities of the representations adopted by the different systems that support the user's activity. The envisioned model must convey in an integrated manner the *profile features* and *social links and roles* of users [10], the characteristics of the *content objects* they produce and consume [3], the elementary *actions and tasks* they perform in virtual or real contexts of interest, the *processes* where such actions and tasks are organized to meet some global, community-wide goal, or special-purpose aspects, as required, e.g., when special tools like *gaming applications* are exploited to better engage users and foster their participation or exchange of opinions. Such a data model should also be capable of expressing the *uncertainty* of data, which is introduced by the automated collection procedures that are normally used to harvest user's features, and in particular *conflicts* due to approximate feature extraction algorithms, contradictory data, or conflicting user's actions. Figure 2 exemplifies the main sub-models and objects that form the social user data model at the base of the system.

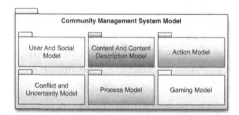

Fig. 2. The social user data model at the base of the system

The User and Social Model: introduces humans into the conceptual model, by expressing the roles they can play as social actors, content producers and consumers. Furthermore, it describes the embedding of users in social networks by modeling their relations to communities and the most common properties that characterize a social activity profile.

The Content and Content Description Model: contains the concepts that denote the assets (e.g., blog posts, tweets, images, videos, entities of interest) associated with the user's activity, and the metadata (a.k.a. *annotations*) that describe such objects and their associations with users.

The Action Model: describes two types of actions that a user can perform: *automatic actions* done by software components like classification algorithms,

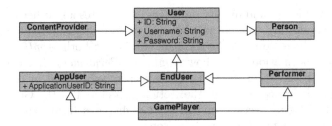

Fig. 3. User Taxonomy Model

and *human actions*, performed by users to detect and resolve conflicts, provide relevant feedbacks, e.g., by rating automatically computed results. These human actions are denoted as *Tasks*, which can be executed with a variety of approaches, from answering a query, to performing work on demand.

The Process Model: focuses on the global aspects of coordinating a set of human and automatic actions to achieve a specific purpose. Such a model could simply be mapped to popular business processes and service orchestration languages, e.g., by BPEL or BPMN, which can be extended to describe cooperative and participative processes enacted by a community of users [6].

The *Gaming Model*: focuses on a specific class of tasks deployed in the form of a game with a purpose (GWAP) and expresses the engagement and rewarding mechanisms typical of gaming (including gaming scores, leaderboards, and achievements). The Gaming Model is related to Action and User Models to denote the assignment of a game session to a player for solving a task.

The *Conflict and Uncertainty Model*: expresses the uncertainty arising from automatically computed social data and content objects' metadata and from conflicting opinions that may arise when humans are requested to perform a piece of work that may entail judgement or errors. The Conflict Model is related to the Action Model, as conflicts are the source of tasks for human solvers.

Figure 3 depicts the user taxonomy at the core of the User and Social Model. The main concept is the *User*, which specializes into *Administrator*, *Content-Provider*, and *End-User*. Administrators and ContentProviders denote roles that serve an internal purpose in the specific human computation platform: the former controls the system, whereas the latter provides *ContentObjects* with associated usage permissions. These internal roles can be extended, to cater for a taxonomy of internal roles depending on the application domain. The *End-User* entity represents social users that interact with the platform consuming or producing resources. When registered in a human computation platform, end-users are further distinguished into *AppUsers*, who interact through an *Application*, i.e., a software module that provides some domain specific functionality; they can be characterized by application-specific properties (e.g., an ApplicationUserID and application-dependent profile data). An *End-User* not registered to the human computation platform can also provide useful information, e.g., by implicitly boosting the relevance of a given content object through share or re-post actions. End-users are denoted as *Performers*, when they are registered explicitly for contributing to managed tasks; they have work-dependent attributes, e.g., their work history and quality data (e.g., error rates and other performance indicators). Games are treated as a special class of applications for implicitly solving a task. Therefore, a *GamePlayer* specializes both *AppUser* and *Performer*. More information about how *AppUsers*, *Performers*, and *GamePlayers* are related with the other entities can be respectively found in the User and Social Model (described next), in the Action Model and in the Gaming Model described later in this Section, and in the Conflict Resolution Model, which is not described in this paper for space reasons.

3.1   The User and Social Model

Figure 4 depicts user's relationships and interactions in the social space. The model refers to the topmost user type of the taxonomy in Figure 3, so to represent people in their social space regardless of their affiliation to the human computation platform. The social space consists of *ConflictResolutionPlatforms*, i.e., platforms where user can perform tasks. For example, *SocialNetworks* (e.g. Facebook, Google+, LinkedIn, Twitter) are specific types of *ConflictResolutionPlatforms*. A *User* can be subscribed to zero or more *ConflictResolutionPlatforms*; each

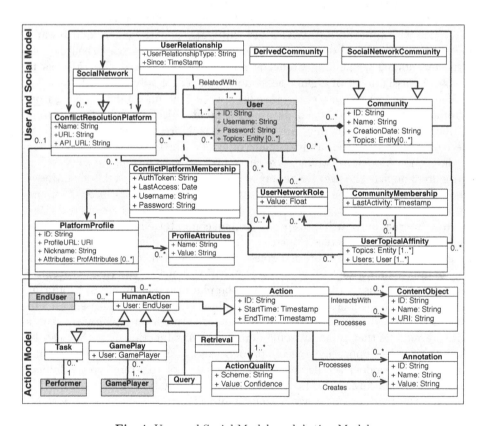

Fig. 4. User and Social Model, and Action Model

subscription goes with a *ConflictResolutionPlatformMembership*, i.e. an entity that contains the main authentication credentials to the social platform, plus some metadata information that describes the User in the platform. Examples of such metadata are: 1) a *SocialPlatformProfile*, i.e. the set of personal user's details stored within the platform, which includes also an open set of *SocialProfileAttributes* (e.g. birthdate, hometown, preferences). 2) A set of *PlatformMetrics* i.e., measures of the importance of the User within the social network space, named *UserNetworkRole*, including classical indicators as Centrality, Prestige, and Authority. 3) A set of *TopicalAffinities*, i.e., relationships with topics. An affinity link is represented by the *UserTopicalAffinity*, which embodies pointer to topics described as Entities of the Content and Content Description model. Users are also related to each other through *UserRelationships* of a given *UserRelationshipType* (e.g., friendship, geographical). Another central concept is that of *Community*, defined as a group of interacting people, living in some proximity (i.e., in space, time, or relationship) and sharing common values. A *Community* is characterized by a *Name*, and by a set of *Topics* that define the common values that tie together its members (*Topics* are described by entities). A *CommunityMembership* denotes the metadata about the community members, including: 1) a set of *CommunityMetrics* i.e., measures of the importance of the *User* within the *Community*; 2) a set of *TopicalAffinities*, i.e., topical relationship with a given (set of) topics. Users may have affinities only to a sub-set of the *Topics* that describe the community, and such affinity can involve other Users. Communities can be real, that is, a proper subgroup of a *SocialNetwork* (denoted as *SocialNetworkCommunities*) or *DerivedCommunities*, i.e. communities that span multiple social platforms according to some criterion (e.g., the union of the Facebook and G+ groups of Star Trek fans). The User and Social Model allows for a definition of *GlobalNetworkMetrics*, i.e., metrics that define the aggregate importance of a *User* across both social networks and communities.

3.2   The Action Model

The Action Model depicted in Figure 4 is strictly related to the User and Social Model, as it represents the spectrum of actions that users can perform on a *ConflictResolutionPlatform*. We define an *Action* as an event (happening in a given time span delimited by a *StartTime* and an *EndTime*) that involves the interaction with, the processing, or the creation of, *Content Objects* and *Annotations*. Actions can be associated with one or more *ActionQuality* values, i.e. values that denote e.g. the correctness or the completeness of an action. For human computation platforms, we distinguish *HumanActions* that fall under three main archetypes: *Retrieval*, *Query* and *Task* actions. The first two are examples of interactions performed in applications, and they involve the querying, consumption, or collection of content items. *Tasks*, instead, relate specifically to human problem solving activities (e.g. rating, tagging, disambiguating, recognizing) and, therefore, are executed by *Performers*. A *GamePlay* is a specific type of *Task* that leverages the entertainment capabilities of online games in order to exploit *Game Players* to solve human computation tasks.

3.3 The Gaming Model

The Gaming Model is depicted in Figure 5. A *Game* is an entertainment application described by a *Title* and characterized by a *Genre* (e.g. Puzzle, Educational), a *Mode* (Single Player, Multi Player), and a *Theme* (e.g. Abstract, Comic, Crime, Science Fiction). A *GamePlay Action* is a human computation action that the user has performed while playing a specific *Game*. A *Game Player* is a type of user described by customization attributes (e.g. *Nickname*, *Motto*) and accomplishments: for instance the *PlayerLevel* attribute represents the proficiency and the experience of a player; the *PlayerTitle* is a special recognition given to the player for his actions (e.g., a chivalry role); the *PlayerType* (e.g. Achiever, Explorer, etc.) is used to associate the player with a particular cluster of gamer type. *GameStats* are stored in order to keep track of the *HoursPlayed* by a player on a specific *Game*, the *Score* he has obtained or other meaningul variables. Games have *Achievements*, i.e. means to foster an entertaining experience for users and a way to profile them. An Achievement is a specific challenge or task that the player can perform in order to get a reward in terms of points or other special features (in-game items, artworks, behind the scene videos); it is defined by a *Category* that specifies which kind of task the achievement was associated with (General, Quest, Exploration, Puzzle solving), and a *PointsGiven* attribute which contains the amount of points to be given if the requirements for the achievement have been met. Once a player reaches the goals of a listed achievement, he will gain a *Badge* related to that specific achievement. A *GameBadge* is used to relate a player with the achievement she has obtained, and it is described by a *CompletionPercentage* attribute that shows how much the player has already achieved in order to complete a specific task.

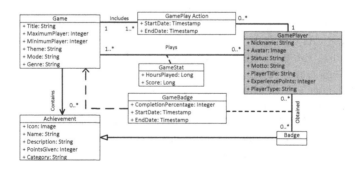

Fig. 5. Gaming Model

4   Overview of the Related Work on Social User Modeling

The need for more interoperable user models has been already identified in the recent work [8], which focuses on context adaptation of applications. This broad survey identifies characteristic dimensions, such as the users' profile, task features, social relations, and the context. Another survey [18] overviews the ontological technologies for user modeling for the purpose to aggregate and align many RDF/OWL user models in a decentralized approach. The **General User Model Ontology** (GUMO) [12] is a uniform interpretation of distributed user profiles models in intelligent environments based on OWL. However, it does not support the modeling of social relationships. The **Cultural User Modeling Ontology** (CUMO) [17] is used to allocate culture dimension to a certain user behavior. Building user models from cross-system platforms [4] is another tentative to aggregate the distributed profiles for the same user in case of obsolete or scattered data. The **Unified User Context Model** (UUCM) [15] advocates the reuse of user profiles in different systems as context passport (e.g., social networks platforms, on line communities, etc.) and minimize the sparse or missing information. **User Role Model** (URM) [21] is another example for modeling users and their access roles to support cross-system personalization. While this model covers social relationships of users, it does not capture profile information. However, the great amount of available user and social representation formats calls for an additional conceptualization effort aimed at providing a unified model that integrates also social features [7]. The **Friend of a Friend** (FOAF, http://www.foaf-project.org) is a project that aims to describe users, their links and activities within Web pages using RDF/XML. However, it lacks the expressive power to represent social interactions (commenting, etc.), social cognition and meta information. The **OpenSocial API** (http://www.opensocial.org) is another recent effort with the goal of providing a common set of APIs to access major social networking applications (such as Myspace, Orkut, Yahoo!, etc.). OpenSocial provides a very abstract and generic data model, so to be able to fit information coming from several social networks. **Semantically-Interlinked Online Communities** (SIOC, http://rdfs.org/sioc/spec), is an RDF/OWL representation to link and describe online community sites (e.g., message boards, wikis, weblogs, etc.). SIOC documents may use other existing ontologies to enrich the information described such as Dublin Core metadata, FOAF, RSS1.0, etc. The literature about recommender systems also proposed user modeling on the social web as a tool for recommendation strategies based on interests and topical affinity . The **ImREAL** (http://www.imreal-project.eu) project or **Grapple** (http://www.grapple-project.org) are such examples. This latter [2] appears very suited to the representation of user profiles and can be freely extended (RDF-based), but does not cover social relationships and social actions. **TheHiddenU** (http://social-nexus.net) project is an attempt in the direction of social user model unification, as it compares several models in terms of their coverage of different user and social concepts. For semantic enrichment and mining of users profiles from the social Web, some frameworks are relevant, such as **USem** [1]. The **U2M** (http://www.u2m.org) project is an example of a user model and context ontology integrating GUMO with UserML for future Web 2.0 extensions. **TweetUM** (http://www.wis.ewi.tudelft.nl/tweetum/) is a Twitter-based User Modeling Framework which allows developers to acquire Twitter-based profiles in RDF format. It creates semantically enriched user profiles inferred from users' tweets, retrieving all topics that the user is interested in, the entities information, the top hash tags or top entities cloud. **GeniUS** (http://www.wis.ewi.tudelft.nl/genius/) is another project that can be used to enrich the semantics of social data: given a stream of messages from the users' status, it can generate the topic and some information about the user. The **Social Web User Model** (SWUM) [9] is a generic model that focuses on the social web domain; its goal is to support data sharing and aggregation of social networks user models by aligning concepts, attributes (e.g., personal characteristics, interests and preferences, needs and goals, knowledge and background), user behaviors (e.g., previous search behavior using Google dashboard), location, and time. User's category or community can be inferred but there is no tracking of the user's actions. Table 6 summarizes and compares the reviewed social and user models in the light of their main characteristics.

With respect to the state of the art, CUbRIK users are not only consumers (searchers) but they can also produce resources to increase the performance of the platform. Therefore, the User and Social model proposed in this paper could be extended to reflect characteristics from SWUM with some enhancement on the human computation side. However, when requested to solve some human computation tasks involving multimedia contents, conflict resolution issues might arise and the part of the model that covers users actions to detect and resolve tasks has not been mentioned in any previous domain (e.g., e-learning, adaptive hypermedia, recommender systems). So, the current social models need

User Model Dimension	GUMO	URM	UUCM	FOAF	OpenSocial	SIOC	GUMF	HiddenU	SWUM	CUbRIK
Demographics	Yes	No	Yes	Yes	Yes	Yes	Yes	Yes	Yes	Yes
Preferences	Yes	No	Yes	No	Yes	No	Yes	Yes	Yes	No
Context-awareness	Yes	No	Yes	No	No	No	Yes	Yes	Yes	No
Skills, Interests	Yes	Yes	Yes	Yes	Yes	No	Yes	Yes	Yes	No
Social Interaction	No	Yes	No	Yes	Yes	Yes	No	Yes	Yes	Yes
Activity, Task History	Yes	Yes	Yes	No	Yes	Yes	No	Yes	Yes	Yes
Games History	No	No	No	Yes	No	No	No	Yes	Yes	Yes
User Behavior	Yes	Yes	Yes	Yes	Yes	Yes	Yes	Yes	Yes	Yes
User Network Role	No	Yes	No	Yes	Yes	Yes	Yes	Yes	Yes	Yes
Resources Capabilities	Yes	No	No	No	Yes	Yes	Yes	Yes	Yes	Yes
Other cognitive patterns	Yes	Yes	Yes	Yes	Yes	Yes	Yes	Yes	Yes	Yes
Topic Affinity	Yes	Yes	Yes	Yes	Yes	Yes	Yes	Yes	Yes	Yes
GeoCultural Affinity	Yes	No	Yes	No	Yes	No	Yes	No	Yes	Yes
User Category	No	Yes	No	No	No	No	No	No	Yes	Yes
User Actions	No	No	No	No	Yes	No	No	No	No	Yes
Conflicts	No	No	No	No	No	No	No	No	No	Yes
Multiple Platforms	No	No	Yes	Yes	Yes	Yes	Yes	Yes	Yes	Yes

Fig. 6. Comparison of different social and user models

to be extended with a *ConflictResolutionPlatforms* to route appropriate tasks to performers also by exploiting serious games, social networks and crowdsourcing markets. In fact, the novelty within CUbRIK resides in the possibility to model Conflict and Uncertainty, Action and Gaming as extensions to the traditional User and Social models.

5   Status of the Implementation and Experience

The illustrated user model is at the base of the implementation effort of the CUbRIK project [11], that aims at building a human computation platform, with the architecture shown in Figure 1, for multimedia content processing tasks. A first version of the Conflict Manager (called CrowdSearcher [5]) has been constructed and tested with Facebook users, to address the human-enhanced resolution of a classical multimedia problem: logo detection in videos. The Conflict Manager takes as input task instances of two types: a first task type consists of a set of candidate logo images automatically retrieved by keyword search using the brand name in Google Images: social users are asked to select the most representative ones to use for matching into the video collection; the second task requires the performers to discover the URL of a new logo image for the same brand. At the moment, the task-to-performer assignment exploits only the work history part of the user model: the more complex URL discovery task is assigned only to those users that have already contributed instances of the simpler logo selection task. Future work will extend the present task allocation policy and use all the features of the illustrated user model: for example, it will consider also profile data of the users, like the country of residence and the topical affinity, to better target the logo selection and discovery tasks to users who are likely to be already familiar with the brand and the local variations of its logo. Furthermore, user social network metrics will be exploited, to send tasks to users that are more likely to re-post it to a large circle of friends.

6   Conclusions and Perspectives

In this paper, we have presented a novel user model that can support human computation applications, defined as applications that make intensive use of human contribution to solve complex tasks. The data model integrates the representation of traditional aspects, like user profiles and roles, with novel features: social information, like membership in multiple communities and centrality metrics, content affinity information, and capabilities. The user model also contains a representation of the actions that users can perform to help problem solving, and the link between actions and problems, expressed by the generic notion of conflict. The illustrated model is at the base of the implementation of the CUbRIK platform, to exploit multiple social networks, crowdsourcing platforms and interaction styles to engage users in difficult multimedia processing tasks. Future work will focus on expanding the reach of the implementation, which is not limited to Q&A on Facebook, LinkedIn, and Twitter, to more interaction styles (e.g., paid work in crowdsourcing markets and GWAPs) and novel platforms (e.g., Mechanical Turk and Microtask.com crowdsourcing markets).

Acknowledgment. This work is partially sponsored by the BPM4People project (www.bpm4people.org), funded by the Capacities and Research for SMEs Program of the Research Executive Agency of the European Community. This work is partially sponsored by the CUbRIK project (http://www.CUbRIKproject.eu/), funded by the European Community Seventh Framework Programme (FP7/2007-2013).

References

1. Abel, F., Celik, I., Hauff, C., Hollink, L., Houben, G.-J.: U-sem: Semantic enrichment, user modeling and mining of usage data on the social web. CoRR, abs/1104.0126 (2011)
2. Aroyo, L., Houben, G.-J.: User modeling and adaptive semantic web. Semantic Web 1(1-2), 105–110 (2010)
3. Axenopoulos, A., Daras, P., Malassiotis, S., Croce, V., Lazzaro, M., Etzold, J., Grimm, P., Massari, A., Camurri, A., Steiner, T., Tzovaras, D.: I-search: A unified framework for multimodal search and retrieval, pp. 130–141 (2012)
4. Berkovsky, S., Kuflik, T., Ricci, F.: Cross-representation mediation of user models. User Model. User-Adapt. Interact. 19(1-2), 35–63 (2009)
5. Bozzon, A., Brambilla, M., Ceri, S.: Answering search queries with crowdsearcher. In: Mille, A., Gandon, F.L., Misselis, J., Rabinovich, M., Staab, S. (eds.) WWW 2012, pp. 1009–1018. ACM (2012)
6. Brambilla, M., Fraternali, P., Vaca, C.: BPMN and design patterns for engineering social BPM solutions. In: Proceedings of the Fourth International Workshop on BPM and Social Software, BPMS 2011 (August 2011)
7. Carmagnola, F., Cena, F., Gena, C.: User modeling in the social web, pp. 745–752 (2007)
8. Carmagnola, F., Cena, F., Gena, C.: User model interoperability: a survey. User Model. User-Adapt. Interact. 21(3), 285–331 (2011)
9. Cena, F., Dattolo, A., De Luca, E.W., Lops, P., Plumbaum, T., Vassileva, J.: Semantic adaptive social web, pp. 176–180 (2011)
10. Kapsammer, E., Mitsch, S., Pröll, B., et al.: A first step towards a conceptual reference model for comparing social user profiles (2011)
11. Fraternali, P., et al.: The CuBRIK project: human-enhanced time-aware multimedia search, pp. 259–262 (2012)
12. Heckmann, D., Schwarzkopf, E., Mori, J., Dengler, D., Kröner, A.: The user model and context ontology gumo revisited for future web 2.0 extensions. In: Proc. of the Int. Workshop on Contexts and Ontologies: Representation and Reasoning, C&O:RR (2007)
13. Howe, J.: The rise of crowdsourcing. Wired 14(6) (2006)
14. Law, E., von Ahn, L.: Input-agreement: a new mechanism for collecting data using human computation games. In: Proc. CHI 2009, pp. 1197–1206 (2009)
15. Mehta, B., Niederée, C., Stewart, A., Degemmis, M., Lops, P., Semeraro, G.: Ontologically-enriched unified user modeling for cross-system personalization, pp. 119–123 (2005)

16. Quinn, A.J., Bederson, B.B.: Human computation: a survey and taxonomy of a growing field. In: Proceedings of the 2011 Annual Conference on Human Factors in Computing Systems, CHI 2011, pp. 1403–1412 (2011)
17. Reinecke, K., Reif, G., Bernstein, A.: Cultural user modeling with cumo: An approach to overcome the personalization bootstrapping problem (2007)
18. Sosnovsky, S.A., Dicheva, D.: Ontological technologies for user modelling. IJMSO 5(1), 32–71 (2010)
19. von Ahn, L.: Games with a purpose. Computer 39, 92–94 (2006)
20. von Ahn, L.: Human computation. In: CIVR (2009)
21. Zhang, F., Song, Z., Zhang, H.: Web service based architecture and ontology based user model for cross-system personalization, pp. 849–852 (2006)

Runtime Adaptation of Architectural Models: An Approach for Adapting User Interfaces

Diego Rodríguez-Gracia[1], Javier Criado[1],
Luis Iribarne[1], Nicolás Padilla[1], and Cristina Vicente-Chicote[2]

[1] Applied Computing Group, University of Almería, Spain
{diegorg,javi.criado,luis.iribarne,npadilla}@ual.es
[2] Dpt. of Info. Communication Technologies, Tech. University of Cartagena, Spain
cristina.vicente@upct.es

Abstract. Traditional techniques of model-driven development usually concern with the production of non-executable models. These models are usually manipulated at design-time by means of fixed model transformations. However, in some situations, models need to be transformed at runtime. Moreover, the transformations handling these models could be provided with a dynamic behavior enabling the adaptation to the current execution context and requirements. In this vein, this paper defines a transformation pattern designed for flexible model transformation that can be dynamically composed by selecting the appropriate transformation rules from a rule repository, which is also represented by a model. The rules in the repository are updated at each step of adaptation to improve later rule selection. We chose the domain of user interfaces, specified as component-based architectural models, as our case study.

Keywords: UI, Adaptive Transformation, Rule Selection, MDE.

1 Introduction

In *Model-Driven Engineering* (MDE), transformations to enable model refinement (commonly, into other models or into code) are usually composed and executed at design-time. Furthermore, models are usually static artifacts and model transformations allows us to provide such elements with a dynamic behaviour. Recently, runtime model transformations are being increasingly used as a means of enabling the so-called *executable models* or *models@runtime*. In this context, transformations are used to adapt the models dynamically, although in most cases, they usually show a static behaviour. Such a static behavior prevents models to adapt to requirements not taken into account *a priori*. In order to enable model transformations to evolve at runtime, we need to provide them with a dynamic behaviour.

In this paper we aim to provide model transformations with such a dynamic behavior that allows them to vary in time according to the context. Specifically, our approach addresses the adaptation of architectural models by means of transformations that are themselves adapted at runtime [1]. Our architectural model

A. Abelló, L. Bellatreche, and B. Benatallah (Eds.): MEDI 2012, LNCS 7602, pp. 16–30, 2012.

definition is described in a previous work [2]. The transformations are are dynamically composed *at runtime* by selecting the most appropriate transformation rules from a rule repository according to the current situation. This repository is also updated at each adaptation stage in order to improve the following rule selection process. The transformation pattern proposed has been made as flexible as possible, enabling designers to instantiate it by adding or removing elements, and thus allowing them to customize their runtime model adaptation processes. An example instance of this pattern for dynamically adapting component-based user interface models is described below to illustrate the proposed approach. It is worth noting that the goals of this research emerge from the previous results obtained in [2], [3], and [4].

To achieve our intended goals, we made use of both M2M and M2T transformations [5]. At runtime, when the system detects a need for adaptation (e.g., when the context properties change, or when the user or the system trigger a certain kind of event), an M2M transformation is invoked. This takes the rule repository and the current model (the one to be adapted) as inputs, and selects the most appropriate rules to be executed from the repository according to the context information available in the model. The generated M2M transformations contain a set of *transformation rules*. These transformation rules are divided into a *Left-Hand-Side* (LHS) and a *Right-Hand-Side* (RHS). The LHS and RHS refer to elements in the source and the target models, respectively. Both LHS and RHS can be represented through variables, patterns, and logic [5].

Then, an M2T process generates an M2M transformation out of the rules selected. Our M2T transformation was implemented using JET[6], and generates M2M transformations defined in ATL [7]. We selected ATL because it enables the adoption of an hybrid (of declarative and imperative) M2M transformation approach. In fact, in ATL it is possible to define hybrid transformation rules in which both the source and the target declarative patterns can be complemented with an imperative block We have also defined a rule metamodel, aimed to help designers: (1) to define correct transformation rules (the metamodel establishes the structure of these rules and how they can be combined), and (2) to store these rules in a repository.

We have chosen the domain of user interfaces as part of a project of the Spanish Ministry to develop adaptive user interfaces at runtime, as there is a recognized and increasingly growing need to provide these artifacts with dynamic adaptation capabilities. Here, user interfaces are specified using component-based architectural models (each UI element is represented by a component). These models may vary at runtime due to changes in the context—e.g., user interaction, a temporal event, visual condition, etc. Hence, our proposal is useful to adapt component-based architecture systems at runtime (such as user interfaces based on components) by means of models and traditional techniques of model-driven engineering. Our approach presents two main **advantages** concerning the adaptation of component-based architectural models: (a) the model transformation applied to the architectural model is not fixed, but dynamically composed at runtime, and (b) this composition is made by selecting the most appropriate set of rules (according to the current context) from those available in a repository, making the adaptation logic for the architectural models be upgradable by changing the rule repository, making it possible to change the adaptation logic by adding/removing/changing the rules in the repository.

The rest of the article is organized as follows: Section 2 introduces the goal of adapting component-based user interfaces. Section 3 presents the proposed transformation pattern. In Section 4 we detail the proposed approach to achieve model transformation adaptation at runtime. Section 5 reviews related work. Finally, Section 6 outlines the conclusions and future work.

2   A Running Example: User Interface Adaptation

The main objective of our proposal is to achieve the adaptation of user interfaces at runtime. Specifically, we are interested in studying the evolution of simple and friendly User Interfaces (UI) based on software components, in a similar way iGoogle widget-based user interfaces do (i.e., a set of UI components). In this context, user interfaces are described by means of *architectural models* containing the specification of user-interface components. These architectural models (which represent the user interfaces) can vary at runtime due to certain changes in the context —e.g., user interaction, a temporal event, visual condition, etc.

For instance, let's suppose two users in the system which are performing a communication task by means of a chat, an email, an audio and a video high quality with other users. Consequently, the graphical user interface offered by the system contains the UI components that provided these services. Let's suppose now that a new user profile role is connected to the system, and which requires the use of new services. This requirement involves the user interface automatically change to adapt its architecture to the new situation: i.e., removing the video high quality while a video low quality component, a blackboard component and a filesharing component are inserted (Figure 1).

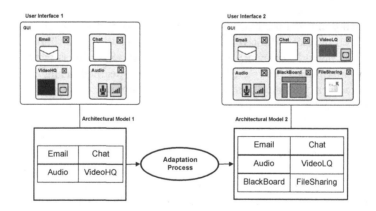

Fig. 1. User Interface Adaptation

Figure 1 illustrates the adaptation process that is performed at the architectural model level representing the user interfaces. Once the new architectural model is obtained (after the adaptation process occurs) a regeneration process is executed to show those software components of the adapted user interface. This regeneration process is not described in this paper, focusing only here on the model transformation process adapting the architectural models, and on how this M2M transformation is dynamically produced from a rule repository (the aims of this paper).

3   Model Transformation Pattern

As previously stated, design-time models are, in principle, static artifacts. Nevertheless, we will define design-time architectural models that will be changed and adapted to the requirements of the system at runtime. In order to modify our architectural models, we follow an MDE methodology so that we can achieve their change and adaptation by M2M transformations. We will design an M2M transformation where both the input and output metamodels are the same: the abstract architectural metamodel (AMM). Therefore, this process will turn an abstract architectural model AM_a into another AM_b (Figure 2).

This *ModelTransformation* process enables the evolution and adaptation of architectural models. Its behaviour is described by the set of rules it contains. Thus, if our goal is to make the architectural model transformation not be a predefined process but a process adapted to the system's needs and requirements, we must get the transformation rules to change depending on the circumstances. In order to achieve this goal, we based on the following conditions: (a) Build a rule repository where all rules that may be applied in an architectural model transformation are stored; (b) Design a rule selection process that takes as input the repository and generates as output a subset of rules; (c) Ensure that the rule selection process can generate different rule subsets, depending on the circumstances; (d) Develop a process that takes as input the selected rule subset and generates an architectural model transformation; (e) Ensure that both the described processes and their elements are within the MDE framework.

The previous steps involved in the adaptation process share a number of similarities. In order to organize and exploit them, we define a transformation pattern. Building a transformation pattern allows us to model the structure and composition of generic elements that may exist in our transformation schema. Such elements provide us with some information about the types of modules

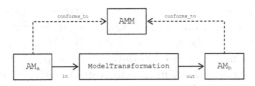

Fig. 2. Architectural Model Transformation

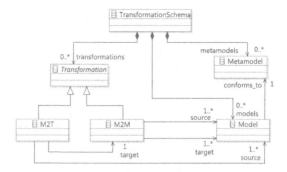

Fig. 3. Transformation Pattern

that can be included in possible transformation configurations and how they connect with the other elements of the schema. Furthermore, this pattern offers us the possibility of changing such schema by creating a different model from the metamodel defined in Figure 3, which has been implemented using EMF [8].

A transformation schema (`TransformationSchema`) is made up of three different types of elements: transformations (`Transformation`), models (`Model`) and metamodels (`Metamodel`). `Metamodel` elements describe the model definitions of the transformation schema. `Model` elements identify and define the system models. `Transformation` elements can be classified into two groups: M2M and M2T. M2M transformations represent model-to-model transformation processes; therefore, they will have one or more schema models associated both as input and output through the `source` and `target` references, respectively. On the other hand, M2T transformations represent the transformation processes that take one or more system models as their input (through `source`) and generate a textual file that, in our case, corresponds to a M2M transformation (through `target`).

4   Adaptive Model Transformation

The transformation schema enabling the runtime adaptation of architectural model, proposed in this paper, is an instance of the transformation pattern described in Section 3. This schema, illustrated in Figure 4, comprises the following three steps (repeatedly executed at each adaptation step):

(a) **RuleSelection**, is the rule selection process that starts when an attribute from a defined class in the initial architectural model (AM_i) takes a specific value (*i.e.,* when the user or the system trigger an event). This process, that is carried out at runtime, is obtained as an instance of the M2M concept. It takes as input the repository model (RRM) and the AM_i (see step #1 in Figure 4), and generates as output (see step #2 in Figure 4) a rule transformation model (RM_i) for architectural models, being $RM_i \subseteq RRM$.

(b) **RuleSelectionLog (RSL)**, is an instance of the M2M concept. Its input is the repository model (RRM) and the selected rule model (RM_i) (step #3),

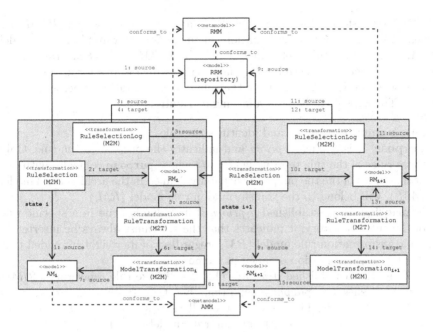

Fig. 4. Transformation Schema

and it generates (step #4) the updated rule repository model for the next adaptation as output.

(c) **RuleTransformation**, is obtained as an instance of the M2T concept. It takes as input (step #5) the rule model (RM_i) and generates as output (step #6) a new transformation process for architectural models at runtime (*ModelTransformation$_i$*).

(d) **ModelTransformation**, is obtained as an instance of the M2M concept and generates as output (step #8) a new architectural model at runtime (AM_{i+1}) starting from the initial architectural model (AM_i).

4.1   Transformation Rules: An Overview

As previously indicated, our goal is to achieve the adaptability of architectural model transformations at runtime. To this end, and given a transformation rule repository for architectural models (RRM), the system generates transformation rule models (RM_i) that adapt to the properties of the system context at runtime. The transformation rules define the degree of adaptability of our system, as such adaptability depends on the ability of the transformation rule model (RM_i) to modify itself from external events of the system. That is why we focus on the description of the transformation rules and the attributes that affect the rule selection process (*RuleSelection*) and the rule repository (RRM), where the transformation rules of the architectural models are stored.

Both the transformation rule model (RM_i) and the rule repository (RRM) are defined according to the transformation rule metamodel for architectural model (RMM). In such metamodel, which defines both RM_i and RRM transformations, we will focus on describing the class (**Rule**) which is directly involved with the rule selection logic belonging to the rule model generation process (*RuleSelection*). The class **Rule** has the following attributes:

— **rule_name**: It is unique and identifies the rule.
— **purpose**: It is defined *a priori* and indicates the purpose of the rule. Only those rules of the rule repository (RRM) whose **purpose** coincides with one of the values of the the **purposes** attribute defined in the architectural model (AM_i), will belong to the transformation rule model (RM_i).
— **is_priority**: It is established *a priori*. If its value is **true** in a specific rule of the rule repository, it indicates that the rule must always be inserted in the transformation rule model (RM_i) regardless of its weight, provided that it satisfies the condition detailed in **purpose**.
— **weight**: It is established *a priori*. That rule in the rule repository (RRM) which satisfies the **purpose** condition, has the attribute **is_priority = false** and has the biggest **weight** of all rules satisfying such conditions, will be inserted in the transformation rule model (RM_i).
— **run_counter**: Indicates the number of times the **purpose** of the rule has matched one of the values of the the **purposes** attribute defined in the architectural model (AM_i).
— **selection_counter**: Indicates the number of times the rule has been selected by the *RuleSelection* process to generate the RM_i.
— **ratio**: Indicates the frequency of using a transformation rule (the result of dividing **selection_counter** by **run_counter**).

The architectural model transformation rules are stored in the rule repository (RRM). It is a model defined according to a rule metamodel (RMM) and is made up of *a priori* transformation rules. As previously mentioned, those rules that fulfil a specific metric are chosen through a rule selection process (*RuleSelection*). Table 1 shows different rules that belong to the rule repository and will be used as an instance in Section 4.2.

4.2   Rule Selection

After an overview of the transformation rules described in Section 4.1, we studied the transformation process known as *RuleSelection* through which rule models (RM_i) are generated from the rule repository (RRM) to get the transformation adaptation at runtime. According to our transformation schema, this process is obtained as an instance of the M2M concept of the transformation pattern (see Section 3). Hence, *RuleSelection* is a model-to-model transformation process that takes as input (**source**) the initial architectural model (AM_i) defined in accordance with an architectural metamodel (AMM), and the rule repository model (RRM) defined in compliance with the rule metamodel (RMM). As

Table 1. Example rule repository (RRM)

rule_name	purpose	is_priority	weight	ratio	run_c	selec_c
Insert_Chat	InsertChat	true	2.0	1.0	3	3
Insert_Audio	InsertAudio	false	4.0	1.0	2	2
Insert_Video1	InsertVideoLowQ	false	11.0	0.5	2	1
Insert_Video2	InsertVideoLowQ	true	6.0	0.5	2	1
Insert_Video3	InsertVideoHighQ	false	9.0	1.0	3	3
Insert_BlackBoard1	InsertBlackBoard	false	6.0	0.5	2	1
Insert_BlackBoard2	InsertBlackBoard	false	4.0	0.5	2	1
Insert_FileSharing	InsertFileSharing	false	3.0	0.0	0	0
Delete_Chat	DeleteChat	true	3.0	0.0	0	0
Delete_Audio	DeleteAudio	true	3.0	0.0	0	0
Delete_Video	DeleteVideo	true	3.0	0.0	0	0
Delete_BlackBoard	DeleteBlackBoard	true	3.0	0.0	0	0
Delete_FileSharing	DeleteFileSharing	true	3.0	0.0	0	0

output (`target`), *RuleSelection* generates the transformation rule model (RM_i) also defined according to the rule metamodel (RMM) (see Figure 4).

The process starts when an attribute of a class defined in the initial architectural model (AM_i) takes a specific value. This class is known as `Launcher`. Then, the RM_i is generated starting from the RRM. Both models are defined in compliance with the rule metamodel (RMM). This new rule model (RM_i) is made up of a subset of rules existing in the rule repository model (RRM); their `purpose` attribute will coincide with one of the `purposes` attribute of the class `Launcher`, defined in the AM_i and they must fulfil a selection metric based on specific values of the `is_priority` and `weight` attributes.

The selection logic is as follows: those rules *a priori* defined as priority (`is_priority = true`) in the RRM will be copied in the selected rules model (RM_i) regardless of the `weight` value assigned at *state i*, provided that the value of the `purpose` attribute of the rule coincides with one of the values of the `purposes` attribute of the architectural model (`AMi!Launcher.purposes contains RRM!Rule.purpose`). Regarding those rules not defined as priority in the rule repository (`is_priority = false`), the process will copy in the RM_i the rule with the biggest `weight` value among all assigned to the rules of the rule repository, where the value of the `purpose` attribute of the rule coincides with one of the values of the `purposes` attribute of the initial architectural model. This selection logic of the *RuleSelection* process is shown in Table 2.

As an example, let us suppose the following architectural model AM_i where `AMi!Launcher.purposes = ['DeleteVideo','InsertVideoLowQ', 'Insert-BlackBoard','InsertFileSharing']`. We assume that the transformation rule repository model (RRM) is the one specified in Table 1. If, for external reasons, the state of the `running` attribute of the architectural model (AM_i) changed into true (`AMi!Launcher.running = true`) at the *state i*, the *RuleSelection* transformation would start. Then, the selected rule model (RM_i) would be generated from the rule repository model (RRM) by selecting the rules with the attribute `purpose = 'DeleteVideo'` or `'InsertVideoLowQ'` or `'InsertBlackBoard'` or `'InsertFileSharing'`, which have the biggest `weight` or which have their attribute `is_priority = true`, as shown in Table 3.

Table 2. Selection Logic

Input: AM$_i$ and RRM Output: RM$_i$
   if AM$_i$!Launcher.running = true **then**
      RuleSelection
   end if

RuleSelection
1: **for** $n = 1 \rightarrow RRM.size$ **do**
2:   **if** AM$_i$!Launcher.purposes[EString$_1$..EString$_n$] contains RRM!Rule$_n$.purpose **then**
3:     **if** RRM!Rule$_n$.is_priority = true **then**
4:       RM$_i$.add(RRM!Rule$_n$)
5:     **else**
6:       **if** $\exists$! j, j $\in$ 1..$RRM.size$/ RRM!Rule$_j$.weight > RRM!Rule$_n$.weight **then**
7:         RM$_i$.add(RRM!Rule$_n$)
8:       **end if**
9:     **end if**
10:   **end if**
11: **end for**

Table 3. Model of selected rules (RM$_i$)

rule_name	purpose	is_priority	weight
Insert_Video2	InsertVideoLowQ	true	6.0
Insert_BlackBoard1	InsertBlackBoard	false	6.0
Insert_FileSharing	InsertFileSharing	false	3.0
Delete_Video	DeleteVideo	true	3.0

4.3   Rule Selection Log (RSL)

When the selected rule model (RM_i) has been acquired by *RuleSelection*, the next step is to update the rule repository execution log. This step is necessary to update the attributes representing the frequency with which the rules are used in the various executions of the system, which is given in the weight attribute of the rule that may be used by *RuleSelection* as explained in Section 4.2. Thus, *RuleSelectionLog* (*RSL*) is an M2M transformation process with the selected rule model (RM_i) and the rule repository model (RRM) as input (**source**), which generates the updated rule repository model as an output (**target**), as shown in Figure 4.

Moreover, *RSL* transformation uses **bonus** and **penalty** coefficients, which add or subtract weight, respectively, and which are defined *a priori*, applying them depending on whether the rule is selected or not. The *RSL* logic is applied to the rule repository (RRM) as shown in Table 4. If the rule is in the selected rule model (RM_i), it is modified in the rule repository model, increasing the process execution counter and the selection counter, and updating the ratio and the weight (lines #3–#6). If the rule is not in the RM_i, but its **action** is the same, it is modified in RRM, increasing the execution counter, and updating the ratio and the weight (lines #9–#11).

Following this logic, the *RSL* highlights transformation rule use frequency (**ratio**), so the **weight** of a rule, although defined *a priori*, is determined by the **ratio** with which the rule has been selected by *RuleSelection* to generate the RM_i. Similarly, not using the rule influences its **weight** negatively. Therefore,

Table 4. *RSL* pseudocode

```
process RSL
 1: for n = 1 → RRM.size do
 2:    if RM_i contains RRM[n] then
 3:       RRM[n].run_counter ← RRM[n].run_counter + 1
 4:       RRM[n].selection_counter ← RRM[n].selection_counter + 1
 5:       RRM[n].ratio ← RRM[n].selection_counter/RRM[n].run_counter
 6:       RRM[n].weight ← RRM[n].weight + RRM[n].ratio * RRM.bonus
 7:    else
 8:       if RM_i.action = RRM[n].action then
 9:          RRM[n].run_counter ← RRM[n].run_counter + 1
10:          RRM[n].ratio ← RRM[n].selection_counter/RRM[n].run_counter
11:          RRM[n].weight ← RRM[n].weight − RRM[n].ratio * RRM.penalty
12:       end if
13:    end if
14: end for
```

Table 5. RRM after RSL

rule_name	purpose	weight	ratio	run_c	selec_c
Insert_Chat	InsertChat	2.0	1.0	3	3
Insert_Audio	InsertAudio	4.0	1.0	2	2
Insert_Video1	InsertVideoLowQ	11.0→10.33	0.5→0.33	2→3	1
Insert_Video2	InsertVideoLowQ	6.0→7.65	0.5→0.66	2→3	1→2
Insert_Video3	InsertVideoHighQ	9.0	1.0	3	3
Insert_BlackBoard1	InsertBlackBoard	6.0→7.65	0.5→0.66	2→3	1→2
Insert_BlackBoard2	InsertBlackBoard	4.0→3.33	0.5→0.33	2→3	1
Insert_FileSharing	InsertFileSharing	3.0→5.5	0→1.0	0→1	0→1
Delete_Chat	DeleteChat	3.0	0.0	0	0
Delete_Audio	DeleteAudio	3.0	0.0	0	0
Delete_Video	DeleteVideo	3.0→5.5	0.0→1.0	0→1	0→1
Delete_BlackBoard	DeleteBlackBoard	3.0	0.0	0	0
Delete_FileSharing	DeleteFileSharing	3.0	0.0	0	0

by this logic, the transformation rules used in *ModelTransformation$_i$* (Figure 4) are adapted to system behavior. Although the attribute values involved in the rule repository model (*RRM*) are set *a priori*, at *state* = i, the values depend on previous system behavior up to that point ($\forall state < i$).

As a practical example, let us assume the rule repository (*RRM*) in Table 1 and the selected rule model (*RM$_i$*) generated by *RuleSelection* (Table 3). The output of this transformation would update the rule repository in Table 5.

4.4   Rule Transformation

The last process required for our adaptive transformation when *RuleSelection* and *RSL* have been executed is called *RuleTransformation*. This process is an instance of the M2T concept in the transformation pattern (Figure 3), in which the source is the selected rule model, and the target is a model-to-model transformation file code (see Figure 4). Thus, the transformation file generated by this process is an instance of the M2M concept (Figure 3) having an architectural model (*AM$_i$*) as the source and generating the new architectural model (*AM$_{i+1}$*)

Fig. 5. Example Rule Model extraction

as output (`target`). Since the rule models in the *RuleSelection* process change depending on the context and system requirements, the *RuleTransformation* process (that takes these models as input) creates runtime architectural model transformations containing the new rules considered to be necessary. Hence, this *ModelTransformation$_i$* process adapts the architectural models at runtime.

For example, Figure 5 shows a rule model extraction generated by *RuleSelection* in which the information dealing with the input and output models is

Table 6. Example of transformation by the *RuleTransformation* process

```
                    Portion of transformation M2T
module t1;
create
<c:iterate var="model_ref" select="/RuleSet/model_ref[@model_type = 'OUT']" delimiter=",">
 <c:get select="$model_ref/@model_name"/> :
 <c:get select="$model_ref/conforms_to/@metamodel_name"/></c:iterate>
from
<c:iterate var="model_ref" select="/RuleSet/model_ref[@model_type = 'IN']" delimiter=",">
 <c:get select="$model_ref/@model_name"/> :
 <c:get select="$model_ref/conforms_to/@metamodel_name"/></c:iterate>;
<c:iterate var="rules" select="/RuleSet/rules">
 <c:if test="$rules[self :: MatchedRule or self :: LazyRule]">
<c:if test="$rules[self :: MatchedRule]">rule</c:if>
<c:if test="$rules[self :: LazyRule]">lazy rule</c:if>
<c:get select="$rules/@rule_name"/>
{
 <c:include template="templates/fromElements.jet" passVariables="rules"/>
 <c:include template="templates/toElements.jet" passVariables="rules"/>
 <c:include template="templates/doBlock.jet" passVariables="rules"/>
}
 </c:if>
</c:iterate>

                     Portion of M2M generated
module t1;
create  AMOUT : AMM from  AMIN : AMM;
rule InsertText
{
 from
 f : AMM!ComplexAbstractComponent in AMIN
 ( f.component_name = 'GUI'
 )
 to
 t1 : AMM!ComplexAbstractComponent in AMOUT
 ( component_name <- f.component_name
 ),
 t2 : AMM!SimpleAbstractComponent in AMOUT
 ( component_name <- 'Text',
   component_parent <- t1
 )
}
```

modeled, as well as the metamodel in which such models are defined, and an example rule. Table 6 shows the *RuleTransformation* code fragment responsible for transforming the rule model extraction. This part of the transformation generates the header section of the ATL transformation file and the content of an example rule. For each element of the rule model (RM_i) there is a part of the M2T transformation process that is in charge of translating the rules and any other necessary information into the ATL code, which constitutes the implementation of the M2M transformation of the *ModelTransformation$_i$* process.

Even though *RuleTransformation* was developed to convert rule models into transformation processes for architectural models, it is extendable to any type of M2M transformation, which is executed on a rule model defined in compliance with the rule metamodel.

5 Related Work

In recent years, several proposals have attempted to achieve adaptive transformation. For example, in [9], the authors propose an incremental update strategy. These transformations are built dynamically from the rules available in a rule repository. The proposal presented in [10] shares some aspects related to the dynamic selection of transformation rules in common with ours. It proposes model refactoring description and execution based on transformation rules, which have formal parameters matched to a model subset. It differs from our proposal mainly in that we use an M2M transformation to implement this rule selection, not a check algorithm.

In [11], the authors propose a meta-transformation approach, in which transformations are defined that accept other transformations as their input and produce (new or modified) transformations as their output. In our approach, although also a meta-transformation, we use JET to generate transformations providing dynamic model adaptability (horizontal transformation), rather than refine Platform-Independent Models (PIM) into Platform-Specific Models (PSM) (vertical transformation). In [12], the architectural models must contain variation and selection criteria so the middleware can automate the transformation. The authors in [13] define variability models to specify the adaptation logic, separating it from the system functionality. In contrast, we propose to store the adaptation logic in a repository of transformation rules.

Some other approaches, also dealing with runtime software adaptation, rely on the use of high-level programming languages. For instance, in [14], the authors propose a Java-based implementation that is executed within an OSGi [15] platform. The main advantage of using M2M transformations instead of high-level programming languages for dynamic adaptation is that they can evolve dynamically (because they can be treated as models), while programs (whether binary or bytecodes) cannot. In this vein, one of the main benefits of using ATL for our M2M transformations is that it enables the use of explicit rule calls internally as a mechanism for rule integration [16]. This way, rules can be dynamically assembled in such a way that each rule calls up the next.

Finally, other proposals make use of composition techniques for dynamic model transformation. For instance, in [17,18], the authors provide a mechanism (a rule-based model transformation language) for making model transformations out of previously created modules. These transformation modules can either be called up from other modules or imported from an ATL file. On the other hand, in [19,20], the authors suggest using M2M transformations to generate transformation models, which could then be adapted or modified. Such models can later be translated into ATL transformation files that behave, in turn, as new transformation modules adapted to the requirements. But unlike our research work, neither of these approaches makes automatic use of composition techniques to adapt model transformation to changes in context.

6 Conclusions and Future Work

In this paper we have described our approach to provide model transformations with a dynamic behavior allowing them to vary in time according to the new application or user requirements. In particular, our proposal focuses on the adaptation of architectural models at runtime. Our scope are architectural models which represent user interfaces made up of UI components [2]. With this aim, we have developed a transformation pattern for modeling the structure and composition of the transformation schema. The transformation schema can also be changed by creating another model conforming the transformation pattern. This provides our proposal with a high degree of flexibility and scalability. We have also developed an M2M process (*RSL*) that updates the transformation rules stored in the rule repository. This way, along with the rule selection process (*RuleSelection*), the transformation rules are able to change depending on the circumstances. Therefore, the transformation rules stored in the rule repository (*RRM*) define the adaptability of our new system, which depends on the ability of the transformation rule repository to modify itself in view of external system events. The scope of adaptability is defined by means of the rule selection logic.

As future work, we intend to achieve a higher degree of adaptability for our proposal. To this end, we suggest providing the generation process of transformation rule models with a more adaptive behavior. Thus, we will take into account, in the selection logic, factors that provide new rule selection criteria to get a higher degree of adaptability in transformations: use frequency of transformation rules, rule weight management policy, etc. We also intend to possibly carry out, through HOT [19], the process by which at runtime we turn rule models into transformation processes applied to architectural models. Once the required adaptability level is reached, and using the scalability degree of our proposal, we'll focus on providing our system with a decision-making technique to be able to manipulate the rule repository so that the system can evolve at runtime and adapt itself to the interaction with the user. Moreover, another improvement we wish to include in our system, is the development of an editing tool for transformation rules in a similar way to that in [14]. On the other hand, this tool would allow us to execute the rule selection process to check which rules are selected from the repository and the context information.

Acknowledgments. This work has been supported by the EU (FEDER) and the Spanish Ministry MICINN under grant of the TIN2010-15588 and TRA2009-0309 projects, and under a FPU grant (AP2010-3259), and also by the JUNTA ANDALUCÍA (proyecto de excelencia) ref. TIC-6114, http://www.ual.es/acg.

References

1. Blair, G., Bencomo, N., France, R.B.: Models@RT. Computer 40(10), 22–27 (2009)
2. Criado, J., Vicente-Chicote, C., Iribarne, L., Padilla, N.: A Model-Driven Approach to Graphical User Interface RT Adaptation. Models@RT, CEUR-WS 641 (2010)
3. Criado, J., Padilla, N., Iribarne, L., Asensio, J.-A.: User Interface Composition with COTS-UI and Trading Approaches: Application for Web-Based Environmental Information Systems. In: Lytras, M.D., Ordonez De Pablos, P., Ziderman, A., Roulstone, A., Maurer, H., Imber, J.B. (eds.) WSKS 2010. CCIS, vol. 111, pp. 259–266. Springer, Heidelberg (2010)
4. Iribarne, L., Padilla, N., Criado, J., Asensio, J., Ayala, R.: A Model Transformation Approach for Automatic Composition of COTS User Interfaces in Web-Based Information Systems. Information Systems Management 27(3), 207–216 (2010)
5. Czarnecki, K., Helsen, S.: Classification of model transformation approaches. In: OOPSLA Workshop on Generative Tech. in the Context of the MDA, pp. 1–17 (2003)
6. Eclipse Java Emitter Templates (JET), http://bit.ly/SdxyWw
7. Jouault, F., Allilaire, F., Bézivin, J., Kurtev, I.: ATL: A model transformation tool. Science of Computer Programming 72(1-2), 31–39 (2008)
8. Gronback, R.: Eclipse Modeling Project: A Domain-Specific Language (DSL) Toolkit. Addison-Wesley Professional (2009)
9. Hearnden, D., Lawley, M., Raymond, K.: Incremental Model Transformation for the Evolution of Model-Driven Systems. In: Wang, J., Whittle, J., Harel, D., Reggio, G. (eds.) MoDELS 2006. LNCS, vol. 4199, pp. 321–335. Springer, Heidelberg (2006)
10. Porres, I.: Rule-based update transformations and their application to model refactorings. Software and Systems Modeling 4(4), 368–385 (2005)
11. Gray, J., Lin, Y., Zhang, J.: Automating change evolution in model-driven engineering. Computer 39(2), 51–58 (2006)
12. Floch, J., Hallsteinsen, S., Stav, E., Eliassen, F., Lund, K., Gjørven, E.: Using Architecture Models for Runtime Adaptability. IEEE Software 23(2), 62–70 (2006)
13. Fleurey, F., Solberg, A.: A Domain Specific Modeling Language Supporting Specification, Simulation and Execution of Dynamic Adaptive Systems. In: Schürr, A., Selic, B. (eds.) MODELS 2009. LNCS, vol. 5795, pp. 606–621. Springer, Heidelberg (2009)
14. Serral, E., Valderas, P., Pelechano, V.: Supporting Runtime System Evolution to Adapt to User Behaviour. In: Pernici, B. (ed.) CAiSE 2010. LNCS, vol. 6051, pp. 378–392. Springer, Heidelberg (2010)
15. OSGi – The Dynamic Module System for Java, http://www.osgi.org/
16. Kurtev, I., van den Berg, K., Jouault, F.: Rule-based modularization in model transformation languages illustrated with ATL. Sci. Comp. Prog. 68(3), 138–154 (2007)
17. Wagelaar, D., Van Der Straeten, R., Deridder, D.: Module superimposition: a composition technique for rule-based model transformation languages. Software and Systems Modeling 9(3), 285–309 (2010)

18. Wagelaar, D., Tisi, M., Cabot, J., Jouault, F.: Towards a general composition semantics for rule-based model transformation. In: MDE Languages and Systems, pp. 623–637. Springer (2011)
19. Tisi, M., Jouault, F., Fraternali, P., Ceri, S., Bézivin, J.: On the use of higher-order model transformations. In: MDA-Found. & Applic., pp. 18–33. Springer (2009)
20. Tisi, M., Cabot, J., Jouault, F.: Improving Higher-Order Transformations Support in ATL. In: Tratt, L., Gogolla, M. (eds.) ICMT 2010. LNCS, vol. 6142, pp. 215–229. Springer, Heidelberg (2010)

Managing Quality of Large Set of Conceptual Schemas in Public Administration: Methods and Experiences

Carlo Batini, Marco Comerio, and Gianluigi Viscusi

University of Milano-Bicocca, viale Sarca 336/14, 20126, Milano Italy
{batini,comerio,viscusi}@disco.unimib.it

Abstract. Information growth asks Public Administrations for an effective control over their information asset. Furthermore, having a global representation of the core concepts of such an asset implies to manage large set of conceptual schemas. At the state of the art, the use of repositories of conceptual schemas aims to provide a structured, global and scalable representation of the core concepts managed in complex large scale information systems. In this paper we discuss several quality properties of repositories, analyzing them within a real, large scale experience.

Keywords: e-Government, Data Governance, Quality, conceptual modeling, repository.

1   Introduction

Organizations currently face the challenge of having and managing hundreds and even thousands databases developed in different times and by different teams. The result is an extremely fragmented view of the overall information managed in the organization, with a consequent increasing relevance of data and information quality issues. In particular, while a great emphasis has been put on the discussion on the central role of data integration in e-Government initiatives [1], at the state of the art the maintenance and evolution of integrated information systems is still a critical issue both at practitioner and academic level [2], [3]. Furthermore, current diffusion of open data initiatives ask for methods and framework enabling access, agile data management and the constant monitoring of the available information asset [4].

In this paper we propose a structured set of conceptual schemas as a repository solution to the above mentioned challenges. In particular, the repository is built and structured by iteratively making use of abstraction (inversely, refinement) primitives for bottom-up/top-down generation of schemas, together with integration/diversification primitives for integration/diversification of schemas characterized by different types of heterogeneities [5]. Even if suitable as solution, repositories of conceptual schemas face quality issues related to maintenance and extension [6]. While wide literature exists on data quality and on schema quality in the context of databases [7], [8], quality dimensions applied to structured set or repositories of conceptual schemas have been poorly investigated.

A. Abelló, L. Bellatreche, and B. Benatallah (Eds.): MEDI 2012, LNCS 7602, pp. 31–42, 2012.
© Springer-Verlag Berlin Heidelberg 2012

This paper aims to investigate and discuss quality dimensions suitable to support the building, structuring and maintenance of large set or repositories of conceptual schemas in particular in public administrations, where the issue of having an up-to-date schema documentation may still represent a challenge. We first introduce and discuss the concept of repository; subsequently, we provide simple formalizations of i) abstraction/refinement primitive, ii) schemas result of an abstraction/refinement process, iii) schemas result of an integration/diversification process, and iv) to some extent also of integration/diversification primitive. We define and use deliberately simple formalisms, since, in order to involve actively users in modelling the data content of an organization, we need to use simple models provided with diagrammatic representations.

The paper is organized as follows. In Section 2 we revisit previous and present research and experiences on structured set of conceptual schemas and repositories of schemas. In Section 3 we provide a formalization of the concepts involved in repositories. Section 4 introduces several quality dimensions and metrics that can be adopted to represent and analyse the quality of a repository. Then (Section 5) we apply such quality model to a real example of large scale repository, the collection of conceptual schemas of an Italian public administration (for sake of privacy statements authors cannot provide further details as to the name of the considered public administration). We conclude the paper discussing results and future work (Section 6).

2   Background and Motivations

Large organizations with a long history and a consequent large set of legacy information systems needs instruments to face schema evolution management and maintenance of very large set of conceptual schemas. At the state of the art, these challenges have been considered in terms of i) *clustering of schemas* [9], ii) *hierarchical structuring of schemas* [10], iii) *methods and techniques for conceptual schema analysis and classification* [11], and iv) *application of integration-abstraction primitives for building dictionaries and repository of schemas* [5], [12].

As for clustering, it can take different names such as typology, numerical taxonomy, and partitioning [13], and applying to different domains such as epidemiology, cellular manufacturing, linguistics, data mining, and economics. Furthermore, at the state of the art Entity-Relationship clustering algorithms and approaches are still mainly semi-automatics, asking for "experts" involvement [14]. As a consequence, there is still a poor clustering assistance in diagramming tool. As for hierarchical structuring of schemas, besides "hierarchical leveling" approach [12], it is worth mentioning the critic by Moody [15] as for the effective improvements of understanding by hierarchical structuring of schemas. Moody points out "connectivity" (i.e. the number of relationships and entity participates in) as a more effective approach to Entity Relationship clustering [15]. As for large set of conceptual schemas structured in a repository, different approaches to repository management have been proposed in the literature. Conceptual modeling languages such as UML are well known in the professional community [16], but are not natively Web compliant. Whereas RDFS and OWL have the advantage of coupling Web compliance and semantics, as onto-logical languages they are difficult to comprehend and use in the large in a cost-effective way [17]. As for methods and techniques for conceptual schema analysis and classification, primitives for schema integration are introduced in [5], where a methodology for schema integration in the Entity Relationship model is presented. Abstractions in conceptual modeling have been studied to support database design and schema summarization [18] and formal characterizations of generic relationships [19]. Finally, as for schema quality dimensions, several papers [15] investigated them in the literature. These quality dimensions are poorly applied to structured set of large set of conceptual schemas. In this paper we consider structured repositories of conceptual schemas [5], [11], where experiences of their usage in Public Administration are presented in [6]. In particular we investigate the issue of quality as a way to challenge the management of the contents of Public Administration data asset, usually unavailable without a previous knowledge of master concepts and acquaintance with administrative procedures [20].

3   Definition of Concepts

A *conceptual schema* S is a set of entities, relationships, generalizations, IS-A relationships in the Entity Relationship model with usual meanings. Without loss of generality, we will consider only binary relationships; an n-ary relationship R_n defined among entities $E_1,..,E_n$ can be transformed in a new entity R_n connected with n binary relationships to $E_1,..,E_n$. We will not consider attributes, cardinalities, other constraints and identifiers. An organization having hundreds and even thousands of databases, may consider feasible to produce an integrated representation of all concepts in databases through a one shot integration process. However, such process is unfeasible, due to the complexity involved in the matching, homogenisation and merging activities related to such a huge number of schemas. For such a reason, the literature proposes several approaches based on the usage, besides *integration*, of a second paradigm usually investigated and adopted to represent complex artefacts, namely *abstraction* [5], [21]. We now show a lightweight formalization of the concept of repository of schemas resulting from the joint usage of the two paradigms.

A *repository of conceptual schemas* is a set of schemas, representing at conceptual level the whole information content of the databases of an organization. A schema may be basic, abstract, or integrated. A *basic schema* is a schema resulting from the conceptualization of a database of the organization.

Besides basic schemas, other schemas in a repository can be generated by two types of *transformations*, namely a. *abstraction*, that has as input a single schema and generates in output a schema, and b. *integration*, that has in input n schemas and generates in output a single schema. We assume that each schema in the repository is in input to only one transformation and there is only one schema that is in input to no transformation (the repository is a tree). Both abstraction and integration have associated refinement and diversification inverse operations, in which the roles of input and output schema(s) are exchanged. An *abstract schema* AS = abstraction (S) is a schema resulting from the application of *abstraction primitives* to a schema S in the repository. Inversely, a *refined schema* RS = refinement (S) is a schema resulting from the application of *refinement primitives* to a more abstract one. An *integrated schema* IS = integration $(S_1, S_2,.., S_n)$ is a schema resulting from the *integration* of *n* schemas $S_1, S_2, .., S_n$. The integration process, deeply investigated in the literature, can be expressed in terms of two activities: 1. discovering heterogeneities by means of schema matching, and 2. applying *integration primitives*, namely transformations performed on schemas to be integrated in order to produce the reconciled integrated schema. We assume that all concepts in $S_1, S_2,.., S_n$ are represented in S. Similarly to abstraction, integration has an inverse conceptual operation, that we call *diversification*, that transforms a schema S into a set of schemas $S_1, S_2,.., S_n$ with a process that makes use of *diversification primitives*, that have a complementary role with respect to integration primitives. A detailed discussion on issues related to integration and diversification primitives is outside the scope of the paper.

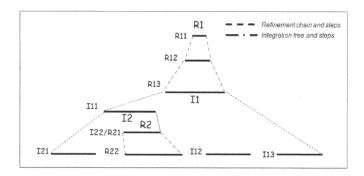

Fig. 1. An example of repository, refinement chains and steps and integration trees and steps

Looking at Fig. 1, we see that, due to our assumption of being a schema involved in only one abstraction or integration, two types of structures can appear in the repository: *refinement chains* (or, inversely, *abstraction chains,* we prefer from now on to adopt the refinement instead of abstraction as the relevant transformation), that can be made of one to n *refinement (abstraction) steps* among schemas (the upper chain in Fig. 1 is made of two refinement steps), and *integration (diversification) trees* and *steps,* with similar meanings. Fig. 1 shows refinement chains and integration steps and trees, whose involved schemas are highlighted with lines having different shapes in the two cases.

Here we discuss the concept of refinement primitive (*r-primitive* in brief); the inverse concept of *abstraction primitive* (*a-primitive*) is quite simple, for reasons of space we omit it. An *r-primitive* is made of two parts, called respectively the *source schema* SS and the *target schema* TS. We assume in the following that SS is made of a unique concept, entity or relationship. When an r-primitive is applied to a schema S, a concept C in S that matches the concept in SS is chosen, and it is substituted by the concepts in TS; the application of the primitive has to specify which concepts in TS inherit the links of SS in S, and the names of concepts in TS.

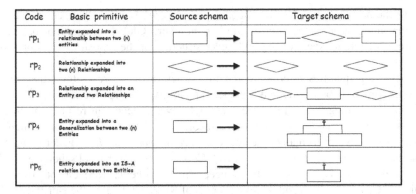

Code	Basic primitive	Source schema	Target schema
rp_1	Entity expanded into a relationship between two (n) entities		
rp_2	Relationship expanded into two (n) Relationships		
rp_3	Relationship expanded into an Entity and two Relationships		
rp_4	Entity expanded into a Generalization between two (n) Entities		
rp_5	Entity expanded into an IS-A relation between two Entities		

Fig. 2. Basic refinement primitives

Among all possible types of r-primitives, we distinguish a subset characterized by a simple structure, and we call them *basic r-primitives* (*br-primitives* in brief). They are represented in Fig. 2. Notice that relationships in rp_1, rp_2, rp_3 may be n-ary, with n $\geq$ 2. Complex r-primitives (*cr-primitives* in brief) are r-primitives whose target schema is any possible E-R schema.

4   Qualities of Repositories

When we move from one schema to a repository of schemas, we may use state of the art quality dimensions for single schemas, while we have to introduce new qualities that characterize the structure of the repository and the generation process of schemas in the repository. Such aspects of the structure and of the generation process concern maintenance and extension of the repository. In this section, we introduce quality dimensions that capture the structure of the repository and the quality of the applied generation process. The quality dimensions are classified according to the distinction between qualities referred to the *high level structure* of the repository (i.e., refinement chains and schemas, integration trees and schemas) and qualities referred to the *full structure* of the repository (i.e., refinement primitives used in refinement steps and concepts involved in refinement primitives).

As for the qualities of high level structure they are a. global schema balancing, b. schema refinement balancing, c. local integration balancing, and d. global integration balancing. *Global schema balancing* requests that abstract and integrated schemas at the same level of the repository have a similar size, where the size can be expressed by the number of concepts (entities, relationships, etc.) in the schema. This quality is not applicable to basic schemas since they have sizes that depend on the historical relevance and evolution of the corresponding databases. *Schema refinement balancing* refers to the homogeneous disposition of schemas in refinement chains. When moving from the top to the bottom of the chain, this quality requests that the increases in the size of the schemas are balanced (i.e., the ratio of consecutive schema sizes is close enough to a constant value). *Local integration balancing* requests that schemas involved in the integration steps are of similar size. It can be seen as a sub-property of global schema balancing. *Global integration balancing* requests that schemas in the different integration steps are of similar number. Global integration balancing captures a different aspect of the high level structure of the repository than previous qualities.

Considering qualities referred to the full structure of the repository, they are a. concept refinement balancing and b. understandability. *Concept refinement balancing* concerns the homogeneous refinement of high level concepts in refinement chains, from abstract schemas to concrete ones. In order to define a metric for refinement balancing we have to formalize the concept of *refinement speed*. Consider a chain of refinements made of schemas S_1, S_2, …,S_m. Consider the upper level schema S_1 in the chain, and let C_{11}, C_{12},.., C_{1n} be the concepts in the schema. Refinement primitives applied to C_{11}, C_{12},.., C_{1n} result in subschemas of S_2, depending on the r-primitive. By iteratively applying refinements to subschemas of S_2 associated to concepts in S_1 we obtain for each concept C_{1i} in S_1 a corresponding chain of schemas CS $(C_{1i}) = [C_{1i}$, TS_{2i}, …, $TS_{ni}]$. Define $\#(S)$ as the number of different concepts in schema S; correspondingly, associated to the chain CS (C_{1i}) we have the list $[1, \#(TS_{2i})$, …, $\#(TS_{ni})]$. We define the *refinement speed* RS associated to CS (C_{1i}) as the list RS $(CS(C_i)) = [\#(TS_{2i}), \#(TS_{2i})/ \#(TS_{3i}), …, \#(TS_{ni-1})/ \#(TS_{ni})]$. A refinement chain has a high concept refinement balancing as far as $RS(CS(C_{1i}))$ for all C_{1i} in the upper level schema contain similar values.

Understandability can be defined as the effort required to the users of the repository to understand the generative process, where low effort corresponds to high understandability. Refinement chains can be generated by a set of refinements made of a mix of r-primitives characterized by different distribution and complexity. As a consequence, a measure of the complexity of primitives is adopted. Given a refinement step $S_1 \rightarrow S_2$, we define *generative complexity* of the refinement step the percentage of cr-primitives compared with the whole set of primitives used to transform $S_1 \rightarrow S_2$, where cr-primitives are weighted according to the number of br-primitives they can be decomposed into, namely that can generate the cr-primitive. As an example, a cr-primitive that can be decomposed into three rp_1 and two rp_5 primitives has weight = 5. Here the hypothesis is that, for each cr-primitive, it is possible to find an equivalent decomposition in terms of br-primitives rp1, rp2, rp3, rp4, rp5, see later for a discussion on this point. Moving from refinement steps to refinement chains we can define the *refinement chain generative complexity* as the average generative complexity of refinement steps in the chain. Finally, we may define the *repository generative complexity* as the average generative complexity of all refinement chains in the repository.

5   Case Study   ·

The authors of the paper have been involved in the past in several projects whose goal has been the production of repositories of schemas for several Italian public admini-strations. This Section describes the case of the repository of 25 basic schemas of the considered Italian public administration (*Fiscal Information System* (FIS) repository in the following). The organizational structure of the considered Italian public administration is made up of four agencies, namely *Revenue Agency*, *Customs Agency*, *Public Land Agency* and *Agency for the Territory*. In 2008 the considered Italian public administration has been committed in a relevant national project, the *Health Card*. In 2009 the considered Italian public administration started the integration of the data bases of the above four main agencies. The following case study is part of the preliminary activities aiming at producing an integrated schema of the available information. The activity involved 40 IT architects skilled in specific domains in the participatory design of a repository of conceptual schemas allowing the management of the available information asset and integration process. The activity started from the results of a previous initiative of the Italian Public Administration that in 1993-1995 realized with a global effort of 3 man/years a repository of schemas based on about 400 basic schemas, with approximately 5.000 entities and a similar number of relationships. Thus, the choice of an approach based on a repository of integrated/abstracted conceptual schemas supports the evaluation of the evolution degrees and the required maintenance activities, by comparing the 2009 available schemas with the complete ones produced in 1993-1995.

In this section we provide several statistics on refinements in the FIS repository. The following measures are used to quantify the refinement activity: 1) number of r-primitives used; 2) number of concepts involved in the refinement; 3) percentage of concept type compared to all the concepts involved in the refinement; 4) refinement speed (RS); 5) average refinement speed (ARS) and 6) refinement speed variance (RSV). Focusing on the measure *number of primitives*, we can evaluate the percentage of br-primitives and cr-primitives used in all the refinement chain of the repository. The cr-primitives are a significant number (46% of the overall primitives). Moreover, the percentage of br-primitives (*rp1, rp2, rp3*) that correspond to aggregation refinements (those refinements involving entities and relationships) is almost the same to the percentage of br-primitives (*rp4, rp5*) referring to generalization refinement. Among the first group, the most frequent primitive is *rp1*, confirming the relevance of the entity concept in the entity relationship model.

Focusing on the percentage of each cr-primitive in all the refinement chains, we notice that it has been possible to find a composition in terms of br-primitives. Moreover, the 38% (*n*rp1* and *n*rp4*) of the cr-primitives uses iteratively one br-primitive, the 56% uses two br-primitives and the 6% uses a combination of three different br-primitives.

The mentioned statistics can be used to measure the generative complexity of the refinement process and to assess the understandability of the generative process according to the approach proposed in Section 4. Due to the high percentage of cr-primitives, in this section we perform an analysis of schema and chain generative complexity and we show examples of how to assess the schema refinement balancing (*sr-balancing* in brief), concept refinement balancing (*cr-balancing* in brief) and understandability of the FIS Repository. According to the definitions in Section 3, sr-balancing is evaluated by means of the *Average Refinement Speed* (ARS) and the *Refinement Speed Variance* (RSV) measures. Vice versa, cr-balancing is evaluated considering the *Refinement Speed* (RS) measure.

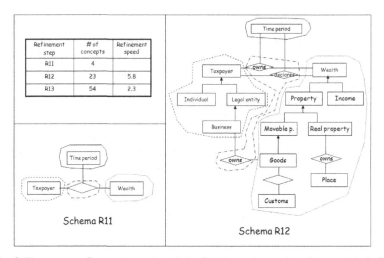

Fig. 3. Figures on refinement speeds and the first two schemas in refinement chain R1

Table 1. Evaluation of refinement speed

Ref. Chain	R1	R2	R3	R4	R5	R6
ARS	4	1.6	1.8	1.7	1.5	1.4
RSV	2.91	0.22	0.57	0	0	0.004

Focusing on the whole repository, we can check sr-balancing and cr-balancing. Table 1 shows ARS and RSV of refinement chains with more than 2 schemas (R1...R6). Notice that the ARS of the refinement chain R1 is an outlier, thus sr-balancing and cr-balancing are very low.

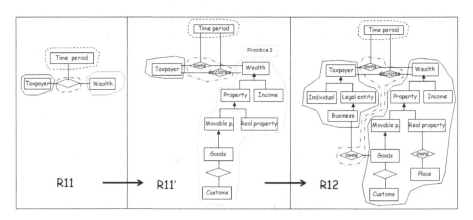

Fig. 4. New refinement chain for R1

In the following, we focus on how to improve these quality dimensions in R1. In the upper left part of Fig. 3 we show the detail for chain R1 where the critical step is R11 → R12, characterized by a high refinement speed (5.8) and low sr-balancing; R11 and R12 are also shown in Fig. 3, together with the sub-schemas in R12 that correspond to concepts in R11. In order to improve sr-balancing of chain R1, we can split the refinement step R11 → R12 in two steps, introducing an intermediate schema R11' (see Fig. 4).

Now we move to cr-balancing. We may evaluate the refinement speed in steps R11 → R11' and R11' → R12 of the four concepts in schema R11.

Table 2. Refinement process for the four concepts in schema R11

Concept	Number of concepts (#) /Refinement Chain (R)			Refinement Speed	
	#R1	#R2	#R3	R11>R11'	R11'>R12
Tax payer	1	1	6	0	6
Time period	1	1	1	0	0
Wealth	1	11	13	11	1.18
Ternary Relationship	1	2	3	2	1.5

The results in Table 2 show that the refinement speeds of *Tax Payer* and *Wealth* are not homogeneous in the analyzed refinement steps. *Tax Payer* is refined only in R11' → R12 and *Wealth* is significantly refined only in R11 → R11'. We may improve cr-balancing anticipating in R11 → R11' the refinement of *Tax Payer* and shrinking in R11' the schema resulting from refinement of the concept *Wealth*. As to the new chain of schemas R11→R11''→R12, Table 3 shows that the number of concepts and the refinement speeds are more homogeneous, thus the resulting cr-balancing is higher.

Table 3. New refinement process for the four concepts in schema R11

Concept	Number of concepts (#) /Refinement Chain (R)			Refinement Speed	
	#R11	#R11''	#R12	R11>R11''	R11''>R12
Tax payer	1	4	6	4	1.5
Time period	1	1	1	0	0
Wealth	1	7	13	7	1.18
Ternary Relationship	1	2	3	2	1.85

As described in Section 4, *understandability* can be assessed focusing on the generative complexity (i.e., percentage of weighted cr-primitives used in the refinement process). Considering the repository generative complexity, moving from the top to the bottom of the repository, the percentage of cr-primitives decreases, although slowly, thus the understandability increases. The critical areas concern chains R5 and R9, characterized by high percentages of weighted cr-primitives (low understandability). In the following, for reasons of space, we focus on chain R1. We observe the generative complexity at a fine grain level for the two refinement steps of chain R1. In Table 4 we see the number of br-primitives and cr-primitives applied in each step, where cr-primitives are expressed in terms of the list of elementary primitives they can be decomposed into. Further, the generative complexity of each refinement step is shown in the last column.

Table 4. Basic and complex r-primitives applied in the first two steps of R1

	Basic Primitives					Complex Primitives		Gen. Complexity
Refin. Steps	rp1	rp2	rp3	rp4	rp5	2*rp4	2*rp1+rp5	
R11>R11"	-	1	-	1	-	1	-	50%
R11">R12	-	1	-	-	1	-	1	60%

We see that the more complex cr-primitive is applied in the step R11'' → R12. We can make the generative process more understandable splitting the step in the two steps, where we have separated the generation of IS-As, now in the step R11'' → R11''', from the generation of relationships, now performed in step R11''' → R12.

6   Conclusion and Future Work

This paper discusses quality dimensions suitable to support the building, structuring and maintenance of large set or repositories of conceptual schemas; in public administrations the issue of having an up-to-date schema documentation may still represent a challenge. The proposed case study discusses the activity carried out in 2009 involving 40 IT architects of the IT department of the considered Italian public administration. The IT architects skilled in specific domains have been involved in the participatory design of a repository of conceptual schemas. The repository provides a clear view of the whole integrated information content of the organization through a generative process; this process is more understandable if the overall structure of such generative process achieves good quality. Moreover, the quality of the structure of the repository also influences its maintenance and extension. Consequently, the contributions of this work concern: (i) the definition of quality dimensions and quality metrics for the structure of repositories of conceptual schemas and their generative processes and (ii) the discussion of a case study resulting from a large scale real project in a Public Administration. This effort aimed at producing a simplified theoretical framework supporting the evaluation of the current conceptual schemas portfolio of one or more Public Administrations. We recognize that a limitation of the proposed approach is in the objective model used for quality dimensions, whereas we do not consider the subjective side, namely quality as perceived by users. In future work, we will investigate the relationships between the two perspectives. Furthermore, many applications of the concept of quality in different domains (e.g., information and data quality) lack in an established formalization for quality measurement. Thus, this formalization is a long-term goal of our proposal as a contribution to the field.

References

[1] Andersen, K.V., Henriksen, H.Z.: E-government maturity models: Extension of the Layne and Lee model. Government Information Quarterly 23, 236–248 (2006)

[2] Tan, B., Leong, C., Hackney, R.: Achieving and Enhancing E-government Integra-tion: Lessons from the Land Data Hub Project of the Singapore Land Authority. In: ICIS 2011 Proceedings (2011)

[3] Lam, W.: Barriers to e-government integration. Journal of Enterprise Information Management 18(5), 511–530 (2005)

[4] Picazo-Vela, S., Gutiérrez-Martinez, I., Luna-Reyes, L.F.: Social media in the public sector: perceived benefits, costs and strategic alternatives. In: Proceedings of the 12th Annual International Digital Government Research Conference (dg.o 2011), pp. 198–203 (2011)

[5] Batini, C., Di Battista, G., Santucci, G.: Structuring primitives for a dictionary of entity relationship data schemas. Software Engineering. IEEE Transactions on Software Engineering 19, 344–365 (1993)

[6] Batini, C., Barone, D., Garasi, M.F., Viscusi, G.: Design and Use of ER Repositories: Methodologies and Experiences in eGovernment Initiatives. In: Embley, D.W., Olivé, A., Ram, S. (eds.) ER 2006. LNCS, vol. 4215, pp. 399–412. Springer, Heidelberg (2006)

[7] Batini, C., Scannapieco, M.: Data Quality: Concepts, Methodologies and Techniques. Springer, Heidelberg (2006)

[8] Duchateau, F., Bellahsene, Z.: Measuring the Quality of an Integrated Schema. In: Parsons, J., Saeki, M., Shoval, P., Woo, C., Wand, Y. (eds.) ER 2010. LNCS, vol. 6412, pp. 261–273. Springer, Heidelberg (2010)

[9] Akoka, J., Comyn-Wattiau, I.: Entity-relationship and object-oriented model auto-matic clustering. Data & Knowledge Engineering 20, 87–117 (1996)

[10] Shoval, P., Danoch, R., Balabam, M.: Hierarchical entity-relationship diagrams: the model, method of creation and experimental evaluation. Requirements Engineering 9, 217–228 (2004)

[11] Castano, S., De Antonellis, V.D., Fugini, M.G., Pernici, B.: Conceptual schema analysis: techniques and applications. ACM Trans. Database Syst. 23, 286–333 (1998)

[12] Campbell, L.J., Halpin, T.A., Proper, H.A.: Conceptual schemas with abstractions making flat conceptual schemas more comprehensible. Data & Knowledge Engineering 20, 39–85 (1996)

[13] Tavana, M., Joglekar, P., Redmond, M.A.: An automated entity-relationship clustering algorithm for conceptual database design. Information Systems 32, 773–792 (2007)

[14] Simperl, E., Sure, Y.: The Business View: Ontology Engineering Costs. In: Hepp, M., Leenheer, P., Moor, A., Sure, Y., Sheth, A. (eds.) Ontology Management, vol. 7, pp. 207–225. Springer, US (2008)

[15] Moody, D.L.: Theoretical and practical issues in evaluating the quality of conceptual models: current state and future directions. Data & Knowledge Engineering 55, 243–276 (2005)

[16] Hepp, M.: Possible Ontologies: How Reality Constrains the Development of Relevant Ontologies. IEEE Internet Computing 11, 90–96 (2007)

[17] Christiaens, S., Leenheer, P., Moor, A., Meersman, R.: Ontologising Competencies in an Interorganisational Setting. In: Hepp, M., Leenheer, P., Moor, A., Sure, Y., Sheth, A. (eds.) Ontology Management, vol. 7, pp. 265–288. Springer, US (2008)

[18] Keet, C.M.: Enhancing comprehension of ontologies and conceptual models through abstractions. In: AI*IA 2007: Proceedings of the 10th Congress of the Italian Association for Artificial Intelligence on AI*IA 2007 (2007)

[19] Dahchour, M., Pirotte, A., Zimányi, E.: Generic Relationships in Information Modeling. In: Spaccapietra, S. (ed.) Journal on Data Semantics IV. LNCS, vol. 3730, pp. 1–34. Springer, Heidelberg (2005)

[20] Ambite, J.L., et al.: Simplifying data access: The energy data collection project. Computer 34(2), 47–54 (2001)

[21] Castano, S., De Antonellis, V.: Global viewing of heterogeneous data sources. IEEE Transactions on Knowledge and Data Engineering 13, 277–297 (2001), ST-Global viewing of heterogeneous data

An MDE-Based Synthesis of Aircraft Safety Models

Sébastien Maitrehenry[1], Sylvain Metge[1], Yamine Aït-Ameur[2], and Pierre Bieber[3]

[1] Airbus Operations S.A.S., Toulouse, France
{sebastien.maitrehenry,sylvain.metge}@airbus.com
[2] ENSEEIHT, Toulouse, France
yamine@enseeiht.fr
[3] ONERA, Toulouse, France
pierre.bieber@onera.fr

Abstract. Ensuring aircraft safety is a huge activity that requires a lot of effort. Today, it is still mostly made from a document management that is very complex and heavy to maintain. Thanks to a Model Driven Engineering (MDE) based approach, new processes and tools, based on models, are introduced at Airbus to overcome this difficulty. In this paper, we present an application of model transformation techniques to automatically generate safety models from design models made by the aircraft architects. We focus on the formalization of our model transformation and address some issues and chosen solutions, in particular concerning annotation, traceability and graph specialization.

Keywords: Model Driven Engineering (MDE), Domain-Specific Modeling Language (DSML), model transformation, annotation, traceability, EXPRESS.

1 Introduction

The development of complex systems, such as aircrafts or nuclear power plants, implies several modeling activities that produce different models expressed in different modeling languages. The choice of the modeling languages depends on the expertise of the engineers, the development practices, the modeled domain, the modeling point of view, the analyses to be performed, and so on. As a consequence, heterogeneous models are produced. This heterogeneity appears at the syntactic and semantic levels. Several attempts targeting the unification of such modeling languages have been proposed in the literature, such as UML and SysML. But, the deployment of these languages is still not a reality.

Other approaches integrate different heterogeneous models. They are based on the definition of several autonomous and local models, expressed in different modeling languages, which are related through model transformations. These transformations are able to embed the needed relevant parts of a source model in a target model. *Model Driven Engineering* (MDE) techniques are set up for this purpose.

This paper studies modeling activities of the second category in the context of aircraft design. Our work consists in deploying MDE-based approaches in order to handle safety analyses from design models. Model transformation is defined and analyses are conducted on real case studies. The paper starts with a presentation of the context

A. Abelló, L. Bellatreche, and B. Benatallah (Eds.): MEDI 2012, LNCS 7602, pp. 43–54, 2012.

and the objectives of our work. Section 3 presents our technical approach, based on the definition of two modeling domains. Then, in section 4, we formalize our approach on our use case. Finally, we describe our prototype on a concrete example.

2   Context of Our Work

Following an MDE approach, more and more models have been developed to assist aircraft design. Each model has its own specificities such as abstraction level (aircraft, system and equipment levels), formalism, simulation and calculation means, in order to match the increasing complexity of the aircraft systems. In order to better federate all activities at aircraft level, including safety ones, aircraft architects initiated recently the *Aircraft Level Functional Approach* (ALFA[1]) project. It aims to provide generic models describing how an aircraft is operated in term of human and aircraft activities. These activity diagrams represent the flow of operations and functions used during a flight scenario (see more details in section 2.1).

In the same way, currently at Airbus, the safety analyses of the aircraft systems are assisted by models defined within the formal language AltaRica [1] [2]. These safety models provide many great results such as failures simulation, fault tree generation and minimal cut set generation. And recently, this kind of technique has been recognized by the airworthiness authorities as a new means to ensure that the aircraft systems fulfil their safety requirements. This paper focuses on a new modeling approach to support one of the first safety activities in the design process: the *Functional Hazard Assessment* (FHA). The produced *Models for FHA* (MFHA) are based on the ALFA diagrams.

2.1   Structure of ALFA and MFHA Models

Both design and safety models have the same structure. They are based on three layers [3], as illustrated on the figure 1.

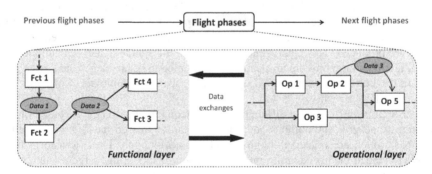

Fig. 1. Structure of operational and functional models

---

[1] Managed by Elio Vecchione, ALFA project leader, Aircraft Architect & Integrator at Airbus.

The functional layer describes the dependencies between functions, through data flow propagation. Here, a function is defined as an activity performed by the aircraft. Some data flows also behave as synchronization: the concerned functions wait for the data before being activated. Based on our case study of the Take-Off roll (TO), we identify three functions dedicated to the guidance of the aircraft on ground: *Sense guidance order*, *Control wheel steering* and *Control aerodynamic yaw*. The first function captures and computes guidance commands. The two last functions control the guidance thanks to the steering and the rudder respectively. We identify for example a dataflow, representing the computed *yaw order*, sent by the sensor function to the two functions which control the actuators.

The operational layer describes the operational flow in the same manner as for the functional flow. An operation is defined as an action performed by a human actor such as the pilots, the cabin crew, the maintenance crew and the passengers. In our case study, the function *Sense guidance order* received an order from the pilot thanks to the operation *Guide the aircraft on ground*. The operational and functional layers are linked by other data flows and synchronizations.

The last and top layer focuses on a specific flight phase, such as the Take-Off. Each flight phase is described by the functions and operations it contains. It is also defined by its interfaces with previous and next flight phases. By this way, we model flight scenario, adapted to the analyses we want to perform.

Some information needs to be added to this model skeleton in order to perform safety analyses. For example, a function is linked to some failure modes, describing which failures can occur for each function and how these failures propagate through the model. Our safety models are detailed in [3].

Furthermore, the ALFA models are designed within the CORE tool by the Vitech Corporation$^{©}$, which does not handle safety analyses. Once the ALFA models are enriched by the relevant information, they are described as MFHA models. The MFHA models are based on the same modeling structure, but they are made with the formal language AltaRica.

2.2   Objectives

As ALFA is a federative project, the ALFA models are used for other analyses domains such as aircraft performance studies. In the same way, the MFHA models should be managed by the ALFA project. Currently, the two models are informally connected or composed. Safety models are set up and provide feedbacks to the ALFA project (see figure 2).

The main objective of this paper is to provide, through MDE-based techniques, a formalization of the links between the ALFA and MFHA models, with the following requirements:

- formalize the connection of the ALFA and of the MFHA views;
- generate automatically the MFHA models from the ALFA models;
- keep the separation between the safety and the design models (no modification of the ALFA models nor of their notations, interface and views);
- trace the transformation in order to provide the safety results to the ALFA world.

3   Our Approach

The MDE approach advocates the use of a different modeling language, namely a Domain-Specific Modeling Language (DSML) [4] [5] [6], for each specific view.

3.1   ALFA and MFHA: Two DSMLs

In our case, we have to create a link between the design domain and the safety one. Therefore, we defined a DSML for the ALFA models and another for our MFHA models. The first step consists in producing the two corresponding metamodels. This step requires a perfect understanding and mastering of all concepts which compose the ALFA and MFHA models.

As a second step, a model transformation may be defined to establish correspondences between objects of the two different domains. Figure 2 gives a global overview of this approach.

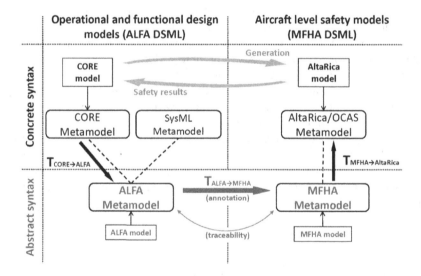

Fig. 2. Methodology of our model transformation

The left part of this figure represents the ALFA domain and the right part is dedicated to the MFHA domain. This figure also shows another important aspect of the MDE approach: the distinction between concrete and abstract syntax. As stated in the literature [4], each DSML is defined as the tuple $\{AS, CS^*, M_{AC}^*, SD^*, M_{AS}^*\}$ where AS is the abstract syntax, CS^* are the concrete syntaxes, M_{AC}^* the mapping of the abstract syntax to each concrete one, SD^* the semantic domains and M_{AS}^* the mapping of the abstract syntax to each semantic domain. The abstract syntax is the heart of the DSML definition. Indeed, even if different tools can be used for model design, the abstract model does not change for a specific domain. For example, the ALFA models are currently designed with the tool CORE only, but aircraft architects also work with SysML for other domain views.

Finally, figure 2 shows the three steps of the model transformation from CORE models to AltaRica ones, through the two abstract syntaxes for the ALFA and MFHA DSMLs: $T_{CORE \rightarrow ALFA}$, $T_{ALFA \rightarrow MFHA}$ and $T_{MFHA \rightarrow AltaRica}$. Even if the development of the two mappings $M_{AC}*$ corresponding to $T_{CORE \rightarrow ALFA}$ and $T_{MFHA \rightarrow AltaRica}$ is complex, due to syntax issues and limitations, the main difficulty of our approach is the transformation between the two domains through the abstract syntaxes.

3.2 $T_{ALFA \rightarrow MFHA}$: A Transformation by Metamodels

This paper focuses on the $T_{ALFA \rightarrow MFHA}$ transformation. Model transformation is the key component of the model-driven approach, representing the process of applying a set of transformation rules on one or more source models to produce target models.

At the top level, we distinguish two kinds of model transformation: the models-to-codes and the models-to-models transformations [4] [7]. In fact, transforming models to codes is the historical special case of the models to models transformation. It consists of writing an output file based on a defined grammar. This is the foundation of code generation, for example from UML to Java code [8]. The models-to-models transformation is more general and consists of applying a set of transformation rules that take one or more source abstract models as input to produce one or more target abstract models as output [7] [9]. $T_{ALFA \rightarrow MFHA}$ is a model-to-model transformation based on two different metamodels. $T_{ALFA \rightarrow MFHA}$ is also a horizontal transformation closely related to a refactoring: the structure of the source model is translated to another structure at the same abstraction level, preserving its behavior [3] [8] [10].

In order to make the transformation more modular and maintainable, we defined it as an instance of a transformation definition at the level of the metamodels. Such transformation definitions are also models, combining all generic transformation rules based on our DSMLs. They can be metamodeled to manipulate a particular generic grammar describing all possible transformation rules instead of describing specific built in transformation rules [7] [9]. Our transformation approach is shown on figure 2, without precising the used models and model transformation languages.

3.3 $T_{ALFA \rightarrow MFHA}$: The Model Annotation

Because the ALFA metamodel does not model all concepts needed to produce the safety models (refer to section 2.1), the transformation requires other information in addition to the source models. However, this information should not be integrated to the source models, in order to preserve the sources of any undesirable information from other domains. As a consequence, our models are annotated [11].

The information added by annotation is formalised in another data model: the annotation model. In many cases, the model transformation is based on a finite number of annotation types to produce the target models. For $T_{ALFA \rightarrow MFHA}$, we identify the failure modes, which can impact each function, and other data needed. However, if the target models evolve, we might add some new annotations or remove some others.

For example, if we analyze human errors in our safety models, we should add also failure modes for operations. Then the model of annotations needs to be modified. As for the transformation, if we wish a modular and maintainable annotation, we have to produce a generic metamodel of annotations. The left part of figure 3 shows the annotation metamodel. The right part illustrates an instance with the failure modes for functions. In this example, an annotation called *Failure_mode_Loss* is applied on two instances of element: *"Function_1"* and *"Function_5"*. A set of failure modes [*total_loss, partial_loss*] is attached to these two functions among all the defined failure modes.

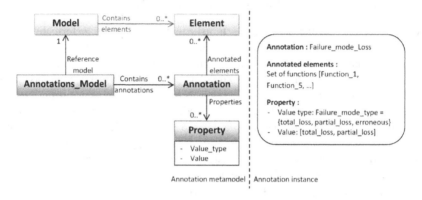

Fig. 3. Annotation Metamodel and one instance example (UML)

3.4   T_ALFA→MFHA : The Traceability

Traceability is another important issue of the MDE. During all the aircraft design process, we have to perform management, evolution and validation of our models, in particular for the design and safety requirements. Furthermore, some results, obtained from safety model analyses, have to be reported to the design. Therefore we need to keep trace of the relationship between the different models and their elements. Following [12] and [7], there are two strategies for storing and managing model-to-model traceability information: directly embedded in the model they refer to, or stored in a separate model. As stated previously, for modularity and maintainability reasons, we choose the second strategy. A metamodel of generic traceability concepts is defined, as for the transformation and the annotation, in order to easily handle different traces for the same model transformation [13]. However dedicated traceability offers also a great advantage thanks to its more precise definition and specificities: the possibility to add constraints and verify some chosen properties. Drivalos and al. [12] present a traceability approach which aims to be generic without losing the precision of a case-specific traceability model.

4   Formalization of Our Approach

In order to perform endogenous transformations [10], the EXPRESS data modeling language has been chosen to describe ALFA and MFHA models, metamodels and model transformations.

4.1   Formalization Language: Express

The EXPRESS language has been defined in the frame of the Standard for Exchange Product model data (STEP) project [14] [15]. Originally, it aims to represent data models in the engineering area but it is now widely used for other data modeling problems. The major advantage of this formal language is its completeness since it offers the capability to model structural, descriptive and behavioral semantics.

This integration avoids the use of different modeling languages that will require mappings between the different models, such as UML combined with a constraint declaration environment like OCL.

The EXPRESS language is based on the notion of ENTITY (see table 1 in section 4.2.1) to structure the data by abstraction. EXPRESS is object oriented: an entity is similar to a class, supporting the definition of specific constraint rules. A second part of EXPRESS models is dedicated to procedures, functions and global constraint rules, defined by a procedural part close to imperative programming languages. [15] provides more details about the definition of this language.

4.2   ALFA and MFHA Models Are Graphs

ALFA and MFHA models look like hierarchical graphs (hypergraphs). Therefore, both models are formalised as specialization of such graphs. A generic model of graphs is defined and reused by specialization. When specialised, DSML specific properties are added (see figure 4 below).

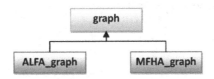

Fig. 4. Specialization of graph to ALFA and MFHA models (UML)

We find a lot of such graph specialization in the literature. The most basic is the graph specialization to trees [16].

Hypergraph Description

A graph G is defined as a pair (V, E) where V is a set of nodes and E a set of edges. Each edge in E is a pair (vx,vy) of vertices in V [16]. This structure is enriched in order to handle graphs with an arbitrarily deep hierarchical structure: the hypergraphs [17] [18] [19].

Figure 5 represents the metamodel of a hierarchical graph based on hypernodes we have modelled in EXPRESS. A graph contains at least one node/hypernode (relationship *nodes*) and may contain edges (relationship *edges*). An edge has exactly an initial node (relationship *init*) and a final node (relationship *final*). Some nodes are hypernodes and contain exactly one subgraph (relationship *sub_graph*). Figure 5 also shows the inverse relationship, marked *(inv)*. For example, the inverse relationship of edges is *in_graph*, modeling the graph where each edge is defined.

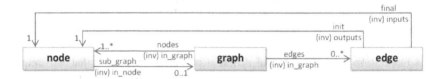

Fig. 5. UML diagram modeling subgraph-based hierarchical graph (UML)

An extract of the EXPRESS code modeling the concept of node is given in table 1.

Table 1. Express code: ENTITY node

```
ENTITY node ABSTRACT SUPERTYPE;
   sub_graph : OPTIONAL graph;
DERIVE
   next : SET OF node := next_nodes(SELF.outputs);
   previous : SET OF node := previous_nodes(SELF.inputs);
INVERSE
   in_graph : graph FOR nodes;
   inputs : SET OF edge FOR final;
   outputs : SET OF edge FOR init;
WHERE
   rule1 : SELF.sub_graph.level :=: SELF.in_graph.level+1;
END_ENTITY;
```

We can also add constraint rules to our definition in order to limit the scope of our model of graph to ALFA and MFHA views. In particular, all our ALFA and MFHA models are directed and connected (global rules).

ALFA and MFHA Models as Graph Specializations
The hierarchical graph specialization to ALFA and MFHA models is depicted on figure 6. All elements which compose the ALFA models (functions, operations and

data flows) are specialized graph nodes. The edges of the ALFA models, named links, are specialized graph edges with a *link_type* and a *name*.

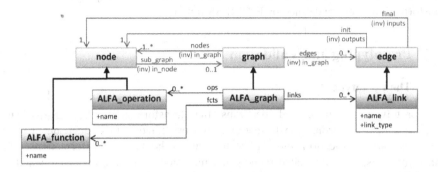

Fig. 6. ALFA models defined as graphs (UML)

The specialized MFHA models follow the same structure as the ALFA models.

4.3   From ALFA Models to MFHA Models: The $T_{ALFA \to MFHA}$ Transformation

The model transformation $T_{ALFA \to MFHA}$ is formalized, by reification, as an entity (table 2). This transformation is based on the source model (relationship *source*), the annotation on the source model (relationship *annotation*) and the traces of the transformation (relationship *traces*). We notice that the resulting trace from the transformation may also be an input for this transformation, as shown in [11]. During the transformation execution, the trace represents the set of already transformed objects at execution time, allowing to verify, for example, that an object is not transformed twice.

Table 2. Entity transformation

```
SCHEMA T_ALFA_TO_MFHA;

REFERENCE FROM ALFA_GRAPH;
REFERENCE FROM MFHA_GRAPH;
[...]
ENTITY transformation;
    source : ALFA_graph;
    annotation : ALFA_graph_annotation;
    traces : SET OF trace;
DERIVE
    target : MFHA_graph := transform_graph(SELF);
END_ENTITY;
[...]
END_SCHEMA;
```

The target model (relationship target) is derived by the *transform_graph* function. Subgraphs are similarly treated by creation of sub-transformations, with the same transformation rules, annotation and set of traces. In our current experimentations, the transformation rules are defined by EXPRESS functional code.

5   Prototyping and Validation

5.1   The Prototype

The prototype we developed performs the transformations $T_{ALFA\rightarrow MFHA}$ and $T_{MFHA\rightarrow AltaRica}$. The second transformation is not presented in this paper, but it is an important part in order to achieve good tests and validate the transformations. The transformations, with associated models and metamodels, have been manipulated in the ECCO toolkit, which support EXPRESS models verification and instantiation.

$T_{ALFA\rightarrow MFHA}$ consists in a generation of all MFHA nodes from each ALFA node, regardless of the transformation order. The MFHA nodes are created with their interface and their entering and exiting links. Thanks to traceability, verification of the link existence is performed. Indeed, a link may be already created from the node located at the other end. In this case, the link is simply upgraded. Then, optionally new nodes are created, such as activation ports, which are not in the ALFA models but needed for the MFHA models. At this time, the graph is completely transformed. Finally, all MFHA nodes are searched to identify those described by subgraph. For each subgraph the same transformation method is applied.

Table 3 shows an instances file of a simple example, which models one operation (#2), one function (#3) and one data flow (#4) from the operation to the function. The top part of table 3 shows the instances of the ALFA model (#1). The instance #7 represents an annotation on the ALFA function (instance #3).

Table 3. Instances files

```
#1=ALFA_GRAPH((#2),(#3),(#4),(#5,#6));
#2=ALFA_OP('Guide_aircraft_on_ground');
#3=ALFA_FCT('Sense_guidance_order');
#4=ALFA_DATAFLOW('Guidance_command');
#5=ALFA_LINK(#2,#4,.data_out.);
#6=ALFA_LINK(#4,#3,.data_trigger.);
#7=ANNOTATION_FAILURE_MODE_LOST(#3,.failure_mode_type.,(.total_loss.);
#1'=MFHA_GRAPH((#2'),(#3'),(#4'),(#5',#6'));
#1''=TRACE_GRAPH_TO_GRAPH(#1,#1');
[...]
#3'=MFHA_FCT('Sense_guidance_order',(.total_loss.),[...]);
#3''=TRACE_FCT_TO_FCT(#3,#3');
[...]
```

The second part of the table shows the result of the model transformation $T_{ALFA \rightarrow MFHA}$. Instances of MFHA elements are created for all instances of ALFA elements. A trace (#1'' and #3'') is also created between the source and target elements. The MFHA function #3' takes into account the annotation #7.

5.2   Validation

During our experiments, we noticed among others that there are two kinds of annotated data: those which might have a direct link with other design data and those very specific to the safety domain. It highlights two remarks about annotations.

- Firstly, the dependencies between existing design data and some of our annotated data are not formalized. For instance, the annotation includes an assessment of the efficiency of each function, whereas this efficiency should be related to the existing performance attribute in the ALFA world. This problem shows that annotating is not the suitable solution in this case. This can be solved in two ways: the evolution, after feedback, of the ALFA metamodel, in order to include concretely the annotated data as a derived attribute, or the use of existing data instead of the annotated data.
- The second remark concerns the automatic generation of the MFHA models. Because of the safety annotated data, the aircraft architects cannot generate and exploit the safety models without the support of safety analysts. Therefore, model generation is only partial, but, as the model analyses need a strong safety expertise, we do not identify this as a limitation, but as a reinforcement of the teamwork design and safety.

6   Conclusion

This paper presented an application of MDE techniques in order to manage the mapping between two engineering domains: the aircraft architecture and the safety domain. The results are encouraging because they respond to a large extent to the identified model transformation issues in the frame of the ALFA project. In particular, we improve the general method, applicable for all domain views (including safety), when developing new models based on the ALFA ones. We reinforce the federative aspect of ALFA by well separating the different domains and the formalization of the connection, thanks to generation rules defined at metamodel level and traces in the transformation. However, because of the annotations, the model transformation is only semi-automatic.

Currently our prototype is not completely modular and easily maintainable because the transformation rules are built thanks to a procedural function. Modeling the transformation rules will be the main part of future development. Because of tool certification issues, our prototype is not dedicated to become an industrial tool for use by safety analysts and aircraft architects. However we expect that this prototype allows formalising the specification of the future tool.

References

1. Arnold, A., Griffault, G., Point, G., Rauzy, A.: The AltaRica formalism for describing concurrent systems. Fundam. Inf. 40(2-3), 109–124 (2000)
2. Point, G., Rauzy, A.: AltaRica – Constraint automata as a description language. European Journal on Automation 33(8-9), 1033–1052 (1999)
3. Maitrehenry, S., Metge, S., Bieber, P., Ait-Ameur, Y.: Toward Model-Based Functional Hazard Assessment at Aircraft Level. ESREL (2011)
4. Jézéquel, J.-M., Combemale, B., Vojtisek, D.: Ingénierie Dirigée par les Modèles, des concepts à la pratique. Ellipse Edition Marketing S.A., 17–23, 35–41 (2012)
5. Taha, W.: Domain-Specific Languages. In: International Conference on Computer Engineering Systems ICCES, pp. xxiii–xxviii (2008)
6. Spinellis, D.: Notable design patterns for domain-specific languages. The Journal of Systems and Software 56, 91–99 (2001)
7. Czarnecki, K., Helsen, S.: Classification of Model Transformation Approaches. In: OOPSLA 2003 Workshop on Generative Techniques in the Context of Model-Driven Architecture (2003)
8. Sendall, S., Kozaczynaki, W.: Model Transformation – the Heart and Soul of Model-Driven Software Development. IEEE Sofware (2003)
9. Yuehua, L.: A Model Transformation Approach to Automated Model Evolution. PhD Thesis (2007)
10. Mens, T., Czarnecki, K., Van Corp, P.: A Taxonomy of Model Transformation. In: International Workshop on Graph and Model Transformation, GraMoT (2005)
11. Vara, J.-M., Bollati, V.-A., Vela, B., Marcos, E.: Leveraging Model Transformations by means of Annotation Models. In: Jouault, F. (ed.) MtATL, pp. 96–102 (2009)
12. Drivalos, N., Paige, R., Fernandes, F., Kolovos, D.: Towards Rigorously Defined Model-to-Model traceability. In: Traceability Workshop, European Conference in Model Driven Architecture, EC-MDA (2008)
13. Vanhoff, B., Van Baelen, S., Joosen, W., Berbers, Y.: Traceability as Input for Model Transformations. In: Traceability Workshop, European Conference in Model Driven Architecture, EC-MDA (2007)
14. Dehainsala, H., Jean, S., Xuan Dung, N., Pierra, G.: Ingénierie dirigée par les modèles en Express : un exemple d'application. Premières Journées sur l'Ingénierie Dirigée par les Modèles (2005)
15. Ait-Ameur, Y., Pierra, G., Sardet, E.: An object oriented approach to represent behavioural knowledge inheterogeous information systems. In: International Conference on Object-Oriented Information Systems (OOIS), pp. 315–339 (2000)
16. Courcelle, B.: Introduction à la théorie des graphes : Définitions, applications et techniques de preuves. Université Bordeaux 1, LaBRI (2004)
17. Drewes, F., Hoffmann, B., Plump, D.: Hierarchical Graph Transformation. Journal of Computer and System Sciences 64, 249–283 (2002)
18. Chimani, M., Gutwenger, C.: Algorithms for the Hypergraph and the Minor Crossing Number Problems. In: Tokuyama, T. (ed.) ISAAC 2007. LNCS, vol. 4835, pp. 184–195. Springer, Heidelberg (2007)
19. Poulovassilis, A., Levene, M.: A Nested-Graph Model for the Representation and Manipulation of Complex Objects. ACM Trans. on Information Systems 12, 35–68 (1994)

Integrating a Formal Development for DSLs into Meta-modeling

Selma Djeddai[1], Martin Strecker[1], and Mohamed Mezghiche[2]

[1] IRIT (Institut de Recherche en Informatique de Toulouse)
Université de Toulouse
Toulouse, France
[2] LIMOSE, Université de Boumerdès
Faculté des Sciences
Boumerdès, Algeria

Abstract. Formal methods (such as interactive provers) are increasingly used in software engineering. They offer a formal frame that guarantees the correctness of developments. Nevertheless, they use complex notations that might be difficult to understand for unaccustomed users. On the contrary, visual specification languages use intuitive notations and allow to specify and understand software systems. Moreover, they permit to easily generate graphical interfaces or editors for Domain Specific Languages (DSLs) starting from a meta-model. However, they suffer from a lack of precise semantics. We are interested in combining these two complementary technologies by mapping the elements of the one into the other.

In this paper, we present a generic transformation process from functional data structures, commonly used in proof assistants, to Ecore models and vice-versa. This translation method is based on Model-Driven Engineering and defined by a set of bidirectional transformation rules. These rules are presented with an illustrating example, along with an implementation in the Eclipse environment.

Keywords: Model Driven Engineering, Model Transformation, Formal Methods, Verification.

1 Introduction

Formal methods (such as interactive proof assistants [13, 19]) are increasingly used in software engineering to verify the correctness of software. They have a solid formal basis and a precise semantics, but they use complex notations that might be difficult to understand for unaccustomed users. On the contrary, Model Driven Engineering (MDE) [3,15] supplies us with visual specification languages as class diagrams [8] that use intuitive notations. They allow to specify, visualize, understand and document software systems. However, they suffer from lack of precise semantics. We are interested in combining these two complementary technologies by mapping the elements of the one into the other, using an MDE-based transformation method.

A. Abelló, L. Bellatreche, and B. Benatallah (Eds.): MEDI 2012, LNCS 7602, pp. 55–66, 2012.

One possible scenario is to define the abstract syntax of a Domain Specific Language (DSL) [20] to be used in the context of a formal verification, and then to generate a corresponding `Ecore` meta-model to be able to use an MDE-based tool chain for further processing. Inversely, the meta-model can than be modified by an application engineer and serve as basis for re-generating the corresponding data types. This operation may be used to find a compromise between the representation of the client's wishes on the meta-model and functional data structures used in the proof. Furthermore, the meta-model can be used to easily generate a textual (or graphical) editor using Xtext (respectively GMF:Graphical Modeling Framework) facilities [9]. This work constitutes a first step towards using MDE technology in an interactive proof development. The illustrating example is a Java-like language enriched with assertions developed by ourselves for which no off-the-shelf definition exists [2]. It constitute a sufficiently complex case study of realistic size for a DSL.

This paper is structured as follows: we start in Section 2 by comparing our approach with related work. Then, we present some preliminaries, to introduce the main components of our work. Section 4 constitutes the technical core of the article; it describes a translation from data models used in verification environments, to meta models in `Ecore` and backwards. We then illustrate the methodology with an example in Section 5, before concluding with perspectives of further work.

2   Related Work

EMF (Eclipse Modeling Framework) [4] models are comparable to Unified Modeling Language (UML) class diagrams [8]. For this reason, we are interested in the mappings from other formal languages to UML class diagrams and back again. Some research is dedicated to establishing the link between these two formalisms. We cite the work of *Idani & al.* that consists in a generic transformation of UML models to B constructs [11] and vice-versa [10]. The authors propose a metamodel-based transformation method based on defining a set of structural and semantic mappings from UML to B (a formal method that allows to construct a program by successive refinements, using abstract specifications).

Similarly, there is an MDE based transformation approach for generating Alloy (a textual modeling language based on first order logic) specifications from UML class diagrams and backwards [1,16].

These methods enable to generate UML components from a formal description and backwards but their formal representation is significantly different from our needs: functional data structures used in proof assistants.

Additionally, graph transformation tools [5, 7] permit to define source and target meta-models all along with a set of transformation rules and use graphical representations of instance models to ease the transformation process. However, the verification functionality they offer is often limited to syntactic aspects and does not allow to model deeper semantic properties (such as an operational semantics of a programming language and proofs by bisimulation).

Our work aims at narrowing the gap between interactive proof and metamodeling by offering a way to transform data structures used in interactive provers to metamodels and vice-versa.

3   Preliminaries

3.1   Methodology

Model Driven Engineering is a software development methodology where the (meta-)models are the central elements in the development process. A metamodel defines the elements of a language. The instances of theses elements are used to construct a model of the language. A model transformation is defined by a mapping from elements of the source meta-model to those of the target metamodel. Consequently, each model conforming to the source meta-model can be automatically translated to an instance model of the target meta-model. The Object Management Group (OMG) [14] defined the Model Driven Architecture (MDA) standard [12], as specific incarnation of the MDE.

We apply this method in order to define a generic transformation processes from datatypes (used in functional programming) to Ecore models and backwards. Figure 1 shows an overview of our approach. For the first direction of the translation, we derive a meta-model of datatypes starting from an EBNF representation of the datatype definition grammar [13]. This meta-model is the source meta-model of our transformation. We also define a subset of the Ecore meta-model [9] to be the target meta-model. In order to perform this transformation, we defined a set of transformation rules (detailed in Section 4.1) that maps components of the meta-model of datatypes to those of Ecore meta-models.

We use the mapping between the constructs of the two meta-models to define the reverse direction transformation rules in order to ensure the bidirectionality of the rules. Bidirectionality [17] is one of the desired options of MDE-based transformations. Indeed, assuming we start from a source model M_S, then we perform a transformation using a function f to get a target model M_T. It is important to derive an equivalent model to M_S, as a result to the application of f^{-1} on M_T. Such a feature requires more restrictions on the Ecore models. The transformation in the reverse direction is given in Section 4.2. The transformation rules of the two sides have been successfully implemented in an application presented with an illustrating example (see Section 5).

3.2   The Datatype Meta-model

Functional programming supplies us with a rich way to describe data structures. However, since some features cannot be supported by Ecore, we have only defined a subset that contains the essential element composing datatypes. Figure 2 depicts the datatype meta-model that is constructed from a subset of datatype's declarations grammar [13, 18]. We point out that we are mainly interested in data structures. It correspond to the static part of the proofs. Except for the case of accessors, the functions are not treated.

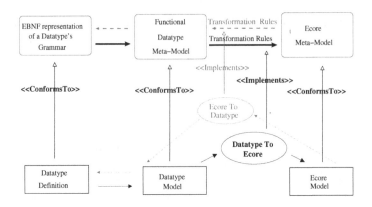

Fig. 1. Overview of the Transformation Method

A *Module* may contain several *Type Definitions*. Each *Type Definition* has a *Type Constructor*. It corresponds to the data types' name. It is also composed of at least one *Constructor Declaration*. These declarations are used to express variant types: a disjoint union of types. *Type declarations* have names, it is the name of a particular type case. It takes as argument some (optional) *type expressions* which can either represent a *Primitive Type* (int, bool, float, etc.) or also a data type defined previously in the *Module*. The *list* notation introduces the predefined data structure for lists. The *type option* describes the presence or the absence of a value. The *ref* feature is used for references (pointers).

We enriched the type definition grammar with a specific function named *Accessor*. It is introduced by the annotation (*@accessor*). It allows assigning a name to a special field of the type declaration. This element is essential for the transformation process, its absence would lead to nameless structural features.

Representing Generic Types in Functional Programming. Parameterized types are important features in functional programming. They are used to express polymorphic data structures. They are comparable to generics in Java and templates in C++. They permit to build different data structures that accept any kinds of values. Each definition of a parameterized type is formed of a *Type Constructor* and a set of *Type Parameters*. The type expressions then can contain a previously defined parameterized type or one of the specified parameters.

3.3   The Ecore Meta-model

Our destination meta-model is a subset of the Ecore meta-model. Ecore is the core language of EMF [4]. It allows to build Java applications based on model definitions and to integrate them as Eclipse plug-ins.

The Meta Object Facility (MOF) set by the OMG defines a subset of UML class diagram [8]. It represents the meta-meta-model of UML. Ecore is comparable to MOF but quite simpler. They are similar in their ability to specify classes, structural and behavioral features, inheritance and packages.

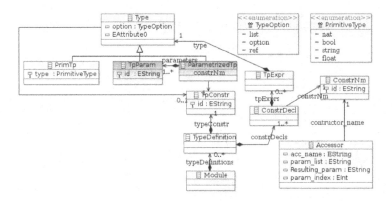

Fig. 2. Datatype Meta-model

We use in the implementation of our approach Eclipse and its core language Ecore. However, it would be possible to choose other solutions [5]. This choice is due to the place that take Eclipse for the development and metamodeling. Also, it offers a wide range of highly integrated tools.

Figure 3 represents a subset of the Ecore language. It contains essentially the elements needed for our transformation process. Its main components are:

- The EPackage is the root element in serialized Ecore models. It encompasses EClasses and EDataTypes.
- The EClass component represents classes in Ecore. It describes structure of objects. It contains EAttributes and EOperations.
- The EDataType component represents the types of EAttributes, either predefined (types: Integer, Boolean, Float, etc.) or defined by the user. There is a special datatype to represent enumerated types EEnum
- EReferences is comparable to the UML Association link. It defines the kinds of the objects that can be linked together. The containment feature is a Boolean value that makes a stronger type of relationships. When it is set to true, it represents a whole/part relationship.

Representing Generics with Ecore. To support parametric polymorphism Ecore was extended. Actually, parameterized types and operations can be specified, and types with arguments can be used instead of regular types. the changes are represented in the Ecore meta-model mainly in two new classes EGenericType and ETypeparameter (they are distinguishable from the others on the Figure 3 by the green color). A parametrized type is then represented by a simple EClass that contains one or more ETypeParameters. An EGenericType represents an explicit reference to either an EClassifier or an ETypeParameter (but not both at the same time). The eTypeArguments reference is used to contain the EGenericTypes representing the type parameters.

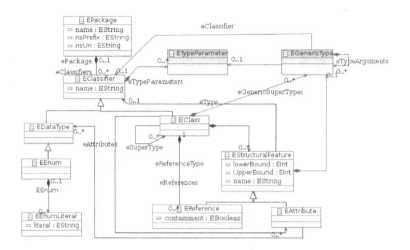

Fig. 3. Simplified subset of the `Ecore` Meta-model

4   From Datatypes to Meta-models and Back Again

This part details the automatic translation from functional datatypes to meta-models, and backwards. The first direction of translation is further developed in Section 4.1 while the reverse direction is presented in Section 4.2. The transformation implementation is spelled out and illustrated by an example(Section 5).

4.1   From Datatypes to Meta-models

Table 1 presents the principal patterns of our recursive translation function. The translation process is detailed and described in a formal notation in [6]. In this table, we proceed with a description by example. The first column represents possible instances of data types, while the second contains the transformation rule applied for this kind of patterns. As for the last one, it shows the results of applying the rule on the instance of data type.

Transforming Generics. In case the datatype definition is polymorphic, , it is translated into the representation of generics in the meta-model. It consists in creating an `EClass` to represent the *Type Constructor* and for each type parameter creating an `ETypeParameter` related to the `EClass` via the `eTypeParameters` reference. Notice that we have to create an `EGenericType` for each class and type parameters (related to their `EGenericType` via `eTypeArguments`) each time we intend to use the `EClass` as a generic. Then, for each *constructor declaration*:

- Create an `EClass` to represent the *Constructor Declaration* which have the same `ETypeParameters` as the *Type Constructor* one.
- Setting its `eGenericSuperType` referring to the generic type representing the *Type Constructor* `EClass`.

Table 1. Table illustrating the transformation rules from datatypes to meta-models

Datatypes	translation description	**Ecore** Diagram Components
datatype *tpConstr*= *Cn1* |*Cn2* |... | *CnN*	Datatypes composed only of *constr-names* (without *typexprs*) are translated to **EEnums** which are usually used to model enumerated types in **Ecore**.	
datatype *tpConstr* = *Cn* **of nat**∗ **string** ∗ ...∗ **bool**	When the datatype is formed of only one constructor, it is translated to an **EClass**. The EClass name is the name of the type constructor. Primitive types give **EAttributes** in the **EClass**. The names of the attributes are given by the accessors names.	
datatype *tpConstr* = *Cn1* **of string** |*Cn2* **of nat** |... |*CnN* **of bool**	When constructor declarations are composed of more than one constructor declaration containing type expressions, a first **EClass** is created to represent the type constructor (*tpConstr*). Then, for each constructor, an **EClass** is created too, and inherits from the *tpConstr* one.	
datatype *tpConstr*= *Cn* **of** *tpConstr2*	When a type expression contains a type which is not a primitive type, the latter has to be previously defined in the Isabelle [13] *theory*. Then, a containment link is created between the current **EClass** and the **EClass** referring to the datatype *tpConstr2*, and the multiplicity is set to 1.	
datatype *tpConstr*= *Cn* **of** *tpConstr2* **option**	The type expression *type* **option** is used to express whether a value is present or not. It returns **None**, if it is absent and **Some** value, if it is present. This is modeled by adopting the cardinality to **0..1**.	

Table 1. *(continued)*

Datatypes	translation description	**Ecore** Diagram Components
datatype *tpConstr=* Cn of *tpConstr2* list	The type expressions can also appear in the form of a *type* list. In this case the multiplicity is set to 0...*.	![TpConstr, Cn, accNm, TpConstr2, 0..*]
datatype *tpConstr=* Cn of *tpConstr2* ref	The last case that we deal with, is *type* ref which is used to represent pointers. It is translated to references without containments.	![TpConstr, Cn, accNm, TpConstr2, 1]

When it comes to use these generics to type **EStructuralFeatures**, we are faced with two scenarios. First, when the type expression is a *type parameter*; the **EStructuralFeature** is typed with an **EGenericType** referring to the **ETypeParameter** of the containing **EClass**. If instead the *type expression* corresponds to a *parameterized type* with *type parameters* it is typed with an **EGenericType** representing the **EClass** with **ETypeParameters**.

To clarify this process, we use the example below. It consists in transforming a parametrized *tree* data type. It has two parameters: the first corresponds to the type of leaves and the second to the type of values contained in a Node. The result after performing the translation is displayed in the arborescent **Ecore** editor. The **EGenericTypes** are not explicitly represented in the **EcoreDiagram**.

Example:

datatype *('s,'t) tree =*
    Leaf 't
    |Node 's (('s,'t) tree) (('s,'t) tree)

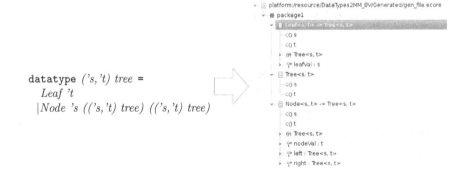

4.2   From Meta-models to Datatypes

To perform the reverse direction of the transformation, we draw heavily on the mapping performed on the forward translation(Section 4.1). In our view, it is important to successfully implement a function that is the inverse of the one from datatype to meta-models. Indeed, the possibility of composing the two functions, apply them on a model and find an equivalent model is paramount. Even if it leads us to set some additional restrictions on the meta-model. For example, the meta-models that contain inheritance of classes on more than one level (degree) (a class that inherits of a class that inherits from another one etc.) are not supported by our transformation rules. Table 2 summarizes the most important features taken into account in our transformation process and their translation in the functional world.

Table 2. Table summarizing the transformation rules from Ecore meta-models to datatypes

Ecore Components	Functional Data Structures
EClass	*Type Constructor + Constructor*
EAttribute	*Type Expression (Primitive Type)*
EReference	*Type Expression*
EEnum	*Type Constructor + Constructors* (without *Type Expressions*)
EEnumLiteral	*Constructor* (without *Type Expression*)
Inheritance	*Type Constructor + Constructors + Type Expressions*
EGenericType	*Parameterized Datatype*
ETypeParameter	*Type Parameter*

5   Implementation and Example

To illustrate our approach, we decided to take as example a description of a DSL. It is a Java-like language enriched with assertions developed by ourselves for which no off-the-shelf definition exists. It represents a real-time dialect of the Java language allowing us to carry out specific static analyses of Java program (details are described in [2]). Our approach is implemented using the Eclipse environment.

Performing the translation for the whole language description would generate a huge metamodel that couldn't be presented in the paper. We thus choose to present a only an excerpt of it, corresponding to a method definition. Figure 4 shows a datatype taken from the Isabelle *theory* where the verifications were performed. A method definition (in our DSL) is composed of a method declaration, a list of variables, and statements. Each method declaration has an access modifier that specifies its kind. It also has a type, a name, and some variable declarations. The *stmt* datatype describes the statements allowed in the method body: Assignments, Conditions, Sequence of statements, Return and the annotation statement (for time annotations). In this example we use Booleans, integers, strings for types and values.

$$
\begin{aligned}
datatype\ binop\ &= BArith|\ BCompar|\ BLogic \\
datatype\ value\ &= BoolV\ bool|\ IntV\ int \\
&\ \ |StringV\ string|\ VoidV \\
datatype\ binding &= Local|\ Global \\
datatype\ var\ &= Var\ binding\ string \\
datatype\ expr\ &= Const\ value \\
&\ \ |VarE\ var \\
&\ \ |BinOperation\ binop\ expr\ expr \\
datatype\ tp\ &= BoolT|\ IntT|\ VoidT|\ StringT \\
datatype\ stmt\ &= Assign\ var\ expr \\
&\ \ |Seq\ stmt\ stmt \\
&\ \ |Cond\ expr\ stmt\ stmt \\
&\ \ |Return\ expr \\
&\ \ |AnnotStmt\ int\ stmt \\
datatype\ accModifier &= \\
Public\ &|Private\ |Abstract|Static\ |Protected\ |Synchronized \\
datatype\ varDecl &= \\
VarDecl\ &(accModifier\ list)\ tp\ int \\
datatype\ methodDecl &= \\
MethodDecl\ &(accModifier\ list)\ tp\ string\ (varDecl\ list) \\
datatype\ methodDefn &= \\
MethodDefn\ &methodDecl\ (varDecl\ list)\ stmt
\end{aligned}
$$

Fig. 4. Datatypes in Isabelle

This part of the *Isabelle theory* was given as input to the implementation of our translation rules presented in Section 4.1. The resulting `Ecore` diagram is presented in Figure 5. As it is shown on the figure, data type definitions built only of type constructors (*Tp, AccModifier, Binop, Binding*) are treated as enumerations in the metamodel. Whereas *Datatype MethodDecl* composed of only one constructor derive a single class. As for type expressions that represent a list of types (like *accModifier list* in *varDecl*), they generate a structural feature in the corresponding class and their multiplicities are set to *(0...*)*. The result of type definitions containing more than one constructor and at least a type expression (*stmt* and *expr*) is modeled as a number of classes inheriting from a main one. Finally, the translation of the *int, bool* and *string* types is straightforward. They are translated to respectively `EInt`, `EBoolean` and `EString`.

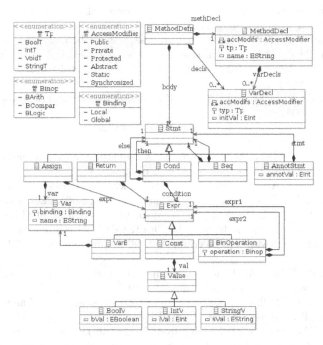

Fig. 5. Resulting Ecore Diagram after Transformation

6   Conclusion

Our work constitutes a first step towards a combination of interactive proof and Model Driven Engineering. We have presented an MDE-based method for transforming data type definitions used in proof assistants to Class diagrams and back again, using bidirectional transformation rules.

The approach is illustrated with the help of a Domain Specific Language developed by ourselves. It is a Java-like language enriched with annotations. Starting from data type definitions, set up for the semantic modeling of the DSL we have been able to generate an EMF meta-model. The generated meta-model is used for documenting and visualizing the DSL, it can also be manipulated in the Eclipse workbench to generate a textual editor as an Eclipse plug-in.

We are working on coupling our work with the generation of provably correct object oriented code from proof assistants.

References

1. Anastasakis, K., Bordbar, B., Georg, G., Ray, I.: UML2Alloy: A Challenging Model Transformation. In: Engels, G., Opdyke, B., Schmidt, D.C., Weil, F. (eds.) MOD-ELS 2007. LNCS, vol. 4735, pp. 436–450. Springer, Heidelberg (2007)

2. Baklanova, N., Strecker, M., Féraud, L.: Resource sharing conflicts checking in multithreaded Java programs (April 2012), http://www.irit.fr/~Nadezhda.Baklanova/papers/FAC2012.pdf

3. Bézivin, J.: Model Driven Engineering: An Emerging Technical Space. In: Lämmel, R., Saraiva, J., Visser, J. (eds.) GTTSE 2005. LNCS, vol. 4143, pp. 36–64. Springer, Heidelberg (2006)

4. Budinsky, F., Brodsky, S.A., Merks, Ed.: Eclipse Modeling Framework. Pearson Education (2003)

5. de Lara, J., Vangheluwe, H.: Using AToM³ as a meta-case tool. In: ICEIS, pp. 642–649 (2002)

6. Djeddai, S., Mezghiche, M., Strecker, M.: A case study in combining formal verification and model-driven engineering. In: Ermolayev, V., Mayr, H.C., Nikitchenko, M., Spivakovsky, A., Zholtkevych, G., Zavileysky, M., Kobets, V. (eds.) ICTERI, CEUR Workshop Proceedings, vol. 848, pp. 275–289 (2012), CEUR-WS.org

7. Ehrig, K., Ermel, C., Hänsgen, S., Taentzer, G.: Generation of visual editors as Eclipse plug-ins. In: Proceedings of the 20th IEEE/ACM International Conference on Automated Software Engineering, ASE 2005, pp. 134–143. ACM, New York (2005)

8. France, R.B., Evans, A., Lano, K., Rumpe, B.: The UML as a formal modeling notation. Computer Standards & Interfaces 19(7), 325–334 (1998)

9. Gronback, R.C.: Eclipse Modeling Project: A Domain-Specific Language (DSL) Toolkit. Addison-Wesley, Upper Saddle River (2009)

10. Idani, A.: UML Models Engineering from Static and Dynamic Aspects of Formal Specifications. In: Halpin, T., Krogstie, J., Nurcan, S., Proper, E., Schmidt, R., Soffer, P., Ukor, R. (eds.) Enterprise, Business-Process and Information Systems Modeling. LNBIP, vol. 29, pp. 237–250. Springer, Heidelberg (2009)

11. Idani, A., Boulanger, J.-L., Philippe, L.: A generic process and its tool support towards combining UML and B for safety critical systems. In: Hu, G. (ed.) CAINE, pp. 185–192. ISCA (2007)

12. Kleppe, A.G., Warmer, J., Bast, W.: MDA Explained: The Model Driven Architecture: Practice and Promise. Addison-Wesley Longman Publishing Co., Inc., Boston (2003)

13. Nipkow, T., Paulson, L., Wenzel, M.: Isabelle/HOL. A Proof Assistant for Higher-Order Logic. LNCS 2283. Springer, Heidelberg (2002)

14. OMG. Meta Object Facility (MOF) Core v. 2.0 Document (2006)

15. Selic, B.: The pragmatics of model-driven development. IEEE Software 20(5), 19–25 (2003)

16. Shah, S.M.A., Anastasakis, K., Bordbar, B.: From UML to Alloy and Back Again. In: Ghosh, S. (ed.) MODELS 2009. LNCS, vol. 6002, pp. 158–171. Springer, Heidelberg (2010)

17. Stevens, P.: A Landscape of Bidirectional Model Transformations. In: Lämmel, R., Visser, J., Saraiva, J. (eds.) GTTSE 2007. LNCS, vol. 5235, pp. 408–424. Springer, Heidelberg (2008)

18. Caml programming language website, http://caml.inria.fr

19. Coq proof assistant website, http://coq.inria.fr/

20. van Deursen, A., Klint, P., Visser, J.: Domain-specific languages: An annotated bibliography. SIGPLAN Notices 35(6), 26–36 (2000)

Transformation of Spatio-Temporal Role Based Access Control Specification to Alloy

Emsaieb Geepalla, Behzad Bordbar, and Joel Last

University of Birmingham, School of Computer Science, UK
{E.M.E.Geepalla,B.Bordbar,jxl745}@cs.bham.ac.uk

Abstract. The recent advances in wireless networks, mobile applications and pervasive computing has prompted an urgent need for the creation of Access Control systems which takes into consideration the location of the user and the time of access. Such systems are even more complex than the conventional Access Control systems. Thus, the need arises for the analysis of the specification of such systems prior to the implementing of the systems. As a result, this paper proposes to use Alloy as a method of automated analysis of Spatio-temporal Role-Based Access Control models (STRBAC). To achieve this, this paper describes a method (AC2Alloy) that allows users to create STRBAC models and transforms them into the required Alloy code automatic, thus allowing for powerful analysis to take place using Alloy analyser utilizing SAT-Solvers. With the help of an example, we show how AC2Alloy convert STRBAC model to Alloy model and verify the resulting model using the Alloy analyser to identify an erroneous design.

Keywords: MDA, Alloy, Spatio-Temporal Access Control.

1 Introduction

The recent advances in mobile computing and other technologies involved in remote accessing of resources has increased the demand for the creation of Access Control systems which take into consideration contextual information such as the location of the users and the time of access. Such information is essential for controlling various spatio-temporal sensitive applications, which rely on the Access Control mechanism in organisations. While spatial constraints limit the access of resources from a particular set of pre-defined locations, temporal constraints put restrictions on the time-limit for accessing these resources. In order to be adaptable to the requirements of such applications and technologies with both spatial constraint and temporal constraint, several Access Control models have been proposed [1], [2], [3], [6], [7], [9], [10].

STRBAC model is one of the Access Control models that have been presented to cater to the need of context information [10]. STRBAC model incorporates multiple rules, such as Role Hierarchy and Separation of Duties constraints. However, it is possible that the different rules of the model might result in conflicts. Existence of conflicting Access Control rules can be because of an error

A. Abelló, L. Bellatreche, and B. Benatallah (Eds.): MEDI 2012, LNCS 7602, pp. 67–78, 2012.

in the specification, resulting in an incorrect implementation of the system. On the other hand, it could be the case that stakeholders of the system are imposing conflicting demands. It is vital that these demands are resolved prior to the development of the system. In both cases, the key challenges are to identify the existence of such inconsistencies. However due to the complexity and size of modern systems, the discovery of such inconsistencies is a formidable task and cannot be carried out manually.

Alloy [5] has been used for analysis of Access Control specification [3], [4], [8] [16]. Alloy is supported by a tool called The Alloy Analyser which is an automated constraint solver that transforms the Alloy code into Boolean expressions, providing the analysis by its embedded SAT solvers [2], [5], [11]. For a small system the creation of model transformation between STRBAC model and Alloy could be mange manually, however due to the complexity and size of modern systems an automated transformation are required. This has promoted us to define a bespoke transformation from STRBAC to Alloy.

In this paper, we present a standalone Eclipse Plug-in application called AC2Alloy. AC2Alloy is a tool for integrating STRBAC and Alloy into a single tool. It enables the user to create STRBAC specification and conduct the analysis via Alloy. The proposed approach can be used in the early phases of the Access Control system development to analyse the design of a system. In particular, the system designer, who might only be familiar with STRBAC and XML, can use the simulation and analysis facilities provided by the Alloy, while he/she is not required to learn Alloy. The user of AC2Alloy has two options to enter the data into the tool. The first option is that the user can enter the STRBAC specification and the XML representation of the STRBAC is automatically generated. The second option is that the user can upload an XML representation of the STRBAC model. The XML representation is automatically transformed into Alloy model. To analyse the STRBAC model, the tool will automatically generate several Alloy checks, so that the user can execute them using Alloy Analyser.

The remainder of this paper is organised as follows. Section 2 provides a review of STRBAC model, Alloy and Model Driven Architecture (MDA). Section 3 describes the outline of our approach, which makes use of MDA techniques to transform from STRBAC to Alloy. In section 4 we introduce a simple example, which will be used to illustrate our approach. Section 5 reviews related work and the paper ends with conclusion.

2   Preliminaries

2.1   Spatio Temporal Role Based Access Control

Spatio-Temporal Role Based Access Control (STRBAC) model is one of the extensions of RBAC [15] that takes into consideration the location of the user and the time of access [10]. Our work is based on the STRBAC model presented on [10]. Due to space considerations, we do not consider some of the elements of STRBAC such as Session in this paper. However such extension can be added to our method.

Definition 1. *STRBAC specification: A STRBAC specification relies on the following sets U, R, P, T, L, RH, LH, URA, PRA, SoDR, SoDP, CC.*

– U, R, P, T, L are, respectively, finite non empty sets of Users, Roles, Permissions, Times and Locations.

– **User Role Assignment** (URA) is a relation defined on users set, roles set, times set and locations set, $URA \subseteq U \times R \times T \times L$.

– **Permission Role Acquire** (PRA) is a relation defined on roles set, permissions set, times set and locations set, $PRA \subseteq R \times P \times T \times L$.

– **Role Hierarchy** (RH) is a partial order on the set of roles which represents which role can inherit another role, $RH \subseteq R \times R \times T \times L$. RH could be unrestricted $rh(r_i, r_j)$, time dependent $rht(r_i, r_j, t)$, location dependent $rhl(r_i, r_j, l)$, or time and location dependent $rhtl(r_i, r_j, t, l)$.

– **Location Hierarchy** (LH) is a partial order on the set of locations which represents which location is inner-location to another location, $LH \subseteq L \times L$.

– **Separation of Duty over Roles** (SoDR) is a constraint over roles, which specifies that users should not assign to exclusive roles $sodr(r_i, r_j)$. SoDR can be unrestricted $sodr(r_i, r_j)$, time dependent $sodrt(r_i, r_j, t)$, location dependent $sodrl(r_i, r_j, l)$, or time and location dependent $sodrtl$ (r_i, r_j, t, l).

– **Separation of Duty over Permissions** SoDP is a constraint over permissions, which specifies the exclusive set of permission $sodp(p_i, p_j)$. SoDP could also be unrestricted $sodp(p_i, p_j)$, time dependent $sodpt(p_i, p_j, t)$, location dependent $sodpl(p_i, p_j, l)$, or time and location dependent $sodptl(p_i, p_j, t, l)$.

– **Cardinality Constraint** (CC) is a constraint over roles, which specifies the restriction on certain roles which can be assigned to a limited number of users. It could also be unrestricted $cc(r_i)$, time dependent $cct(r_i, t)$, location dependent $ccl(r_i, l)$, or time and location dependent $cctl(r_i, t, l)$.

To represent such models we make use of XML. The use of XML in security policies is not new. Ferriaolo et al. used XML and Schema languages to represent RBAC framework [15]. Another contribution proposed by Joshi et al is XML based RBAC policy framework X-RBAC [14]. A recent similar work presented by Mondal and Sural [13] is an XML based policy specification framework for a spatio-temporal RBAC model. For further details about STRBAC we refer the reader to [4], [10].

2.2 Alloy

Alloy is a language used for modelling and specification of object-oriented systems. It is based on first-order logic. Alloy allows analysis of the model via Alloy Analyser, which is SAT-Solver based [5]. Figure 1 presents a subset of Alloy metamodel adapted from [12]. For the purposes of this paper, we have not considered the whole features of Alloy language.

An Alloy model consists of a set of modules. Each module consists of one or more paragraphs. The paragraphs of a module can be either **signatures**, **facts**, **predicates**, or **check** commands. **Signatures** are used to define new sets of atoms. Constraints such as **facts** and **predicates** are used to specify constraints and expressions. A `fact` is a constraint that always holds and it consists of an optional name, while a `predicate` is a constraint that can be instantiated in different contexts and has a name. Commands such as `check` are an instruction to the Alloy Analyser to perform an analysis. A `check` command helps to search for a counterexample showing that the model is inconsistent. For further details on Alloy and the meaning of elements in Figure 2, we refer the reader to [5].

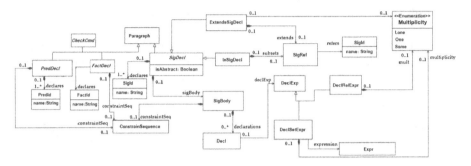

Fig. 1. A Subset of Alloy Metamodel adapted from [12]

2.3 Model Driven Architecture (MDA)

The method adopted in this paper makes use of Model Driven Architecture (MDA) [17] techniques for defining and implementing the transformations from models captured in the XML representation of STRBAC into Alloy. Central to the MDA is the notion of metamodels [36]. A metamodel defines the elements of a language, which can be used to represent a model of the language. In the MDA a model transformation is defined by mapping the constructs of the metamodel of a source language into constructs of the metamodel of a destination language. Then every model, which is an instance of the source metamodel, can be automatically transformed to an instance of the destination metamodel with the help of a model transformation framework [17].

3 Model Transformation from STRBAC to Alloy

This section presents a brief description to our work. An outline of our approach is presented in Figure 2. In order to use MDA methodology to transform a STR-BAC model to Alloy, we need to construct a metamodel for STRBAC to specify the elements of STRBAC that will be mapped to the subset of Alloy features presented in Figure 1. To conduct the model transformation, a set of transformation rules has been defined. The rules map various elements of the source metamodel into the elements of the destination metamodel. The rules have been implemented into an Eclipse Plugin application called AC2Alloy. If a STRBAC model is provided as input to AC2Alloy, an Alloy model is automatically generated by the tool, and then the produced Alloy model could be analysed using Alloy Analyser.

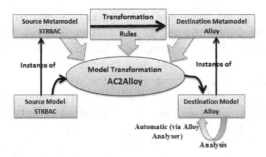

Fig. 2. The Outline of The approach

Figure 3 depicts a simplified metamodel we constructed for STRBAC. It shows that STRBAC relies on the elements Users, Roles, Permissions, Times, Locations, URA, PRA, RH, LH, SoDR, SoDP and CC. The Users, Roles, Permissions, Times and Locations are sets of atoms that represent users, roles, permissions, times and locations. User Role Assignment (URA) and Permission Role Acquire (PRA) are sets of relations between the atoms. Role Hierarchy (RH), Location Hierarchy (LH), Separation of Duty over Roles (SoDR), Separation of Duty over Permission (SoDP) and Cardinality (CC) are constraints over the atoms and relations. For further details on elements STRBAC appearing in Figure 3 we refer the reader to the STRBAC specification presented in [4].

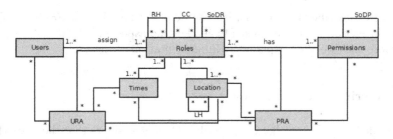

Fig. 3. Simplified STRBAC Metamodel

3.1   Transformation Rules

This section presents a brief overview of the transformation rules from STRBAC to Alloy. It provides an informal correspondence between elements of the STRBAC and Alloy. Figure 4 depicts the correspondence between the model elements in the STRBAC and Alloy. It shows that there are twelve transformation rules used to define how various elements of STRBAC map to Alloy. These rules can be divided into three categories. The first category contains five rules which are: T1, T2, T3, T4 and T12. All the rules from this category are straight-forward as it will be seen in section 4.1. The rules T1, T2, T3 and T4 transform Users, Permissions, Times and Locations respectively into Alloy **signatures**, while T12 transforms the Cardinality constraints into checks. The second category contains a combination of five rules: T5, T6, T7, T8 and T9. The rule T5 transforms the Roles into snippets of Alloy, consisting of signatures which embody both fact and predicates. The Transformation rules T6, T7, T8 and T9 inject new assignment information to the predicates within the Alloy code for Roles, so that the predicates will be updated. The third category contains two transformation rules T10 and T11. The rule T10 maps Separation of Duty over Permissions (SoDP) to predicates that specify the constraints and checks that will be used to verify the constraints. The rule T11 maps Separation of Duty over Roles (SoDR) to predicates that specify the constraints and checks that will be used to verify the constraints.

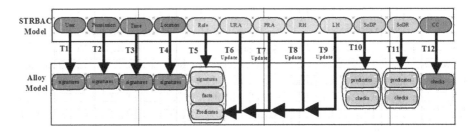

Fig. 4. Overview on the Transformation Rules and their Relationship

We shall describe these rules with the help of example of a *SECURE Bank System* in section 4.1 to demonstrate challenging aspects of the transformation, but before that we shall explain the implementation of the tool.

3.2   Description of AC2Alloy

Figure 5 depicts a screen shot of the tool AC2Alloy. It shows that there are three panels. The left panel allows the user to add the elements of STRBAC or modify them. The middle panel produces XML representation and readable English descriptions for the specification of STRBAC uploaded. It also allows users to upload XML files. The third panel presents automatic creation of Alloy model. It also allows the user to modify the model if needed before the analysis is applied.

AC2Alloy makes use of several distinct technologies. First it transforms the description of STRBAC specification to XML representation at the Eclipse GUI level. Second, it uses JAXB to take the XML representation of the STRBAC specification and produces Java objects for the STRBAC specification. It then makes use of Simple Transformer (SiTra) to transform the generated Java objects for STRBAC to Alloy code. SiTra implements a tracing mechanism by producing a hash-map between Access Control specification and Alloy. This hashing can be used to transform the outcome of the analysis conducted by Alloy back to Access Control representation so that the user can see the outcome of the analysis.

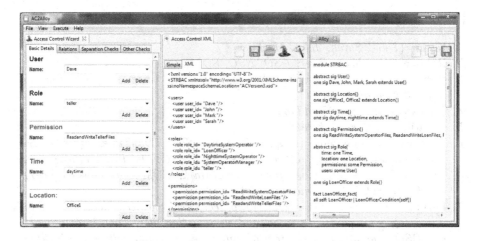

Fig. 5. Snap Shot of AC2Alloy

4   Example: *SECURE Bank System (SBS)*

This section provides a brief introduction to the *SECURE Bank System (SBS)* adapted from [10] to demonstrate the transformation from STRBAC to Alloy via AC2Alloy. The specification of *SBS* is as follow:

1. The organisation has four users: Dave, Sarah John and Mark.
2. The organisation consists of five roles: teller, loan officer, DayTime system operator (DSO), NightTime system operator (NSO), system operator manager (SOM).
3. The user Dave can have the role teller only at office1 during DayTime.
4. The user Sarah can have the role loan officer only at office1 during DayTime.
5. The user John can have the role DSO only at office2 during DayTime and the role NSO only at office2 during NightTime.
6. The user Mark can have the role SOM only at office1 or office2 during DayTime.
7. The teller can read and write teller files only from office1 during DayTime.
8. The loan officer can read and write loan files only from office1 during DayTime.
9. The DayTime system operator (DSO) can read and write system operator file from office2 during the DayTime.
10. The NightTime system operator (NSO) can read and write system operator file from office2 during NightTime.
11. The system operator manager (SOM) rights consist of all rights from teller, loan officer, DayTime system operator and NightTime system operator.
12. The same person cannot read and write teller files and loan files at office1 during the DayTime.

The above specification could be represented using STRBAC as follows:

1. Users={*Dave, Sarah, John, Mark*}
2. Roles={*teller, loan officer, DSO, NSO, SOM*}
3. Permissions={*read and write teller files, read and write loan files, read and write system operator file*}
4. Times={*DayTime, NightTime*}
5. Locations={*ofiice1, office2*}
6. User Role Assignment={ura*(Sarah, loan officer, DayTime, office1)*, ura *(Dave, teller, DayTime, office1)*, ura*(John, DSO, DayTime, office2)*, ura *(John, NSO, NightTime, office2)*, ura*(Mark, SOM, DayTime, office1)*, ura*(Mark, SOM, DayTime, office2)*}
7. Permission Role Acquire={pra*(loan officer, read and write loan files, Day-Time, office1)*, pra*(teller, read and write teller files, DayTime, office1)*, pra*(DSO, read and write system operator file, DayTime, office2)*, pra*(NSO, read and write system operator file, NightTime, office2)*}
8. Role Hierarchy={rh*(SOM, teller)*, rh*(SOM, loan officer)*, rh*(SOM, DSO)*, rh*(SOM, NSO)*}
9. Separation of Duty Over Permissions={sodptl*(read and write teller files, read and write loan files, DayTime, office1)*}

4.1 Transformation of the SECURE Bank System to Alloy: Description of the Transformation Rules

In order to apply our approach to the *SECURE Bank System* example, we need to follow the following three steps. The first step is to translate the STRBAC specification to XML representation. The second step is to translate the XML representation of STRBAC to Alloy. Last but not least, the produced Alloy model will be analysed using Alloy Analyser. Here we will assume that the specifications of STRBAC have been uploaded and transformed into XML representations correctly. The rules T1, T2, T3 and T4 presented in section 3.1 transform the sets of Users, Permissions, Times and Locations in the *SECURE Bank System* to Alloy signatures as follows:

Rule T1: abstract sig Users{}
   one sig Dave, Sarah, John, Mark extends Users{}
Rule T2: abstract sig Permissions{}
   one sig ReadWriteTellerFiles, ReadWriteLoanFiles,
      ReadWriteSystemOperatorFiles extends Permissions{}
Rule T3: abstract sig Times{}
   one sig DayTime, NightTime extends Times{}
Rule T4: abstract sig Locations{}
   one sig office1, office2 extends Locations{}

Marking a signature as an abstract signature means it has no atoms except those belonging to its extension. For example, the abstract sig User {} has no atoms except *(Dave), (Sarah), (John)* and *(Mark)*.

As described in section 3.1 the transformation rules T5, T6, T7, T8 and T9 are considered as a combination of rules. For example, when the rules T6, T7, T8 and T9 are not applied yet, the rule T5 will transform the Roles *(teller)* and *(system operator manager (SOM))* to Alloy signatures, facts and predicates as can be seen from the following Alloy code.

<u>Rule T5:</u> abstract sig Role{ time: one Times, location: one Locations,
       permissions: some Permissions, users: some Users}
  one sig teller extends Role{}
  fact tellerFact{all self:teller | tellerCondition[self]}
  pred tellerCondition[self:teller]{((self.permissions=none)&&
     (self.location=none)&&(self.time=none)&&(self.users= none))}
  one sig SOM extends Role{}
  fact SOMFact{all self:SOM | SOMCondition[self]}
  pred SOMCondition[self:SOM]{((self.permissions=none)&&
     (self.location=none)&&(self.time=none)&&(self.users=none))}

The four relations inside the abstract signature body are empty sets because of the use of the constant none. This means that there is no assignment between users, roles, permissions, times and location at this stage. When the rule T6 is applied, the User Role Assignment will be transformed, so that the predicates within the Alloy code for Roles will be injected with new assignment information. For example, the transformation of ura*(Mark, SOM, DayTime, office1)* will inject the predicate SOMCondition with new assignment information and the updated predicate will be as follows:

<u>Rule T6:</u> pred SOMCondition[self:SOM]{((self.permissions=none)&&
     (self.location=none)&&(self.time=none)&&(self.users=Mark))}

The rule T7 presented in section 3.1 transforms the Permission Role Acquire. It also updates the predicates within the Roles code with new assignment information. For example, the transformation of pra*(teller, read and write teller files, DayTime, office1)* will inject the predicate tellerCondtion with new assignment information.

<u>Rule T7</u> pred tellerCondition[self:teller]{
     ((self.permissions=ReadWriteTellerFiles)&&(self.location=none)&&
     (self.time=none)&&(self.users= none))}

The rule T8 presented in section 3.1 is used to transform the Role Hierarchy and it also updates the Roles predicates. For example, the transformation of rh*(SOM, teller)* will update the predicate SOMCondition with new assignment information as can be seen in the following Alloy predicate.

<u>Rule T8</u> pred SOMCondition[self:SOM]{
     ((self.permissions=ReadWriteTellerFiles)&&(self.location=none)&&
     (self.time=none)&&(self.users= Mark))}

Because of the Role Hierarchy the senior role *(system operator manager (SOM))* inherits the permission *(read and write teller files)* which is assigned by the junior role *(teller)*.

The transformation rules T10 and T11 presented in section 3.1 transform the Separation of Duty over Roles and Separation of Duty over Permissions into predicates and checks. For example, the rule T10 will transform sodptl *(read and write teller files, read and write loan files, DayTime, office1)* into the following Alloy predicate and check. The check was created to validate the predicate.

Rule T10 pred SODP[p1, p2:Permission, l:Location, t:Time]{all r1:Role |
    ((p1 in r1.permissions)&&(t in r1.time)&&(l in r1.location))⇒
    ((p2 not in r1.permissions)&&(t in r1.time)&&(l in r1.location))}
SoDP1 :check {SODP[ReadandWriteTellerFiles, ReadandWriteLoanFiles,
    DayTime, Office1]}

The rules T9, T11 and T12 are not presented here because the specification of the *SECURE Bank System* does not have any Location Hierarchy, Separation of Duty over Roles or Cardinality constraints. Due to shortage of space we have not extended the specification of *SECURE Bank System* to consider such information.

4.2 Analysis of the SECURE Bank System via Alloy

The analysis of the produced Alloy model will be carried out using the latest version of the Alloy Analyser (version 4.2 release candidate 3, which can be downloaded from http://alloy.mit.edu/alloy/download.html). The generated Alloy model for the *SECURE Bank System* contains only one check that is presented in section 4.1. This check was create to find out whether or not there is a role that has the two conflicted permissions *(read and write teller files)* and *(read and write loan files)* during the *(DayTime)* and at location *(office1)*.

The execution of the Alloy shows that Alloy Analyser picked up a counterexample as depicted in Figure 7. The Figure shows that the violation has arisen because the role *(system operator manager (SOM))* has both conflicted permissions *(read and write teller files)* and *(read and write loan files)* while at location *(office1)* and during the time *(DayTime)*. This is because the role *(SOM)* is a senior role to the roles *(tellers)* and *(loan officer)*, and the role *(teller)* is assigned to the permission *(read and write teller files)*, while the role *(loan officer)* is assigned to the permission *(read and write loan officer files)* during the *(DayTime)* at the *(office1)*, so that, the role *(SOM)* can inherit the two conflicted permissions.

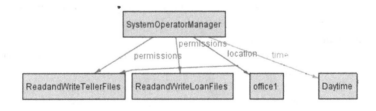

Fig. 6. Inconsistency Caused by SoDP Identified by Alloy

5   Related Work

There is a plethora of works using automated techniques for analysis of Access Control policies such as [3], [4], [8], [16]. Some of the approaches do not particularly address STRBAC, like RBAC-96 [2]. In [8], Jackson et al. demonstrate how to use Alloy to verify the internal consistency of RBAC-96 Schema. This work has demonstrated that using Alloy has sufficient expressive power to prescribe implementation independent specification of Access Control systems. However this work has not considered the environment information such as time and location that is needed in many applications today. Additionally, the transformation between RBAC and Alloy was carried out manually.

In [3], Samuel et al. illustrates how GST-RBAC can be specified in Alloy. They describe how the various GSTRBAC rules, that is, user-role assignment, role-permission assignment, and user-role activation, can be specified by Alloy. However, the transformation between GST-RBAC was carried out manually. Manual transformation is tedious and might pose errors especially when the Access Control specification is very large.

The analysis of STRBAC models with Alloy has been extensively studied by Indrakshi et al. [4], [16]. In our earlier work [16] with Indrakshi, we used UML2Alloy to automate the transformation between STRBAC and Alloy. However, UML2Alloy [12] is a general purpose tool that translates UML Class Diagrams enriched with OCL constraints to Alloy. Furthermore, the transformation of STRBAC using UML2Alloy requires the user to be familiar with OCL, so that he/she could manually write the statements that he/she wants to validate. In contrast, AC2Alloy was developed specifically for the transformation of STRBAC to Alloy, so that there is no need for the user to be an OCL expert. In addition, our tool AC2Alloy will automatically generate several checks to analyse the produced Alloy model.

6   Conclusion

This paper describes a method that supports automatic transformation between STRBAC specification and Alloy Model. STRBAC to Alloy transformation is based on several transformation rules. The presented approach is fully automated, as the user provides only the input STRBAC specification, and then the automated transformation will generate an XML representation for that specification and finally an Alloy model will be created. The suggested transformation is implemented in an Eclipse Plug-in called AC2Alloy. The paper also makes the use of Alloy Analyser to analyse the Alloy code produced by AC2Alloy. The suggested method and the involving transformation are described with the help of an example.

References

1. Chen, H.-C., Wang, S.-J., Wen, J.-H., Huang, Y.-F., Chen, C.-W.: A Generalized Temporal and Spatial Role-Based Access Control Model. JNW 5(8), 912–920 (2010)

2. Ray, I., Toahchoodee, M.: A Spatio-temporal Access Control Model Supporting Delegation for Pervasive Computing Applications. In: Furnell, S.M., Katsikas, S.K., Lioy, A. (eds.) TrustBus 2008. LNCS, vol. 5185, pp. 48–58. Springer, Heidelberg (2008)

3. Samuel, A., Ghafoor, A., Bertino, E.: A Framework for Specification and Verification of Generalized Spatio-Temporal Role Based Access Control Model. Technical report, Purdue University, CERIAS TR 2007-08 (February 2007)

4. Toahchoodee, M., Ray, I.: On the Formal Analysis of a Spatio-Temporal Role-Based Access Control Model. In: Proceedings of the 22nd Annual IFIP WG 11.3 Working Conference on Data and Applications Security, pp. 17–32 (July 2008)

5. Daniel, J.: Software Abstractions Logic, Language, and Analysis. The MIT Press, Cambridge (2006)

6. Bertino, E., Catania, B., Damiani, M.L., Perlasca, P.: GEO-RBAC: a spatially aware RBAC. In: Proceedings of the 10th ACM Symposium on Access Control Models and Technologies, Stockholm, Sweden, pp. 29–37 (June 2005)

7. Chen, L., Crampton, J.: On Spatio-Temporal Constraints and Inheritance in Role-Based Access Control. In: Proceedings of the 2008 ACM Symposium on Information, Computer and Communications Security, Tokyo, Japan, pp. 205–216 (March 2008)

8. Zao, J., Wee, H., Chu, J., Jackson, D.: RBAC Schema Verification Using Lightweight Formal Model and Constraint Analysis (2002), http://alloy.mit.edu/publications.php

9. Joshi, J.B.D., Bertino, E., Latif, U., Ghafoor, A.: A Generalized Temporal Role-Based Access Control Model. IEEE Transactions on Knowledge and Data Engineering 17(1), 4–23 (2005)

10. Ray, I., Toahchoodee, M.: A Spatio-temporal Role-Based Access Control Model. In: Proceedings of the 21st Annual IFIPWG11.3 Working Conference on Data and Applications Security, Redondo Beach, CA, pp. 211–226 (July 2007)

11. Jackson, D., Schechter, I., Shlyakhter, I.: Alcoa: the alloy constraint analyzer, In: International Conference on Software Engineering (ICSE 2000), pp. 730–733 (2000)

12. Bordbar, B., Anastasakis, K.: UML2Alloy: A tool for lightweight modelling of Discrete Event Systems. In: IADIS International Conference in Applied Computing 2005, Algarve, Portugal, pp. 209–216 (2005)

13. Mondal, S., Sural, S.: XML-based policy specification framework for spatiotemporal access control. In: SIN 2009, pp. 98–103 (2009)

14. Bhatti, R., Joshi, J., Bertino, E., Ghafoor, A.: Access Control in Dynamic XML-Based Web-Services with X-RBAC. In: Proceedings of ICWS 2003 (2003)

15. Ferraiolo, D.F., Richard Kuhn, D., Chandramouli, R.: Role Based Access Control, 2nd edn (2007)

16. Ray, I., Bordbar, B., Toahchoodee, M., Anastasakis, K., Georg, G.: Ensuring Spatio-Temporal Access Control for Real-World Applications, pp. 978–971. ACM, doi: 978-1-60558-537-6/09/06

17. Akehurst, D.H., Bordbar, B., Evans, M.J., Howells, W.G.J., McDonald-Maier, K.D.: SiTra: Simple Transformations in Java. In: Wang, J., Whittle, J., Harel, D., Reggio, G. (eds.) MoDELS 2006. LNCS, vol. 4199, pp. 351–364. Springer, Heidelberg (2006)

Modular Ontological Warehouse
for Adaptative Information Search

Nesrine Ben Mustapha[1,2], Marie-Aude Aufaure[1],
Hajer Baazaoui Zghal[2], and Henda Ben Ghezala[2]

[1] Ecole Centrale Paris, MAS Laboratory, Business Intelligence Team,
Grande Voie des Vignes 92295 Chatenay-Malabry
{nesrine.ben-mustapha,marie-aude.aufaure}@ecp.fr
[2] Laboratory RIADI, ENSI, La Manouba, Tunisia
hajer.baazaouizghal@riadi.rnu.tn}@riadi.rnu.tn

Abstract. With the growth rate of information repositories, most of the
current research effort are focusing on improving the accuracy in search-
ing and managing information (especially text data), because of lacking
of adaptive knowledge representation to the information content of these
systems. Besides, domain knowledge is evolving and consequently, ontologies should be automatically built and extended. Thus, introducing
modularity paradigm in ontology engineering is now important to tackle
scalability problems. In this paper, we address the problem of representing modular ontologies at an abstract level that can improve the
traditional information system with higher efficiency, in the context of
previous work aiming at integrating ontology learning in traditional Information Retrieval systems on the web. The contribution consists in
organizing ontology elements into semantic three-layered ontology warehouse (topic classification, domain knowledge representation, and module representation). The proposed model has been applied for textual
content semantic search and relevance improvement has been observed.

Keywords: ontology, modularization, knowledge representation,
graph-based modeling.

1 Introduction

With the growth rate of information volume, information access and knowledge
management has become challenging traditional Knowledge management Sys-
tem.Domain ontologies are a fundamental form of knowledge representation of a
domain of knowledge or discourse [8]. A well constructed ontology can help developing knowledge-based information search and management system, such as
search engine, automatic text classification system, content management system,
etc, in a more effective way. Then, the performance of these systems depends
mainly on two aspects: *Domain vocabulary coverage* of ontologies and *Adaptive ontology representation* for search process over textual data. These aspects
have been explored in an anterior work [1] that aims to propose an enhanced

A. Abelló, L. Bellatreche, and B. Benatallah (Eds.): MEDI 2012, LNCS 7602, pp. 79–90, 2012.
© Springer-Verlag Berlin Heidelberg 2012

multi-domain information search system based on the integration of incremental ontology learning from users'queries and web snippets. Consequently, additional considerations that have to be taken into account, deal with the scalability of incrementally ontology built and the contextual information requested to use these fragment for Information Retrieval process (IR) (especially query expansion, document filtering and classification). The main objective of this work consists in proposing a modular model of ontologies built from texts, with the aim of using them for multi-domain search on the web. To manage distributed knowledge in a dynamic setting, we need flexible knowledge representation formalism to meet the following requirements for information retrieval: How to define an ontology module according to the semantic of content ? and How to organize multiple networked, distributed and dynamic ontologies over multiple knowledge domains?

In this paper, we propose an abstract syntax of modular knowledge by three-layered ontology warehouse (topic classification, domain knowledge representation, module representation) and definitions of functions that supports navigation between the proposed layers. Since, graphs are a natural way of representing and modeling heterogeneous information in a unified manner (structured, semi-structured and unstructured ones), we choose this structure to design ontology modules. The main advantage of using graphs resides in its dynamic aspect and its capability to represent relations, even multiple ones, between objects. It also facilitates querying and analysis using graph operations. Besides, as there exists a bijection between graphs and DL formalism, then we choose graph-based formalism as an abstract level of modular knowledge representation. The proposed graph-based model is inspired from *attributed Typed graph model* [10] in order to specify a modular ontology by an *attributed typed graph of ontologies*. In the remainder of this paper, we present in section 2, an overview of related works on ontology modularization. Section 3 describes the proposed modular ontological knowledge warehouse for knowledge management systems where formal definitions of the different layers are explained. Section 4 describe the main statements of the graph-based formalism of modular ontologies. Section 5 is concerned with the applicative case study of the proposed model with the aim of performing an adaptative information search. In the next section, the experimentation results are discussed. Finally, we conclude and discuss directions for future research.

2   Modular Ontologies

Modularization, in its generic meaning, denotes the possibility to perceive a large knowledge repository (an ontology) as a set of modules, i.e. smaller repositories that, in some way, are parts of and compose the whole knowledge [5]. Several definitions of Ontology Module (OM) exist in the literature, but a consensual definition has not been proposed yet. Therefore, according to some recent works, an OM is seen as a reusable component of ontology, which is self-contained but bears definite relationships to other OM. On one hand, scalability and interpretability of ontologies have generated a significant interest in ontology modularization from the semantic web community. Recently, there has been growing interest in the topic of modularity in ontology engineering [5]. Ontology modularization is the process of decomposition of a whole large ontology into smaller modules. As a motivating example, we consider one of the case studies of the *NeOn project* [6]- a fishery case study in the Food and Agriculture Organization (FAO) of the United Nations (UN). This case study aims to improve the interpretability of FAO information systems in the fishery domain. However, since the definition for a good software module is already vague [13], there is no well-define agreement on the criteria for decomposing an ontology into modules. Indeed, the definition of an ontology module is still subjective [7] and is intrinsically dependent on the application scenario in which ontology modules are used. Moreover, a number of studies have been carried out on different aspects of modularization (languages for modular ontologies, techniques to extract modules from ontologies, etc.). However, these elements tend to be disconnected from each other and no complete modularization framework have yet been proposed for ontologies, within the application scenario of information retrieval. For these reasons, we intend to provide a generic formalism that would gather under a common framework the different aspects of ontology modularization with the aim of meeting the requirements of a broad range of information search application on the web.

On the other hand, in order to tackle problems of mapping between the ontology vocabulary and the terms contained in textual results, vocabulary and distributional information of terms extracted from documents should be taken into account in ontology representation. In this context, the experimental results of the thesis of Stein L.Tomassen [12] has confirmed the underlying assumption of this work that aims to propose the construction of vectors of context (a set of weighted terms extracted from documents) with the use of domain ontology. The use of these vectors could improve the accuracy of these search systems based on ontologies of 10 %. This proves that the terms extracted from documents indexed can contextualize the search and improve the accuracy of results, despite the presence of a domain ontology. Therefore, information on the distribution of terms in documents are important to be encapsulated in the ontology.

3 Modular Ontological Knowledge Warehouse for Knowledge Management Systems

Multi-domain ontology modeling is a crucial point due to terminological ambiguity, semantic heterogeneity, knowledge scalability and reuse. In this section, we have defined a modular knowledge representation model, based on three layers (topic level, ontology layer and Module layer).The first layer represents the topic ontology which is a based on a taxonomy of thematic concepts. Each topic is linked to a set of modular domain ontologies (second layer). The second layer represents a set of modular domain ontologies as a network of *Ontology modules* (OM). The third layer is made up with ontology modules definition. An ontology module is an ontology fragment that includes only the concepts and relations that are relevant for a granular knowledge on close concepts. Hence, it is possible to structure a user query by a conceptual graph made of concepts belonging to a same module. OM can share some concepts and some relations with other Ontology modules.

A Modular Knowledge Warehouse (τ) is defined as:

$$\tau = <\mathcal{T}, Mo_d, \mathcal{M}, \mathcal{R}, \sigma_o, \sigma_d > \tag{1}$$

Where:

- $\mathcal{T}$ is the topic ontology definition;
- Mo_d is the modular ontology definition;
- $\mathcal{M}$ is the set of module definition composing the modular ontology Mo_d;
- $\mathcal{R}$ is a set of Resources' URI;
- σ_o is a function associating to each thematic concept of the topic ontology ($\mathcal{CT}$), a modular ontology definition (Mo_d);
- σ_d is a function providing for each instance of module definition (Mo_d) with a set of resources ($\mathcal{R}$) (ie. Document URL, Product's URI..).

3.1   Topic Ontology Definition

In this ontology, concepts refer to categories of knowledge domain (Art, Business, Health, computer sciences, etc.) linked by mainly subsumption relationships, as proposed by the definition 2.

A **topic ontology** (T) is defined as:

$$T = <\mathcal{CT}, \mathcal{RT}, \sigma_o > \tag{2}$$

Where :

- $\mathcal{CT}$ is a class definition of topics (domain of knowledge);
- $\mathcal{RT}$ is the signature of an overlapping relationship between thematic concepts $\mathcal{CT}$;
- $\leq^{CT} : \mathcal{CT} \times \mathcal{CT}$ it is a partial order on thematic concepts CT which defines the hierarchy of $\mathcal{CT}$;
- σ_o is a function allowing the connection between topic layer and modular ontologies layer by associating to each thematic concept ($\mathcal{CT}$), a modular domain definition (MO$_d$).

This ontology doesn't contain any objects. Only concept and relation definitions are specified. Based on the given definition, an illustration of a topic ontology is described as following:

- $\mathcal{CT}$ = {"Medicine", "Sciences", "Arts", "Business", "E-Commerce", "Home", "Software", "Tourism" , "Health", "Internet", "Notebook", "Employment", "Diseases", "News", "Sport"}
- Examples of relations between thematic concepts are $\sigma_{\mathcal{R}}\mathcal{T}$(Medicine, Sciences) and $\sigma_{\mathcal{R}}\mathcal{T}$(Medicine, Health).
- σ_o(Medicine)="Medicine.owl"; σ_o(health)="health.owl"; σ_o(Sciences)="Sciences.owl", etc.

3.2 Modular Domain Ontology: Definition

Domain knowledge associated to each thematic concept of the topic ontology (such as human anatomy, human diseases, etc.) is specified by a composition of ontology fragments related to fine-grained areas (etc, head, neck and lung cancers etc.). However, most of existing ontologies follow a monolithic approach, which makes this representation impossible. In our case, a modular domain ontology is composed of modules and inter-module relations. We distinguish two types of relationships: taxonomic and conceptual ones. Because of the general structure of any domain ontology based on a hierarchy of concepts, we propose to define a taxonomic structure of modules by two types of composition: a static and a dynamic composition. The aggregation of ontological modules is called in the literature, "composition". Since the definition of ontological modules is based on the "pivotal concepts", it is possible to deduce the hierarchy of modules from taxonomic relationships between pivotal concepts, basin on an existing domain ontology. Thus, this composition is called "static" because it is based on the predefined hierarchy in the ontology used. Dynamic composition of ontology modules were explored in [11] with the aim of proposing an hierarchical classification of modules based on web-based similarity between pivotal concepts. Inter-module relations are defined using conceptual relations between concepts belonging to overlapped ontology modules. These relationships are characterized by connection interface.

A **modular domain ontology** (MO$_d$) is defined as:

$$MO_d =< \mathcal{ID}_{Mo}, \mathcal{M}_{i=1..n}, \mathcal{R}_o, \mathcal{H}_{\mathcal{M}}, \mathcal{R}_{\mathcal{M}} > \tag{3}$$

Where: $\mathcal{ID}_{Mo}$ is the identifier of the modular domain ontology; $\mathcal{M}_{i=1..n}$ is simply a set of module definitions (described by the formula 4) that are connected by external definitions; $\mathcal{R}_o$ is a set of roots of ontology modules; $\mathcal{H}_{\mathcal{M}}$ is a set of taxonomic relationships linking the set of roots $\mathcal{R}_o$ of Module definition ($\mathcal{M}$); $\mathcal{R}_{\mathcal{M}}$ is an external relation definition between ontology modules $\mathcal{M}$.

Example of Modular Ontology. An example of modular domain ontology "E-Commerce" is described in Figure 1.

This ontology is described by the following features:

- $\mathcal{ID}_{Mo}$="Ontology_ E-Commerce";
- The set of modules $\mathcal{M}_{i=1..4}$= "person_Module", "customer_Module", "product_Module","payment_Module";
- The set $\mathcal{R}_o$ of pivotal concepts=pivotalConcept_ person, pivotalConcept_ customer, pivotalConcept_ payment;
- Taxonomic inter-module relations are defined as followings:
  - $Racine\_E - commerce \leq^M person\_Module$;
  - $Racine\_E - commerce \leq^M Product\_Module$;
  - $Racine\_E - commerce \leq^M payment\_Module$;
  - $Module\_Personne \leq^M customer\_Module$.

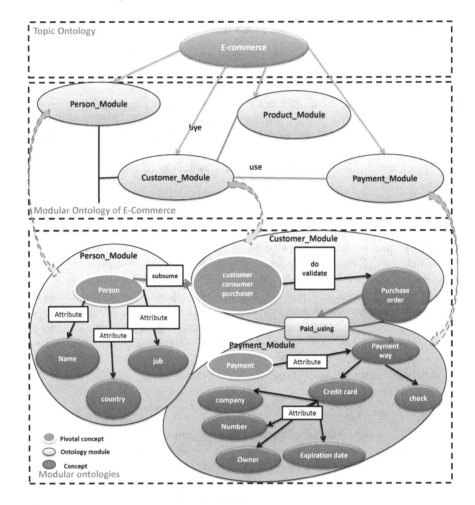

Fig. 1. "Example of modular domain ontology "*E-Commerce*

Conceptual relations consist of:

- $\mathcal{I}_M(Module\_Person, Module\_customer) = Concept\_Person$
- $\mathcal{I}_M(Module\_customer, Module\_payment) = Concept\_type - of - payment.$

We remind that interface connection between ontology modules is a concept belonging to the linked modules.

3.3   Ontology Module Definition

An ontology module (OM) is seen as a ontology fragment that has a "*meaning*", from the viewpoint of applications or users. In the literature, several criteria should be met to comply with the notion of ontological module include: (1) small module size for easy maintenance; (2) independence from the other modules: so that the addition or the removal of a module will not affect many others; and (3) understandability.An OM consists of ontological concepts (referenced by a set of terms) strongly linked by relations (referenced by a set of terms). Each module ontology is characterized by a basic concept, called "*pivotal concept*" that encapsulates the basic meaning of the granule of knowledge concerned. We define an ontological module by a cluster of related concepts (C) and conceptual relations (CR). The OM encapsulates the ontology of commonsense knowledge elements.

An **OM** is defined as follows 4.

$$M = < \mathcal{ID}_{\mathcal{M}}, \sigma_o^{-1}, \mathcal{C}, \mathcal{R}, \mathcal{O} > \tag{4}$$

where: $\mathcal{ID}_{\mathcal{M}}$ *is the identifier of ontology module;* σ_o^{-1} *is the inverse function de* σ_o *that provide a set of thematic concepts (CT) associated to the OM;* $\mathcal{C}$ *is a set of identifiers of domain concepts making up the OM;* $\mathcal{R} : C \times C$ *is a set of relations between the internal concepts of the OM;* $\mathcal{O}$ *is a set of objects described by the OMs.* Besides, we define the signature of $(\mathcal{C}, \mathcal{R}, \mathcal{O})$ ʃ⟩}$(\mathcal{C}, \mathcal{R}, \mathcal{O})$ to be a triple $(\mathcal{CN}, \mathcal{RN}, \mathcal{ON})$ where $\mathcal{CN}$ is a set of all names (terms) of concepts defined in $\mathcal{C}$, $\mathcal{RN}$ is a set of all names (terms) of relations defined in $\mathcal{R}$, $\mathcal{ON}$ is a set of objects names.

Since the proposed modularization approach is to enhance knowledge search and management, the notion of query is very important to express connection between OMs. This issue is explained in the following subsection.

3.4   Internal and External Definitions

In contrast with ontology definition, concept and relation inside an OM have local (internal) meaning and distributed (external) meaning. For instance, the meaning of the concept *measure* in the OM related to "*body mass Index*" in the medical topic is different from its meaning in the chemical topic. Therefore, concept and relation have internal and external definitions.

Module-based Query is defined as follows: Let $\mathcal{VQ}$ be a set of variables disjoint from ON . A module-based query Q over an OM $\mathcal{M} = (C, R, O)$ is an expression of the form of $q_1, ..., q_n$, where q_i are query terms of the form $\mathcal{C}(x)$ or $\mathcal{R}(x, y)$ are such that:

$$x, y \in \mathcal{VQ} \bigcup ON, C \in \mathcal{CN} and R \in \mathcal{RN}.$$

An **internal concept definition** $\mathcal{CI}$ is the axiom of the form: $\mathcal{CNI} \equiv \mathcal{D}, \{M_i\}_{i:1..n}$ where $\mathcal{CNI} \subseteq \mathcal{CN}$, $\mathcal{D}$ is the domain ontology and $\{M_i\}_{i:1..n}$ is a set of OMs that have in common the concept C.

An **external concept definition** is an axiom of the form: $C \equiv M : Q$ where M is an OM and Q is an module-based query over the signature of M with exactly one free variable.

An **external relation definition** is an axiom of the form: $R \equiv M : Q$ Where M is an OM and Q is an ontology-based query over the signature of M with exactly two free variable.

As aforementioned, we intend to provide a generic graph-based formalism that would gather under a common framework the different aspects of ontology modularization with the aim of meeting the requirements of a search application on the web.

4   Graph-Based Framework for Modular Ontologies: Typed Attributed Graph of Ontologies

At an abstract level, since it exists a bijection between graphs and ontology languages, we choose graph-based formalism as an abstract level of modular ontology definition. Since the OMs are supposed to be extracted from unstructured text, as explained in [4], the discovered concepts and relations are not validated at one step. The ontological representation should take into account change management and automatic update. In our work, we propose to define a general structure of a ontological knowledge base (networked OMs classified by domain) independent of a concrete language. The proposed Ontological knowledge warehouse include a graph-based modeling and functional operators for inter-level navigation. For this reason, we choose to rely on typed attributed graph as it is powerful enough to represent an ontology written in RDF, OWL or DAML+OIL. Besides, typed attributed graph is the model implemented in the ACG library for graph transformation. Details about attributed graph are described in [10].

A **typed attributed graph** representation of the OM $\mathcal{AG_M}$ is a pair $(\mathcal{N}_G, \mathcal{E}_G)$, where $\mathcal{N}_G$ is a set of attributed nodes and $\mathcal{E}_G$ is a set of attributed edges. A **typed attributed node** $\mathcal{N}_G = (T_N, AV_N)$ has a type T_N and a set of attribute values AV_N where Tn is the set of terms referring CN to a concept C and AV_N is the set of score's values assigned to each of the terms belonging to CN. A **typed attributed edge** $\mathcal{EG}_M = (T_E, \mathcal{RN}, AV_E, O_E, D_E)$ has a type T_E, a set of attribute values AV_E, an origin node O_E and a destination node D_E, where T_E denotes the type of a relation (hyponymy, meronymy, possession, etc.) and $\mathcal{RN}$ is a set of terms referring to the relation defined in $sig(\mathcal{R})$. A **typed attribute value** AV_E is a pair $(\mathcal{RN}, score)$ associating score's value $score$ to a term of $(\mathcal{RN})$.

In this framework, we propose the following statements:

- Topic ontology is specified by classic typed attributed graph of thematic concepts;
- Modular domain ontology is represented by a typed attributed graph of OMs;
- OM is defined by a typed attributed graph of concepts (ontology definition);
- Each concept is a typed attributed graph of terms.

Furthermore, we propose the model of *typed attributed graph of ontologies* where The nodes and edges are of several types, as follows. The *Term* node (T): is the smallest conceptual unit extracted in the form of a nominal expression. The *Concept* node (C): is a typed attributed graphe of *Term* nodes (T) connected by arcs typed as *Terminological relations* (TR) and is a conceptual unit of the *module* (M) graph. The **Module** node (M): is a graph of nodes *Concept* (C) connected with the *conceptual relationships* (CR). The **Ontology** node (GO): is the largest unit defined as a typed attributed graph of of *Module* node (M) connected with the *inter-module* interface (I).

5 Adaptative Information Search Based on Modular Knowledge Warehouse

In this view, the user can navigate through the multi-layer warehouse by selecting the corresponding thematic concept and the suitable OM or formulate a query as a set of keywords or a question in natural language. The query analysis module (1) processes the request according to its type. We distinguish two main cases:

- the absence of an ontology or an OM covering the ontological terms of the request or the response expected (2.*a*);
- The existence of an OM corresponding to the user query (2.*b*).

In the first case, the first iteration takes place only by invoking the results delivered by the conventional search engine (ie yahoo, google, etc.) (2.*A*1 and 2.*A*2). Then a new case is created in the base case (2.*A*3) where the query and the results viewed by the user are inserted. This event will trigger the operation of

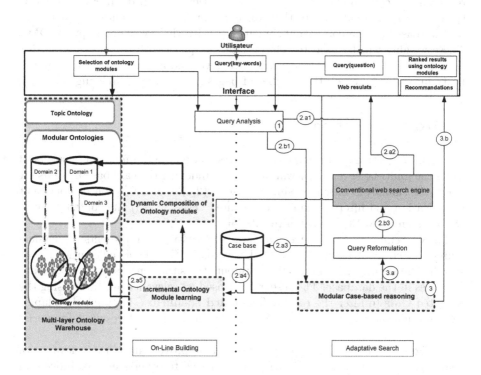

Fig. 2. Adaptative information search based on modular knowledge warehouse

the second component responsible for the learning modules of ontologies from the web (2.$A4$) [4]. This OM builds the ontology to be displayed in the search interface to allow the user to refine his search. Adding or updating an OM (2.$A5$) causes the update of the dynamic composition of the modular ontology [11] corresponding modular domain. Therefore, the approach to the *dynamic composition of modules of ontologies* is called to reorganize the concepts being overlap between the different OMs of ontologies and update the hierarchy of OMs based on a semantic similarity measure [11](3.b). In the second case, the component relating to research based on case-based reasoning and modular ontologies can learn a relevance descriptor based on similar cases whose structure depends on the corresponding OM (3). This descriptor will be used to reformulate the query (3.$A1$) based on semantic proximities (which are calculated based on the number of pages returned ("*hit*") by the conventional search engine) (3.$A2$). The results for the reformulated query are provided to the user (3.$A1$). Simultaneously, the relevance descriptor is used to classify the recommendations relating to OMs semantically close to the current OM and to rank them (3.b).

This application is characterized by its adaptivity, for the following reasons. First, it uses ontologies are built incrementally and one based on the needs of users who are looking for information (made by queries). Second, the web search engine will be able to adapt the changement occurring in the areas of knowledge and cooperate users in an indirect way to build the fragments ontologies that represent the common needs of information retrieval **in a modular way**.Finally, the concepts and relationships that make up any OM are weighted by their similarities based on the contextual concurrence with the pivotal concepts of OMs. These weights will be used to reformulate the query with the closest concepts (belonging to the same OM) at a semantic level and at a statistical level (similarity measures based on the number of pages returned by search engines web).

6   Experimentation

The main objective of this experiment aims to observe the following aspects of using the multi-layer ontology warehouse: (1) Indexing the case base by OMs for query reformulating based on similar cases , (2) the contribution of document classification and filtering using the weighted OMs [3] , (3) the contribution of OM enrichment with the search results [4].

Three *scenarios* were conceived. The **scenario** $A1$: represents a classical search, which involves the search for keywords on Google, as conventional web search. The **second scenario** $B1$ represents the situation where there are similar cases in the database. The research is based on relevance indicator using the weighted OMs to filter the results. The **third scenario** $C1$ represents adaptative information search based on OM enrichment from search results and queries (case base).

In Figure 3, the results show a significant improvement of the relevance of results of returned in third scenario $C1$ compared to other scenarios.Indeed, in the second scenario (B1), we see a significant increase in the accuracy rate for

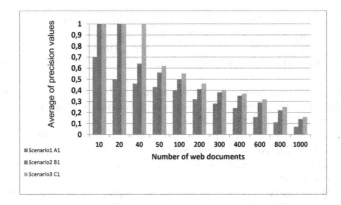

Fig. 3. L'valuation de la prcision moyenne du module CBRModSearch

the first twenty documents. In addition, we also note a significant improvement in results accuracy in the third scenario. This result shows the impact of the reformulation of the query and filtering of documents based on updated OM.

7   Conclusion

In this paper, we focus on the necessity of introducing modularity to support the partial reuse of ontologies for semantic annotation in knowledge management systems. We outline some related works of ontology modularization approaches in order to fix the main requirements of the proposed model of modular ontological knowledge. The main propositions described in this paper are: three-layered ontology warehouse (topic classification, domain knowledge representation, module representation). The proposed three-layered ontological warehouse were designed and developed for CBR-based content management where ontology modules are used to annotate cases and compute similarity between cases and recommend similar content. An improvement of results relevance and content recommendation was observed as described in a previous works. The ongoing work concerns modular and semantic indexing in digital libraries by ontology modules.

References

1. Ben-Mustapha, N., Baazaoui-Zghal, H., Aufaure, M.-A., Ben-Ghezala, H.: Combining semantic search and ontology learning for incremental web ontology engineering. In: Sixth International Workshop on Web Information Systems Modeling (WISM 2009), Held in Conjunction with CAISE 2009, pp. 1036–1049 (2009)
2. Ben-Mustapha, N., Baazaoui-Zghal, H., Aufaure, M.-A., Ben-Ghezala, H.: Semantic search using modular ontology learning and case-based reasoning. In: Proceeding of EDBT/ICDT Workshops (2010)
3. Ben-Mustapha, N., Baazaoui-Zghal, H., Aufaure, M.-A., Ben-Ghezala, H.: Enhancing semantic search using case-based modular ontology. In: Proceedings of the 2010 ACM Symposium on Applied Computing, SAC 2010, pp. 1438–1439 (2010)

4. Ben-Mustapha, N., Aude-Aufaure, M., Baazaoui-Zghal, H., Ben-Ghezala, H.: Contextual Ontology Module Learning from Web Snippets and Past User Queries. In: König, A., Dengel, A., Hinkelmann, K., Kise, K., Howlett, R.J., Jain, L.C. (eds.) KES 2011, Part II. LNCS (LNAI), vol. 6882, pp. 538–547. Springer, Heidelberg (2011)
5. Stuckenschmidt, H., Parent, C., Spaccapietra, S. (eds.): Modular Ontologies: Concepts, Theories and Techniques for Knowledge Modularization. LNCS, vol. 5445. Springer, Heidelberg (2009)
6. Dzbor, M., Motta, E., Studer, R., Sure, Y., Haase, P., Gómez-Pérez, A., Richard, V.B., Waterfeld, W.: Neon Lifecycle Support for Networked Ontologies (Overview and Objectives). In: Integration of Knowledge, Semantics and Digital Media Technology, pp. 451–452 (2005)
7. d'Aquin, M., Schlicht, A., Stuckenschmidt, H., Sabou, M.: Ontology Modularization for Knowledge Selection: Experiments and Evaluations. In: Wagner, R., Revell, N., Pernul, G. (eds.) DEXA 2007. LNCS, vol. 4653, pp. 874–883. Springer, Heidelberg (2007)
8. Gruber, T.R.: Toward principles for the design of ontologies used for knowledge sharing. Technical report, Technical Report KSL-93-04 (1993)
9. Stuckenschmidt, H., Klein, M.: Structure-Based Partitioning of Large Concept Hierarchies. In: McIlraith, S.A., Plexousakis, D., van Harmelen, F. (eds.) ISWC 2004. LNCS, vol. 3298, pp. 289–303. Springer, Heidelberg (2004)
10. Ehrig, H., Ehrig, K., Prange, U., Taentzer, G.: Fundamental Theory for Typed Attributed Graphs and Graph Transformation based on Adhesive HLR Categories. Journal of Fundam. Inf. 74(1), 31–61 (2006)
11. Elloumi-Chaabene, M., Ben-Mustapha, N., Baazaoui-Zghal, H., Moreno, A., SAnchez, D.: Semantic-based composition of modular ontologies applied to web query reformulation. In: Proceedings of the 6th International Conference on Software and Data Technologies ICSOFT, pp. 305–308. SciTePress (2011)
12. Tomassen, S.L.: Conceptual Ontology Enrichment for Web Information Retrieval. Phd, Norwegian University of Science and Technology NTNU (2011)
13. Parnas, D.L.: On the Criteria To Be Used in Decomposing Systems into Modules. Communications of the ACM 15(12) (December 1972)

Ontological Re-classification of Individuals: A Multi-viewpoints Approach

Meriem Djezzar[1], Mounir Hemam[1,2], and Zizette Boufaida[1]

[1] LIRE Laboratory, Mentouri University of Constantine, Algeria
[2] Department of Computer Science, University of Khenchela, Algeria
{djezzar.meriem,mounir.hemam,zboufaida}@gmail.com

Abstract. A multi-viewpoints ontology confers to the same universe of discourse, several partial descriptions, where each one is relative to a particular viewpoint. Moreover, these partial descriptions share at global level, ontological elements and semantic bridges constituent a consensus between the various viewpoints. In this paper, we define, firstly, a multi-viewpoints knowledge model based on viewpoint and ontology notions. The multi-viewpoints knowledge model is used to formalize the multi-viewpoints ontology in description logics. Then, based on developed model, we propose a process for the relocation of an individual in a multi-viewpoints ontology. The Individuals relocation concerns the reclassification of an individual, already classified, who sees its data change. The reclassification is necessary when the knowledge of the individual evolves. This evolution may be the result of an enrichment (adding knowledge to the individual), a impoverishment (removing knowledge), and/or modification (changing knowledge).

Keywords: Viewpoint, Ontologies, Description Logics, Instance Classification.

1 Introduction

An ontology is a conceptual representation of a domain, allowing the actors (human and software) to share knowledge. It provides a way of expressing the meaning of concepts by organizing them hierarchically and defining their properties in a formal knowledge representation language. It can also includes axioms and be populated. In the latter case, it also includes instances of concepts (i.e. individuals).

Since there are generally several ways of apprehending knowledge of a domain, the representation of ontologies is therefore not an easy task. This is due primarily to the difficulty of finding consensus definitions of concepts in a domain satisfying the definition of each user, which reflect his viewpoint on the domain.

The difficulty of representing ontologies is mainly related to the existence of several user communities who can be interested in the same domain but with different viewpoints. These communities evolving in a multidisciplinary environment, coexist and collaborate among themselves. Each community has its own interests and perceives differently the conceptual entities of the same universe of discourse.

A. Abelló, L. Bellatreche, and B. Benatallah (Eds.): MEDI 2012, LNCS 7602, pp. 91–102, 2012.

In this work, we are interested in the problem of representing an ontology in hete-rogeneous organization by taking into account different viewpoints and different ter-minologies of various users, groups or even communities in the organization. Such ontology, that we call multi-viewpoints ontology, is defined in [1], [2] as an ontology witch confers to the same universe of discourse, several partial representations; where each one is relative to a particular viewpoint. In addition, these partial representations share at global level, ontological elements and bridges constituent a consensus be-tween the various viewpoints.

For defining multi-viewpoints ontology, we were inspired by works that deal with viewpoint notion in the area of knowledge representation [3], [4], [5]. For this, we use a sub-language of the description logic $\mathcal{SHOQ}$(D) [1] to express notions inherent to viewpoints such as global and local concepts, bridges, stamps, …

In this paper, we are interested in classification reasoning based on the multi-viewpoints ontologies representation model. Our main goal is to propose a multi-viewpoints individual relocalisation process which takes advantage of the model originalities.

Classification reasoning [6], [7] is one of the main reasoning mechanisms asso-ciated with description logics. In fact, structuring knowledge in classes, subclasses and instances promotes the use of the classification to retrieve implicit knowledge, relations between a new situation and situations already known. The term of *classifi-cation* supports two distinct mechanisms: (i) classification of classes (also called cate-gorization) which consists of organizing and maintaining a hierarchy of classes, by inserting new classes in their place and (ii) classification of instances which consists of finding, in a hierarchy of classes, the most specific classes of an individual.

Intuitively, instance classification consists in connecting an individual to a more specialized class than its creation class. Classifying an individual is thus to bring him down as low as possible in the hierarchy of specialization by comparing the descrip-tions provided by subclasses.

The relocalisation of individuals, which is an extension of the classification of in-stances, concerns the reclassification of an individual, already classified, who sees its data change. The reclassification is necessary when the knowledge of the individual evolves. This evolution may be the result of an enrichment (i.e. adding knowledge to the individual), a impoverishment (i.e. removing knowledge), and / or modification (i.e. changing knowledge).

In our study, relocating an individual in the multi-viewpoints ontology is due to the addition or modification of an attribute value. Moreover, the relocation process con-sists of recalculating, in each viewpoint, the most specific local concept for the mod-ified individual.

The remainder of this paper is organized as follows. Section 2 provides an overview of the multi-viewpoints approach. In Section 3, we first recall the multi-viewpoints ontology representation model then how to use it in the individuals classification process. Section 4 presents an extension of the classification, namely the relocation of an individual in a multi-viewpoints ontology. Finally Section 5 concludes the paper and suggests some future work.

2   Multi-viewpoints Approach

For a given domain of knowledge, several criteria can be used to observe an object. These different perceptions of the world are called viewpoints or perspectives. In computer science, most of data modelling systems don't deal with the variety of perceptions related to the same universe of discourse and develop tools to create a single model for a single vision of the observed world. The viewpoint approach is opposed to this monolithic approach and makes it possible to model the same reality according to different points of view.

Several interpretations of viewpoint notion are possible. One of the first references to viewpoints was proposed by [8]: viewpoints correspond to different perceptions of an object with respect to observer's position. The second interpretation is a knowledge domain one: viewpoints correspond to the different ways to translate knowledge with respect to the social position, know-how and competence of an expert. In this interpretation, a viewpoint includes context, and the perception of a person or group of persons. Examples of systems that implement viewpoints in object representations are [9], [10], [11], [12]. A good overview is given in [3]. [13] introduces viewpoints in the conceptual graph model, in a "corporate memory" context.

In the following, we identify the main objectives in integrating viewpoints into computer systems. Note that there is no single use of this concept that includes all of these objectives.

The viewpoint as a means of providing multiple descriptions of an entity: the viewpoint concept seems to naturally result from the multiple views of objects of a specific study. As a matter of fact, a real world entity can have many behavioural contexts and many states from which the notion of multiple descriptions has been derived. In this case it is defined as the fact of conferring several partial descriptions to the same universe of discourse each of which describes it in a given viewpoint.

The viewpoint as a means of mastering system complexity: several research works are based on the viewpoint concept with the principal objective of explicitly taking into account the complexity of the system. The result of the study is then held by dividing it into partial descriptions according to different and complementary aspects.

The viewpoint as an approach for the modelling and distributed development of systems: many authors state that the modelling of complex systems as defined in [14] cannot be handled with the same techniques as used for simple systems. Different works suggest a distributed development approach based on viewpoint notion. Hence, every development process can be represented by correlated viewpoints.

For the purpose of this research work on multi-representation ontologies, we adopt the term multi-viewpoints ontology to emphasize the importance of viewpoint notion in (i) to solve the multiple representation problems, (ii) to provide a better visibility and access to ontological elements (concept, roles, individual), (iii) to allow a collaborative modular development among diversified communities in the same domain and (iv) to benefit from the multi-viewpoints representation of knowledge to allow their evolution. In the framework of this study, we are interested in ontologies represented by the description logics language. In addition, in order to take into account the notion of a viewpoint on ontology, we suppose that the various viewpoints on the same universe of discourse are partial but complementary vision of it. Their union produces a complete and coherent representation vocabulary.

3   Multi-viewpoints Ontology Representation

Description logics (DL) [15], [16] are a family of knowledge representation languages that can be used to represent the knowledge of an application domain in a structured and formally well-understood way. The basic modelling elements in DL are concepts, roles and individuals. Concepts are only variable-free unary predicates represented as classes, and used to group individuals with similar properties. So, a class is used for a set of objects that have shared properties. In DL, roles are also variable-free binary predicates and are used to associate any two concepts or any two individuals.

For our requirements of multi-viewpoints ontology representation, we introduce in description logics the following notions:

Multi-Viewpoints Ontology: Is a multiple description of the same universe of discourse according to various viewpoints. It is defined as a 4-tuple of the form $O = (C^\mathcal{G},$ $\mathcal{R}^\mathcal{G}, \mathcal{V}p, \mathcal{M})$, where $C^\mathcal{G}$ a set of global concepts, $\mathcal{R}^\mathcal{G}$ a set of global roles, $\mathcal{V}p$ a set of viewpoints, and $\mathcal{M}$ a set of bridge rules.

Viewpoint: Is defined as a triple $\mathcal{VP}_\mathcal{X} = (C^L, \mathcal{R}^L, \mathcal{A}^L)$, where C^L a set of local concepts, $\mathcal{R}^L$ a set of local roles, and $\mathcal{A}^L$ a set of local individuals.

Global Concept: Is used to represent a concept or entity of the real word which is observed from two or several viewpoints, at the same time, with basic and common properties (i.e. attributes).

Local Concept: Is used to represent a concept which is viewed and described locally according to a given point of view.

Global Role: It's a relationship between two local concept defined in two different viewpoints.

Local Role: It's a relationship between two local concepts defined in the same point of view.

Stamps: We adapt the stamping mechanism used in [4] to allow multiple representations of concepts. In our approach, stamps (i.e. labels) permits each ontological element (i.e. concepts, roles, individuals) to be known by the viewpoint that it belong to.

Local Hierarchy: Under a viewpoint VP_i, a local hierarchy, denoted vpi/$\mathcal{H}$, is defined by the triplet $(C^L, \partial, \sqsubseteq)$ where : C^L is a set of local concepts, ∂ is a function from C^L to C^G which associates each root concept (i.e. more general concept) S $\in C^L$ to one global concept $C^\delta \in C^G$ and $\sqsubseteq$ is the subsumption relationship used to explicitly express a partial ordering relation according to the two following forms:

vpi: D $\sqsubseteq$ vpi: C   (1)
C and D are two local concepts defined in the same viewpoint VP_i.

$vp_i: S \sqsubseteq C^\delta$

S is the more general local concept defined in VP_i and C^δ is global concept name. (2)

Multi-Instantiation: The multiple instantiation mechanism used to now permits an individual to belong to more then one local concept according to different viewpoints. In the context of our work we address the following individual property:

Property: An individual is an instance of a global concept and instance of one or several local concepts defined in one or several viewpoints respectively. Thus, an individual has a basic description (*i.e.* global description) and may be described according to different viewpoints simultaneously.

Bridge Rule: The particularity of the multi-viewpoints representation is the existence of a communication channel among various viewpoints. This communication channel, called bridge rule, allows representing links between local concepts of different viewpoints. A bridge rule is a statement of one of the four following forms:

$vpi: X \xrightarrow{\sqsubseteq} vpj: Y$ (inclusion bridge rule) (1)

Means that an individual which is an instance of the source concept X under the VP_i is also an instance of the target concept Y under the VP_j.

$vp1: X_1 \sqcap ... \sqcap vpk: X_k \xrightarrow{\sqsubseteq} vpj: Y$ (*inclusion bridge rule with several sources*) (2)

Means that an individual which is an instance of each of the source concepts under disjoint viewpoints is also an instance of the destination concept.

$vpi: X \xleftrightarrow{\equiv} vpj: Y$ (bi-directional inclusion bridge rule) (3)

Means that the sets of possible extensions of the two local concepts under different viewpoints are equal.

$vpi: X \xleftrightarrow{\perp} vpj: Y$ (bi-directional exclusion bridge rule) (4)

Means that the two concepts X and Y cannot be at the same time representations of the same individual.

Formally, the interpretation of bridge rules is associated with a set of *domain relations*. A domain relation $r_{ij} \subseteq \Delta^{I_i} \times \Delta^{I_j}$ states, for each individual of Δ^{I_i}, the individual of Δ^{I_j} its corresponds to. The notation $r_{ij}(A^{I_i})$ denotes the interpretation of the local concept A, defined in the viewpoint vp_i, as considered in the interpretation domain of the viewpoint vp_j. Then, the semantics of bridge rule is given with respect to domain relations:

- $\langle \mathcal{I}_i, r_{ij}, \mathcal{I}_j \rangle \models vp_i: X \xrightarrow{\sqsubseteq} vp_j: Y$, if $r_{ij}(X^{I_i}) \subseteq Y^{I_j}$

- $\langle \{\mathcal{I}_1,..., \mathcal{I}_k\}, r_{ij}, \mathcal{I}_j \rangle \models vp_1: X_1 \sqcap ... \sqcap vp_k: X_k \xrightarrow{\sqsubseteq} vp_j: Y$, if $r_{1j}(X_1^{I_1}) \cap ... \cap r_{kj}(X_k^{I_k}) \subseteq Y^{I_j}$

- $\langle \mathcal{I}_i, r_{ij}, \mathcal{I}_j \rangle \models vp_i: X \xleftrightarrow{\equiv} vp_j: Y$, if $r_{ij}(X^{I_i}) \subseteq Y^{I_j}$ and $r_{ji}(Y^{I_j}) \subseteq X^{I_i}$

- $\langle \mathcal{I}_i, r_{ij}, \mathcal{I}_j \rangle \models vp_i: X \xleftrightarrow{\perp} vp_j: Y$, if $r_{ij}(X^{I_i}) \cap r_{ji}(Y^{I_j}) = \varnothing$

3.1   Simple Modeling Example

We illustrate our multi-viewpoints knowledge model through a simple modelling example. It concerns the representation of real estate domain. In this example, three viewpoints are considered: Size, Finance and Localisation, designed by vp1, vp2 and vp3 respectively. Each one contains only information that is relevant to it. In addition, the global level is simplified to a unique global concept Apartment.

Global Concept

Apartment $^{\delta}$ ≡ ($\forall_{vp1}$ roomNumber.Number) ⊓ ($\forall_{vp2}$ rent.Number) ⊓

($\forall_{vp1, vp2, vp3}$ hasAdress.String)

Defines a global concept *Apartment* with an attribute *roomNumber* according to vp_1, an attribute *rent* according to vp_2 and a common attribute *hasAddress* according to vp_1, vp_2 and vp_3.

Local Concept

vp_1: SmallApartment ≡ Apartment $^{\delta}$ ⊓ (roomNumber. {1, 2})

Defines a local concept *SmallApartment*, under the viewpoint vp_1, as a sub-concept of the global concept *Apartment* and the value of the attribute *roomNumber* is one of {1, 2}.

Subsumption relationship

vp_2: CheapApartment ⊑ Appartement $^{\delta}$

Expresses a subsumption link between the local concept *CheapApartment*, defined in the viewpoint vp_2, and the global concept *Apartment*.

vp_2 : HLM ⊑ vp_2: CheapApartment

Expresses a subsumption link between two local concepts defined in the same viewpoint vp_2. In fact, under Finance viewpoint, all HLM apartments are not expensive.

Local /Global Role

vp_2: live_by (ExpensiveApartment, Rich-Tenant)

Defines a local role between two local concepts defined in the same viewpoint vp_2

live $^{\delta}$ (vp_2: Rich-Tenant, vp_3: DowntownApartment)

Defines a global role between two local concepts defined under two different viewpoints.

Bridge Rule

vp_2 : HLM ←$\xrightarrow{\equiv}$ vp_3: ApartmentSuburbs

States that the two local concepts *HLM* and *ApartmentSuburbs*, defined under Finance VP and Localisation VP respectively, are equivalent. In fact, all HLM apartments are in the suburbs and all suburbs apartments are HLM.

Multi-instanciation

vp_1: SmallApartment (at-john) vp_3: ApartmentSuburbs (at-john)

Says that the individual *at-john* is an instance of *SmallApartment* in vp_1 and is an instance of *ApartmentSuburbs* in vp_3

3.2   Classification of Individuals in a Multi-viewpoints Ontology

The two fundamental mechanisms based on the multi-viewpoints knowledge model are *instantiation* and *classification* [17]. Instantiation creates an individual, possibly incomplete, by providing its global concept, its local concept in each viewpoint and values for the attributes satisfying the constraints defined in the global concept and in the local concepts. The classification mechanism allows an individual to migrate from its current local concept to a more specific one. It takes place in each viewpoint and uses bridge rules.

The implementation of the multi-viewpoints classification process is held according to the following algorithm:

```
Input:
    - The individual I to classify
    - The global concept Cᵟ to which I belongs
Output:
In each viewpoint VPᵢ the individual I is attached to his
more specialized local concept
begin
    for each VPᵢ ∈ [VP₁...VPₙ] do
        while (Actif (VPᵢ) ) do
            Matching;
            Marks_Propagation;
            Update;
        end_while
    end_for /* all viewpoints were explored */
    Attachement;
end.
```

Fig. 1. Multi-viewpoints classification algorithm [17]

The multi-viewpoints classification process is based primarily on a matching mechanism between an individual and a local concept. First an individual I is created from a global concept C^{δ}. Then, if the global concept C^{δ} has specializations, we tries to match the individual I with each sub local concepts SC_i of C^{δ}. Matching mechanism characterize local concepts in three categories :

- admissible local concept for which a given individual satisfies all the constraints on all the attributes that exist in this local concept;
- potential local concept for which no decidable constraint is violated, but where a given individual may bear unknown values;
- prohibited local concepts for which individuals bear constraint violations.

The matching results are used to mark the sub local concepts of C^{δ} as *admissible*, *potential* or *prohibited*. We then repeated the classification from admissible local concepts until the more specialized local concepts are explored.

It should be noted that this multi-viewpoints classification leads to a "parallel" vision of the descent of the individual in different viewpoints. Indeed, through the use of bridges, several viewpoints can be changed "simultaneously". In addition, bridges are exploited as short cut in order to fasten the classification of the individual in different involved viewpoints.

So, the procedure *Marks-Propagation* proceeds a propagation of labels *admissible*, *potential* or *prohibited* on local concepts of different viewpoints. This marking, based on the semantics of bridge rules, reduces future matching. For example, in the case of an *inclusion bridge rule* between two local concepts *A* and *B*: if the source local concept *A* is marked *admissible* for the individual *I*, then the target local concept *B* must also be. Inversely, if the target local concept *B* is marked *prohibited* then the source local concept *A* must also be.

4   Multi-viewpoints Individuals Relocation Process

Individuals relocation consists in reclassifying an instance, already classified, who sees its data change. These changes may be due to the deletion of the value of an attribute, the addition of an attribute value not valued or the modification of the value of an attribute. In each unstable viewpoint, relocation process must then to ascend, in the local hierarchy, the modified individual to find the first admissible local concept, then descend it towards more specialized admissible local concepts to witch the modified individual can be attached (Fig. 2).

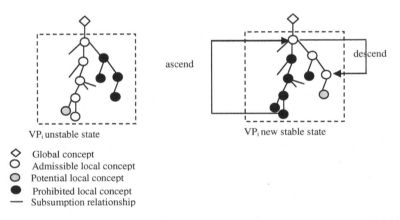

VP$_i$ unstable state   VP$_i$ new stable state

◇ Global concept
○ Admissible local concept
◉ Potential local concept
● Prohibited local concept
— Subsumption relationship

Fig. 2. Relocation of an individual *I* inside the viewpoint PV$_i$. *I* no longer satisfied the constraints of its smaller admissible local concept, then it rose along its membership local concepts until the first local concept to which it satisfies the constraints, then it has fallen, by classification to its new smaller admissible local concept.

4.1   Addition or Modification of the Value of an Attribute

An individual already classified has two types of knowledge: one hand the list of its more specific admissible local concepts (one in each viewpoint) and the other hand the list of attribute-value pairs. When modifying the value of an attribute or when adding an attribute value which was unknown, two cases are possible:

- The individual with its new attribute value satisfies all the constraints for this attribute, described in its current more specialized admissible local concepts. In this first case, the individual is in a stable state and is not required to ascend in any of the local hierarchies of the different viewpoints. Moreover, it is possible that the new attribute value allows the individual to migrate from its current admissible local concept to a more specific one. Thus, for this first case, a simple classification (Sect. 3.2) is revived with the new value of the attribute and from the current admissible local concepts of the individual.
- The modified individual does not satisfy the type of the attribute in at least one of its current local concepts. In this second case, there is an inconsistency. To deal with this contradiction, a relocation procedure is invoked whose objective is to find, in each unstable viewpoint, the more specific local concept in which the modified individual is susceptible to be an instance. So, we can define the relocation as the procedure which, from an unstable state (an instance of a global concept that no longer satisfies the types of its current admissible local concepts), restores the stability of the multi-viewpoints ontology by updating the list of the more specific local concepts.

In the following, we will explain the relocation of an individual in an unstable viewpoint, then the impact of this relocation to other viewpoints, through the use of bridge rules.

Ascent of the Individual. Let a be the modified attribute of the individual I, $v0$ its ancient value in I and $v1$ its new value; finally, let C_min0 be the more specialized admissible local concept of I before the modification of a, in the concerned viewpoint. So the ascent of I is required when $v1$ does not satisfy the type of a in C_min0. The ascent of I is done, by following the path of its admissible super-concepts from C_min0 until the first concept C_min1 for which $v1$ satisfies its type for a (Fig. 3).

The ascent of the individual is done independently in all unstable viewpoints for which the type of the more specific admissible local concept is no longer valid for I. The result of the ascent is a new smaller admissible concept for I, **C_min1**, which is necessarily a super-concept of the ancient smaller admissible concept of I, **C_min0**. In addition, the mark of all local concepts between C_min0 and C_min1 (without including C_min1) changed form admissible to prohibited.

The second step of the relocation process concerns the propagation of these change of marks to the other viewpoints, through the use of bridge rules.

Propagation of the Ascent. When an individual is raised in a viewpoint, certain of its ancient admissible local concepts become prohibited. So, this second step consists, at first, to identify the list of bridges for which at least one of its concepts (source or target) has changed mark form admissible to prohibited. Then, for each of these bridges the step propagation of the ascent proceeds a propagation of the prohibited

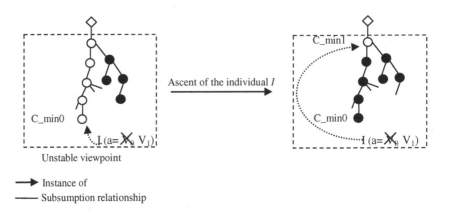

Ascent of the individual *I*

Unstable viewpoint

→ Instance of
── Subsumption relationship

Fig. 3. Ascent of the individual *I* when its value for *a* has changed from V_0 to V_1

mark on local concepts of different viewpoints. Propagation of the prohibited mark, after the ascent of the modified individual, obeys the following two rules:

1. Case of bridge with a single source: if the target concept is marked prohibited then the source concept becomes prohibited.
2. Case of bi-directional inclusion bridge: if one of the two concepts of this bridge is marked prohibited the other must be marked also prohibited.

Finally, the step propagation of the ascent may include, in addition to the propagation of the prohibited mark, the deletion of some bridges (i.e. removing a bridge from the list of active bridges). A bridge (uni or bidirectional) becomes inactive, if it no longer serves to make propagation marks. Two particular cases (see Fig. 4) are distinguished:

– A uni-directional inclusion bridge rule (with several sources) is inactive if one of its source concepts is marked prohibited.
– A bi-directional exclusion bridge rule is inactive if one of its concepts is marked prohibited.

Therefore, no new mark for a potential concept does not allow to make new inferences.

⊘ admissible, potential or prohibited concept

● prohibited concept

Fig. 4. Bridges in an inactive state

Descent of the Individual. Once the ascent and propagation of marks completed, relocation tries to descend the individual to the maximum in the different viewpoints. This descent part of a stable state and consists to invoke, from this state, the classification procedure (Sect. 3.2).

4.2   Suppression of the Value of an Attribute

When the value of an attribute is removed in the individual I (it becomes unknown to I), the more specific admissible local concepts of I, which establish restrictions for this attribute a, must change their mark from admissible to potential. So, in the viewpoints of those concepts, the individual rises to the first concept not describing a. Unlike the preceding case, once the ascent is finished (i.e. the new smaller admissible local concept C_min1 for I has been found), the algorithm does not try to descend individual to the sub-concepts of C_min1. In fact, knowledge of I having impoverished and not enriched. For this, no further descent is possible.

5   Conclusion

In this paper, we have proposed an approach for representing and reasoning with multiple viewpoints in description logic ontologies. The underlying key of our approach is to allow the description of such ontology, without eliminating heterogeneity but by merging heterogeneity (at local level) and consensus (at global level). For each viewpoint corresponds a local representation. In addition, the different viewpoint share at a global level, ontological elements and bridge rules. These last, allow to link different local concepts from different viewpoints and thus to infer information from a viewpoint based on those known in another. The merit of this approach is to allow reasoning mechanisms to operate locally on each viewpoint, or on assemblies of these viewpoints. The reasoning mechanism that we have used is the re-classification of individual. This re-classification takes into account the characteristics of the multi-viewpoints model: global concept, viewpoint and bridge.

As future work, we intend to validate and test the proposed approach in the domain of urbanism where we expect a wide range of viewpoints like transportation, land use, urban planning, etc. Furthermore, a link with the Ontology Web Language -OWL-will be established in the future phase of our study.

References

1. Hemam, M., Boufaida, Z.: Représentation d'ontologies multi-points de vue: une approche basée sur la logique de descriptions. Journées Francophones d'Ingénierie des Connaissances, Tunisia (2009)
2. Hemam, M., Boufaida, Z.: MVp-OWL: A Multi-Viewpoints Ontology Language for the Semantic Web. Int. J. Reasoning-based Intelligent Systems, Inderscience Publishers 3(3/4), 147–155 (2011)

3. Mariño, O.: Raisonnement classificatoire dans une représentation à objets multi-points de vue. PhD thesis, Université Grenoble 1, France (1993)
4. Benslimane, D., Vangenot, C., Roussey, C., Arara, A.: Multirepresentation in Ontologies. In: 7th East-European Conference on Advances in Databases and Informations Systems, pp. 4–15. Springer (2003)
5. Benslimane, D., Arara, A., Falquet, G., Maamar, Z., Thiran, P., Gargouri, F.: Contextual Ontologies. In: Yakhno, T., Neuhold, E.J. (eds.) ADVIS 2006. LNCS, vol. 4243, pp. 168–176. Springer, Heidelberg (2006)
6. Simon, A., Napoli, A., Lieber, J., Ketterlin, A.: Aspects de la classification dans un système de représentation des connaissances par objets. Sixièmes rencontres de la Société Francophone de Classification, Montpellier, 205–209 (1998)
7. d'Aquin, M., Lieber, J., Napoli, A.: Decentralized Case-Based Reasoning for the Semantic Web. In: Gil, Y., Motta, E., Benjamins, V.R., Musen, M.A. (eds.) ISWC 2005. LNCS, vol. 3729, pp. 142–155. Springer, Heidelberg (2005)
8. Minsky, M.: A framework for representing knowledge. In: Winston, P. (ed.) The Psychology of Computer Vision. McGraw Hill, New York (1975)
9. Bobrow, D., Winograd, T.: An overview of KRL, a knowledge representation language. Cognitive Science 1, 3–45 (1977)
10. Stefik, M., Bobrow, D.: Object-oriented programming: Themes and variations. The A.I. Magazine 6, 40–62 (1985)
11. Carre, B.: Méthodologie orientée objet pour la représentation des connaissances. PhD thesis, Laboratoire d'Informatique Fondamentale de Lille, France (1989)
12. Davis, H.: VIEWS: Multiple perspectives and structured objects in a knowledge representation language. Bachelor and Master of Science Thesis. MIT (1987)
13. Ribière, M., Matta, N.: Virtual enterprise and corporate memory. In: ECAI 1998 Workshop on Building, Maintaining and Using Organizational Memories (1998)
14. Benchikha, F., Boufaida, M.: The Viewpoint Mechanism for Object-oriented Databases Modelling, Distribution and Evolution. Journal of Computing and Information Technology 15(2), 95–110 (2007)
15. Baader, F., Calvanese, D., McGuinness, D., Nardi, D., Patel-Schneider, P.F. (eds.): The Description Logic Handbook: Theory, Implementation, and Applications. Cambridge University Press (2003)
16. Baader, F., Horrocks, I., Sattler, U.: Description Logics. In: van Harmelen, F., Lifschitz, V., Porter, B. (eds.) Handbook of Knowledge Representation, ch. 3. Elsevier (2007)
17. Hemam, M., Boufaida, Z.: Raisonnement par classification sur une ontologie multi-points de vue. Journées Francophones sur les Ontologies, Poitiers France, 149–156 (2009)

Transformation and Validation with SWRL and OWL of ODM-Based Models*

Jesús M. Almendros-Jiménez and Luis Iribarne

Dpto. de Lenguajes y Computación University of Almería
04120-Spain
{jalmen,luis.iribarne}@ual.es

Abstract. In this paper we present an approach for the specification of transformations and validations of ODM models. Adopting a SWRL/OWL based approach we will show how transform and validate models. Model-to-model transformations are described with SWRL rules, and validation of source and target models is achieved by SWRL.

1 Introduction

The *Ontology Definition Metamodel (ODM)* proposal [18] of the *Object Management Group (OMG)* [15] aims to define an ontology-based representation of UML models. ODM is an standard for representing UML models by OWL in which, among others, UML classes are mapped into ontology concepts, UML associations are mapped into ontology roles, and multiplicity restrictions of UML are mapped into cardinality restrictions in roles. ODM is itself a UML meta-model in which UML models can be accommodated. Following the ODM proposal, a UML model can be represented with an ontology in which the **TBox** (i.e. the *terminological box*) contains the UML meta-model while the **ABox** (i.e. the *assertional box*) contains the instance of the UML meta-model which represents the model.

On the other hand, *SWRL (Semantic Web Rule Language)* [9] has been adopted as rule language on top of OWL. SWRL permits the specification of relationships between semantic data. SWRL is inspired in Datalog and some other formalisms of logic programming. SWRL uses the logic implication as mechanism for expressing that a certain conjunction of SWRL atoms (i.e. the antecedent) entails a conjunction of SWRL atoms (i.e. the consequent). While OWL is able to express relationships between semantic data, SWRL offers a rule-based mechanism for expressing the relationships. However, SWRL is equipped with the so-called SWRL built-ins that enable to express more complex relations. For instance, SWRL permits to use *add*, *multiply* for integers, *concatString*, *subString*, for strings, among others. It makes SWRL suitable for semantic data inference when complex relations are handled.

* This work has been supported by the Spanish Ministry MICINN and Ingenieros Alborada IDI under grant TRA2009-0309. This work has been also supported by the EU (FEDER) and the Spanish Ministry MICINN under grants TIN2010-15588, TIN2008-06622-C03-03, and the JUNTA ANDALUCIA (proyecto de excelencia) ref. TIC-6114.

A. Abelló, L. Bellatreche, and B. Benatallah (Eds.): MEDI 2012, LNCS 7602, pp. 103–115, 2012.
© Springer-Verlag Berlin Heidelberg 2012

Model validation is a key element of Model Driven Development (MDE). Firstly, source and target models must conform to the corresponding meta-models. Source and target meta-models describe the *syntactic structure* of source and target models. However, some *semantic requirements* have to be imposed on source and target models. Secondly, *pre-conditions* and *post-conditions* and *invariants* are imposed on transformations. While source and target models can be well-formed with regard to meta-models some extra requirements can be required. We can distinguish two specific cases: *source and target model requirements*, and *transformation requirements*. The first case covers requirements on source and target models in isolation. The second case covers requirements on target models with regard to the source models.

In this paper, we present an approach for the specification of transformations and validations of ODM models. Adopting a SWRL/OWL based approach we will show how transform and validate models. Properties to be validated range from structural and semantic requirements on models (pre and post conditions) to properties of the transformation (invariants). The approach has been applied to the well-known example of model transformation: the Entity-Relationship (ER) to Relational Model (RM) transformation.

1.1 Ontology Driven Model Transformation and Validation

In UML, the *Meta Object Facility (MOF)* [16] serves as meta-meta-model, while semantic requirements are usually expressed in the *Object Constraint Language (OCL)* [17], and the *ATLAS Transformation Language (ATL)* [10] is used for transforming models. Our proposal can be seen as an *Ontology Driven Method for Model Transformation and Validation*. The use of OWL and SWRL in ODM based transformations can be seen as an alternative to the use of ATL and OCL in MOF based transformations. Here SWRL and OWL play the role of validation mechanisms of source and target models as OCL plays in MOF transformations. SWRL plays also the role of OCL as query language as well as the role of ATL as transformation language. Our approach is based on the use of SWRL for transformation and validation of models. Particularly, we propose the use of SWRL enriched with *built-ins* for the handling of *URIs*, and handling of *collections* of OWL elements: individuals, data-types and URIs.

Additionally, when handling transformations of ODM models, SWRL/OWL can be also used for the *completion* of source and target models to facilitate the transformation and the validation. We propose an *early step* in the transformation in which the source model is completed. *Completion* means to extend the model with new classes and properties that facilitates the transformation and validation. Moreover, we propose a *later step* in the transformation in which the target model is completed, including extra semantic information with the same purpose. Completion of the target model enables to define a *partial transformation* of the source model into the target model. In the completion stage the partial transformation is completed with elements that can be automatically derived from the target model.

In the context of ODM models, model-to-model transformations are OWL to OWL transformations. It means that instances of a certain **TBox** are transformed into instances of another **TBox**. From a MDA perspective, the **TBox**es play the role of source and target meta-models while ODM plays the role of meta-meta-model. OWL to OWL

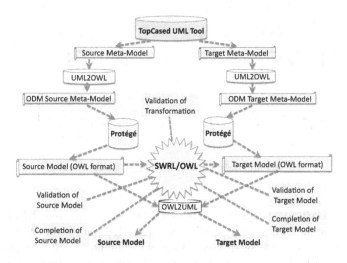

Fig. 1. Integration with UML/OWL tools

transformations can be achieved by SWRL following our approach. SWRL has been designed for expressing relations between individuals of one or more ontologies (thanks to the use of name spaces). However, some more is required to be used as transformation language. Model transformations are constructive in nature. Transformations create a target model from a source model. SWRL is not equipped with mechanisms for creating new individuals. Nevertheless, we can extend SWRL with this end, by incorporating a built-in called *newURI* for building URIs. On the other hand, some transformations can require to handle collections of OWL elements. Typically, $n - 1$ and $n - m$ transformations construct the target model from n source models, and $1 - 1$ transformations can also require to build one element of the target model from n elements of the source model. With this aim, we also propose the introduction of SWRL built-ins called *makeSet* and *makeBag* for collecting OWL elements. Additionally, some SWRL built-ins are required: *element, notElement* for handling members of sets and bags, as well as typical set operators: *union, intersection* and *difference*.

In the ODM context, one can argue that the use of OWL as modeling language provides a suitable framework for validation of properties. OCL can be replaced by OWL when specifying requirements imposed on models. OWL reasoning ranges from *ontology consistence checking* to *ontology-based inference* (i.e. derivation from ontology axioms). While the topic can be applied to ODM, model validation in transformations is a wider topic of research. *Model validation* involves ontology consistence checking and ontology-based inference, as well as cross validation of ontologies (i.e. ontology merging and reasoning). Moreover, certain requirements cannot be checked with OWL. OWL has a limited expressivity power which SWRL aims to overcome.

Our approach has been implemented and tested with some examples. We have developed our own SWRL reasoner on top of *SWI-Prolog*, called *OTL: Ontology based Transformation Language*, that includes the cited built-ins. For practical reasons, we have integrated our tool with other UML and OWL tools (see Figure 1). We have used

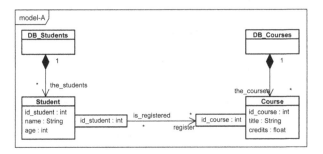

Fig. 2. Entity-relationship modeling of the Case Study

the *TopCased* UML tool [20] to design the source and target meta-models. In addition, we made use of an UML2OWL transformer (available from [8]) in order to have the ODM-based representation of source and target meta-models. We have also adopted the *Protégé* tool [12] to define the instance of the source meta-model as well as for exporting the source model (i.e., meta-model+instance) to an OWL document. After, SWRL/OWL are used, to complete and validate the source model, and for transforming the instance of the source model into the instance of the target model. Once the target model is computed, SWRL/OWL are used for completing and validating the target model, and for validating the transformation. After, the *Protégé* enables the exporting of the target model (i.e., meta-model+instance) to an OWL document. Finally, we made use of an OWL2UML transformer to get the UML target model from the ODM-based representation.

The structure of the paper is as follows. Section 2 will introduce the elements of model transformation through a case study. Section 3 will describe the SWRL/OWL based approach. Section 4 will discuss related work. Finally, Section 5 will conclude and present future work.

2   Case Study

This section describes the elements of model transformation through a case study. The case study is a well-known example of model transformation. Basically, the entity-relationship (ER) model (model A) is transformed into the relational model (RM) (model B). Let us suppose that the modeler (developer) has drawn the model of Figure 2, for representing a database by an ER style UML diagram, and the modeler wants to obtain the model of Figure 3, a RM style UML modeling of the same database. The developer has adopted the following nomenclature.

In the ER modeling of Figure 2 *Entities* are represented with classes (i.e., *Student* and *Course*), including attributes; *Containers* are defined for each entity (i.e., *DB_Students* and *DB_Courses*); Containers are composed of entities[1]; *Relationships* are represented

---

[1] In traditional ER modeling containers are omitted, however in a UML-based modeling are incorporated.

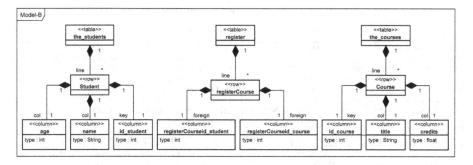

Fig. 3. Relational modeling of the Case Study

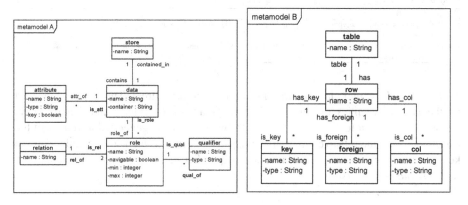

Fig. 4. Meta-model of the Source/Target Models

with UML associations. Association roles are defined for relationships and container/entity associations (i.e., *the_students*, *the_courses*, *is_registered* and *register*). Relationships can be adorned with *qualifiers* and *navigability*. Qualifiers specify the key attributes of each entity taken as foreign keys of the corresponding relationship. In the RM modeling of Figure 3, tables are composed of rows, and rows are composed of columns. The model introduces the stereotypes: << *table* >>, << *row* >> and << *column* >>. *line* is the role of the rows in the tables, and *key*, *foreign* and *col* are the roles of the key, foreign and non key attributes in the rows, respectively. Finally, each column has an attribute called *type*. Figure 4 shows the ER and RM meta-models (meta-models A and B). In the first case, *DB_Students* and *DB_Courses* are instances of the class *store*, while *Student* and *Course* are instances of the class *data*, and the attributes of the classes *Student* and *Course* are instances of the class *attribute*. In the second case, tables, rows, keys, cols and foreigns of the target model are instances of the corresponding classes.

Now, the goal of model transformation is to describe how to transform a class diagram of the type A (like Figure 2) into a class diagram of type B (like Figure 3). The transformation is as follows. The transformation generates two tables called *the_students* and *the_courses* both including three columns that are grouped into rows.

108   J.M. Almendros-Jiménez and L. Iribarne

Table 1. Model validation: requirements

Model A	
(v1) Attributes of a data have distint names (SR) (WF)	(v2) Data have a unique key attribute (SR) (TR)
(v3) Data have a key attribute (SR) (TR)	(v4) Attributes are associated to exactly one data (SC) (WF)
(v5) Data are contained in exactly one store (SC) (WF)	(v6) Data have distinct names (SR) (TR)
(v7) Data have distinct containers (SR) (TR)	(v8) Qualifiers are associated to exactly one role (SC) (TR)
(v9) Qualifier names of a role are distinct (SR) (TR)	(v10) Qualifiers are key attributes (SR) (WF)
(v11) Relations have two roles (SC) (WF)	(v12) Relation names are distinct (SR) (WF)
(v13) Roles are associated to exactly one relation (SC) (TR)	(v14) Roles are associated to exactly one data (SC) (TR)
(v15) Role names of a data are distinct (SR) (TR)	(v16) Stores are associated to exactly one data (SC) (WF)
Model B	
(v17) Col names of a row are distinct (SR) (WF)	(v18) Foreign names of a row are distinct (SR) (WF)
(v19) Key names of a row are distinct (SR) (WF)	(v20) Foreigns of a row are keys of another row (SR) (WF)
(v21) Tables are associated to exactly one store (SC) (WF)	(v22) Rows are associated to exactly one table (SC) (WF)
(v23) Keys are associated to exactly one row (SC) (TR)	(v24) Cols are associated to exactly one row (SC) (WF)
(v25) Foreigns associated to exactly one row (SC) (TR)	(v26) Table names are distinct (SR) (WF)
(v27) Row names are distinct (SR) (WF)	(v28) Rows have exactly one key (SC) (TR)
(v29) Rows have either keys and cols or foreigns (SR) (TR)	
Models A and B	
(v30) Key and col names and types are names and types of attributes	(v31) Table names are either container names or role names
(v32) Row names are data names or concatenations of role and data names	(v33) Foreign names are concatenations of role, data and key names

Table *the_students* includes the attributes of *Student* of Figure 2. The same can be said for the table *the_courses*. Given that the association between *Student* and *Course* is navigable from *Student* to *Course*, a table with two columns is generated to represent the assignments of students to courses, using *register+Course* as name of the table. Foreign keys are named as role name + class name + qualifier name: *registerCourseid_student*, *registerCourseid_course*.

2.1 Model Validation

While source and target meta-models impose *structural constraints (SC)* on source and target models, several *semantic requirements (SR)* on source and target models (i.e., pre and post-conditions) can be usually specified in a transformation. In addition, some *cross requirements* (i.e., invariants) on models can be described. In Table 1 we can see requirements imposed on the case study, classified as (SC) and (SR). Some requirements express conditions on *well-formed models (WF)*, while some of them are required by the transformation, that is, they are *transformation requirements (TR)*.

For instance, case v2 requires that each data has an unique key attribute. This is a semantic requirement. Key attributes are attributes having *key* set to *true*. This requirement is a pre-condition of the transformation because key attributes are used as foreign keys of the target model. Case v5 is an structural constraint of well-formed models: each data is associated to an store. It is not required by the transformation and can be expressed in the UML diagram with a cardinality constraint. Cases v6, v7, v9, v12 and v15 are related to the name of elements of the source model, and therefore they are semantic requirements. Case v29 is entailed by the transformation which assigns either keys and cols, or foreigns to rows. Therefore, it is a post-condition. Finally, cases v30-v33 are invariants that describe the relationship between names of the target model and names of the source model.

Table 2. Completion of Model A

Case	SWRL Rule
(c1)	*mmA:attribute(?C) ∧ mmA:key(?C,?D) ∧equal(?D,true) ∧ mmA:name(?C,?N) ∧ mmA:type(?C,?T)* → *mmA:keyAttribute(?C)∧ mmA:key_name(?C,?N) ∧ mmA:key_type(?C,?T)*
(c2)	*mmA:attribute(?C) ∧ mmA:key(?C,?D) ∧ equal(?D,false) ∧ mmA:name(?C,?N) ∧ mmA:type(?C,?T)* → *mmA:nonkeyAttribute(?C) ∧ mmA:nonkey_name(?C,?N) ∧ mmA:nonkey_type(?C,?T)*
(c3)	*mmA:data(?A) ∧ mmA:role_of(?A,?C) ∧ mmA:navigable(?C,?E) ∧ equal(?E,true) ∧ mmA:rel_of(?C,?D) ∧* *mmA:is_rel(?D,?D2) ∧ owl:differentFrom(?D2,?C) ∧ mmA:qual_of(?D2,?D3) ∧* *mmA:name(?D3,?N) ∧ mmA:type(?D3,?T)* → *mmA:navigable_role(?C) ∧ mmA:inv_qualifier_name(?C,?N) ∧ mmA:inv_qualifier_type(?C,?T)*

It is worth observing that the requirements on source and target models in isolation are not enough for the soundness of the transformation. For instance, source and target models can both have keys, but a cross requirement is needed: the keys of the target models are the keys of the source model.

3   SWRL/OWL for Model Transformation and Validation

In this section we show how SWRL can be used for defining transformation and validation rules in our approach. We can consider the following steps: (a) *Completion of the source model.* Completion procedure adds new classes and properties to the source model as well as fills them with individuals. Completion incorporates derived concepts and relationships from the source model. A particular case of completion is the introduction of the OWL relationships: *owl:sameAs, owl:differentFrom* for individuals. Completion facilitates the transformation and the validation; (b) *Validation of the source model.* OWL and SWRL rules are used to validate the source model; (c) *Transformation of the source model into the target model.* Target model elements are obtained from the elements of the completed source model. Usually, a *partial transformation* is defined, assuming that the completion step of the target model will obtain a completed target model; (d) *Completion of the target model.* Completion of the target model is similar to completion of the source model. Completion also facilitates the validation of the target model; (e) *Validation of the target model.* OWL and SWRL rules are used to validate the target model; and (f) *Cross validation of source and target models.* OWL and SWRL rules are used to validate source and target models. Cross validation involves ontology merging.

With the goal to use SWRL for model transformation, completion and validation, SWRL is equipped with the built-ins *newURI, makeSet, makeBag, element, notElement, union, intersection* and *difference*. In the following, we will show how the proposed approach is used in the case study. It is worth observing that there will be some completion and validation tasks that can be achieved by OWL constructors and OWL reasoning.

(a) Completion of the Source Model: The first step of the proposed method consists in the completion of the source model. Basically, new classes and properties are defined in terms of the source model elements. Completion is particular for each transformation, and therefore the transformation guides the definition of new classes and properties. Moreover, some requirements can be easier specified on completed models, and therefore validation also guides the introduction of new concepts and roles.

Table 3. Validation of Model A

Case	SWRL Rule
(v1)	*mmA:attr_off(?Data,?Att1) ∧ mmA:attr_off(?Data,?Att2) ∧ mmA:name(?Att1,?Name1) ∧* *mmA:name(?Att2,?Name2) ∧ owl:differentFrom(?Att1,?Att2) ∧ equal(?Name1,?Name2)* *→ val:duplicated_attribute_name(?Att1) ∧ val:duplicated_attribute_name(?Att2)*
(v6)	*mmA:data(?Data1) ∧ mmA:data(?Data2) ∧ owl:differentFrom(?Data1,?Data2) ∧* *mmA:name(?Data1,?Name1) ∧ mmA:name(?Data2,?Name2) ∧ equal(?Name1,?Name2)* *→ val:duplicated_data_name(?Data1) ∧ val:duplicated_data_name(?Data2)*
(v7)	*mmA:data(?Data1) ∧ mmA:data(?Data2) ∧ owl:differentFrom(?Data1,?Data2) ∧* *mmA:container(?Data1,?Name1) ∧ mmA:container(?Data2,?Name2) ∧ equal(?Name1,?Name2)* *→ val:duplicated_data_container(?Data1) ∧ val:duplicated_data_container(?Data2)*
(v9)	*mmA:qual_off(?Role,?Qualifier1) ∧ mmA:qual_off(?Role,?Qualifier2) ∧ mmA:name(?Qualifier1,?Name1) ∧* *mmA:name(?Qualifier2,?Name2) ∧ owl:differentFrom(?Qualifier1,?Qualifier2) ∧ equal(?Name1,?Name2)* *→ val:duplicated_qualifier_name(?Role)*
(v10)	*mmA:qualifier(?Qualifier) ∧ mmA:name(?Qualifier,?Name) ∧ mmA:key_name(?Key,?KeyName) ∧* *makeSet(?KeyName,?Names) ∧ notElement(?Name,?Names)* *→ val:qualifier_non_key_Name(?Qualifier)* *mmA:qualifier(?Qualifier) ∧ mmA:type(?Qualifier,?Type) ∧ mmA:key_type(?Key,?KeyType) ∧* *makeSet(?KeyType,?Types) ∧ notElement(?Type,?Types)* *→ val:qualifier_non_keyType(?Qualifier)*
(v12)	*mmA:relation(?Rel1) ∧ mmA:relation(?Rel2) ∧ owl:differentFrom(?Rel1,?Rel2) ∧* *mmA:name(?Rel1,?Name1) ∧ mmA:name(?Rel2,?Name2) ∧ equal(?Name1,?Name2)* *→ val:duplicated_relation_name(?Rel1) ∧ val:duplicated_relation_name(?Rel2)*
(v15)	*mmA:data(?Data) ∧ mmA:role_off(?Data,?Role1) ∧ mmA:role_off(?Data,?Role2) ∧* *owl:differentFrom(?Role1,?Role2) ∧ mmA:name(?Role1,?Name1) ∧ mmA:name(?Role2,?Name2) ∧* *equal(?Name1,?Name2)* *→ val:duplicate_role_data(?Data)*

In the case study, we define the concepts and roles of Table 2. The *keyAttribute* concept of c1 identifies the *attributes* of the source model in which *key* is set to *true*. In addition, the concept *navigable_role* of c3 is a type of *role* of the source model in which *navigable* is set to *true*. In the completion of the source model, *register* is a *role* as well as a *navigable_role*. Finally, completion includes the filling of the OWL relationships *owl:sameAs* and *owl:differentFrom*. All the individuals are declared as distinct when correspond to different objects and declared as the same, otherwise. Rules c1 and c2 can be also expressed with OWL constructors, while c3 has to be defined with SWRL.

(b) Validation of the Source Model: In this step the validation rules of the source model (see Table 1) are defined with SWRL (see Table 3). In order to use SWRL as model validator the idea is to define a concept for each requirement. The concept will be populated with the individuals that violate the requirement. When the concept is empty the requirement is preserved. In Table 3 the concepts are (v1) *duplicate_attribute_name*, (v6) *duplicate_data_name*, etc. SWRL rules classify the elements of the source model, and whenever a requirement is violated a certain individual is assigned to the corresponding class. Case v10 uses the proposed *makeSet* and *notElement* SWRL built-ins.

Some of the requirements can be specified with OWL constructors. This is the case of rules v2, v3, v4, v5, v8, v11, v13, v14 and v16, which can be specified with the cardinality constraints of OWL (i.e., *at most, at least, exactly*). It is worth observing that the introduction of *owl:differentFrom* is vital for using OWL as consistence checker. When a cardinality constraint is violated in OWL the underlying reasoning mechanism identifies the involved elements, but when they are declared as distinct, the ontology reasoner reveals a consistence error.

(c) Transformation of the Source Model to the Target Model: Next step consists in the specification of the transformation with SWRL rules (see Table 4). Firstly,

Table 4. Transformation of the Source Model into the Target Model

Case	SWRL Rule
(r1)	mmA:data(?A) ∧ mmA:container(?A,?B) ∧ newURI(?A,'table1',?C) → mmB:table(?C) ∧ mmB:name(?C,?B)
(r2)	mmA:navigable_role(?C) ∧ mmA:name(?C,?B) ∧ newURI(?C,'table2',?D) → mmB:table(?D) ∧ mmB:name(?D,?B)
(r3)	mmA:data(A) ∧ mmA:name(?A,?B) ∧ newURI(?A,'row1',?C) → mmB:row(?C) ∧ mmB:name(?C,?B)
(r4)	mmA:navigable_role(?C) ∧ mmA:name(?C,?D) ∧ mmA:is_role(?C,?DT) ∧ mmA:name(?DT,?B) ∧ concatString(?D,?B,?F) ∧ newURI(?C,'row2',?G) → mmB:row(?G) ∧ mmB:name(?G,?F)
(r5)	mmA:data(?A) ∧ mmA:attr_of(?A,?B) ∧ mmA:nonkeyAttribute(?B) ∧ mmA:name(?B,?N) ∧ mmA:type(?B,?T) ∧ newURI(?B,'col',?D) → mmB:col(?D) ∧ mmB:name(?D,?N) ∧ mmB:type(?D,?T)
(r6)	mmA:data(?A) ∧ mmA:attr_of(?A,?B) ∧ mmA:keyAttribute(?B) ∧ mmA:name(?B,?N) ∧ mmA:type(?B,?T) ∧ newURI(?B,'key',?D) → mmB:key(?D) ∧ mmB:name(?D,?N) ∧ mmB:type(?D,?T)
(r7)	mmA:navigable_role(?C) ∧ mmA:name(?C,?B) ∧ mmA:is_role(?C,?DT) ∧ mmA:name(?DT,?H) ∧ mmA:is_att(?C,?Q) ∧ mmA:name(?Q,?F) ∧ concatString(?B,?H,?Aux) ∧ concatString(?Aux,?F,?K) ∧ mmA:type(?Q,?T) ∧ newURI(?C,'foreign1',?D) → mmB:foreign(?D) ∧ mmB:name(?D,?K) ∧ mmB:type(?D,?T)
(r8)	mmA:navigable_role(?C) ∧ mmA:name(?C,?B) ∧ mmA:is_role(?C,?DT) ∧ mmA:name(?DT,?H) ∧ mmA:inv_qualifier_name(?C,?F) ∧ concatString(?B,?H,?Aux) ∧ concatString(?Aux,?F,?K) ∧ mmA:inv_qualifier_type(?C,?T) ∧ newURI(?C,'foreign2',?D) → mmB:foreign(?D) ∧ mmB:name(?D,?K) ∧ mmB:type(?D,?T)
(r9)	mmA:data(?A) ∧ newURI(?A,'table1',?T) ∧ newURI(?A,'row1',?R) → mmB:has(?T,?R) mmA:navigable_role(?C) ∧ newURI(?C,'table2',?T) ∧ newURI(?C,'row2',?R) → mmB:has(?T,?R)
(r10)	mmA:data(?A) ∧ mmA:attr_of(?A,?B) ∧ mmA:nonkeyAttribute(?B) ∧ newURI(A,'row1',R) ∧ newURI(B,'col',CL) → mmB:is_col(R,CL)
(r11)	mmA:data(A) ∧ mmA:attr_of(A,B) ∧ mmA:keyAttribute(B) ∧ newURI(?A,'row1',?R) ∧ newURI(?B,'key',?K) → mmB:is_key(?R,?K)
(r12)	mmA:navigable_role(?C) ∧ newURI(?C,'row2',?R) ∧ newURI(?C,'foreign1',?F) → mmB:is_foreign(?R,?F)
(r13)	mmA:navigable_role(?C) ∧ newURI(?C,'row2',?R) ∧ newURI(?C,'foreign2',?F) → mmB:is_foreign(?R,?F)

name spaces *mmA* and *mmB* are used to distinguish the source from the target model. Secondly, the proposed SWRL built-in *newURI* is used. The behavior of the proposed built-in is very simple. *newURI(URI,String,NewURI)* concatenates *URI* with *String* obtaining the *NewURI*. It makes possible to build new URIs from the source model URIs. When a certain source model element is mapped to a certain target model element the URI of the target model is built from the URI of the source model element and a certain string. For instance, r1 defines an element of the class *table* of the target model whose URI is built from the URI of an element of the class *data* of the source model plus the string *'table1'*. The same happens with r2 and *'table2'*. It works when a 1-to-1 model mapping is accomplished. When the mapping is *n*-to-1, *n* calls to *newURI* would generate a target model URI from the *n* URIs of elements of the source model. In the case of a 1-to-*n* mapping, there will be *n* rules assuming that each rule uses a different string.

On the other hand, r2, r4, r7, r8, r12 and r13 make use of the completion of the source model in which we have defined the concept of *navigable_role*. Rules from r1 to r8 define the elements of the target model: *table*, *row* and *key*, *foreign*, *col*, while rules from r9 to r13 are specific for defining the roles of the target model: *has*, *is_col*, *is_key*

Table 5. Completion of Model B

Case	SWRL Rule
(c4)	mmB:has(?B,?A) → mmB:table(?A,?B)
(c5)	mmB:is_key(?B,?A) → mmB:has_key(?A,?B)
(c6)	mmB:is_foreign(?B,?A) → mmB:has_foreign(?A,?B)
(c7)	mmB:is_col(?B,?A) → mmB:has_col(?A,?B)

Table 6. Validation of Model B

Case	SWRL Rule
(v17)	mmB:row(?Row) ∧ mmB:col(?Row,?Col1) ∧ mmB:col(?Row,?Col2) ∧ mmB:name(?Col1,?Name1) ∧ mmB:name(?Col2,?Name2) ∧ owl:differentFrom(?Col1,?Col2) ∧ equal(?Name1,?Name2) → val:duplicate_col_name(?Row)
(v18)	mmB:row(?Row) ∧ mmB:foreign(?Row,?Col1) ∧ mmB:foreign(?Row,?Col2) ∧ mmB:name(?Col1,?Name1) ∧ mmB:name(?Col2,?Name2) ∧ owl:differentFrom(?Col1,?Col2) ∧ equal(?Name1,?Name2) → val:duplicate_foreign_name(?Row)
(v19)	mmB:row(?Row) ∧ mmB:key(?Row,?Col1) ∧ mmB:key(?Row,?Col2) ∧ mmB:name(?Col1,?Name1) ∧ mmB:name(?Col2,?Name2) ∧ owl:differentFrom(?Col1,?Col2) ∧ equal(?Name1,?Name2) → val:duplicate_key_name(?Row)
(v27)	mmB:row(?Row1) ∧ mmB:row(?Row2) ∧ owl:differentFrom(?Row1,?Row2) ∧ mmB:name(?Row1,?Name1) ∧ mmB:name(?Row2,?Name2) ∧ equal(?Name1,?Name2) → val:duplicate_row_name(?Row1) ∧ duplicate_row_name(?Row2)
(v29)	mmB:key(?Row,?Key) ∧ mmB:foreign(?Row,?Foreign) → val:bad_row_key_foreign(?Row) mmB:col(?Row,?Col) ∧ mmB:foreign(?Row,?Foreign) → val:bad_row_col_foreign(?Row)

Table 7. Cross Validation of Models A and B

Case	SWRL Rule
(v30)	mmB:key(?Key) ∧ mmB:name(?Key,?Name) ∧ mmA:key_name(?Key,?NameKey) ∧ makeSet(?NameKey,?Names) ∧ notElement(?Name,?Names) → val: bad_key_name(?Key) mmB:key(?Key) ∧ mmB:type(?Key,?Type) ∧ mmA:key_type(?Key,?TypeKey) ∧ makeSet(?TypeKey,?Types) ∧ notElement(?Type,?Types) → val: bad_key_type(?Key) mmB:col(?Col) ∧ mmB:name(?Col,?Name) ∧ mmA:col_name(?Col,?NameCol) ∧ makeSet(?NameCol,?Names) ∧ notElement(?Name,?Names) → val: bad_col_name(?Col) mmB:col(?Col) ∧ mmB:type(?Col,?Type) ∧ mmA:col_type(?Col,?TypeCol) ∧ makeSet(?TypeCol,?Types) ∧ notElement(?Type,?Types) → val: bad_col_type(?Col)
(v31)	mmB:table(?Table) ∧ mmB:name(?Table,?Name) ∧ mmA:table_name(?Table,?NameTable) ∧ makeSet(?NameTable,?Names) ∧ notElement(?Name,?Names) → val:bad_table_name(?Table)
(v32)	mmB:row(?Row) ∧ mmB:name(?Row,?Name) ∧ mmA:row_name(?Row,?NameRow) ∧ makeSet(?NameRow,?Names) ∧ notElement(?Name,?Names) → val:bad_row_name(Row)
(v33)	mmB:foreign(?Foreign) ∧ mmB:name(?Foreign,?Name) ∧ mmA:foreign_name(?Foreign,?NameForeign) ∧ makeSet(?NameForeign,?Names) ∧ notElement(?Name,?Names) → val:bad_foreign_name(?Foreign)

and *is_foreign*. Let us remark that Table 4 is a *partial transformation* of the source into the target model. There are elements that can be derived from this partial transformation, particularly, the inverse roles *table*, *has_col*, *has_key* and *has_foreign*. In a OWL based transformation, partial transformations are completed in the step of completion of the target model.

(d) Completion of the Target Model: Next step consists in the completion of the target model. In the case study (see Table 5) it adds the inverse roles of the roles defined by the partial transformation. Let us remark that inverse roles can be also obtained from OWL constructors and OWL reasoning. We can also complete the target model with OWL by adding cardinality constraints ('1' and '*') in order to obtain the target model shown in Figure 3.

(e) **Validation of the Target Model:** Next step consists in the validation of the target model following the requirements of Table 1. In Table 6, we have defined the concepts *duplicate_col_name*, *duplicate_key_name*, etc.

(f) **Cross Validation of Source and Target Models:** Finally, cross validation of models A and B is achieved by the rules of Table 7. Cross validation requires ontology merging. The concepts defined by the rules are *bad_key_name*, *bad_key_type*, etc. using the proposed SWRL built-ins *makeSet* and *notElement*.

4 Related Work

Model transformation is a widely studied topic of research in which many frameworks and tools have been developed (see [7,11,21]). However, the use of the ODM representation for model transformation as well as the adoption of SWRL have not been explored enough. We have shown that SWRL has to be equipped with some built-ins with this end. Our proposed built-ins (except *newURI*) are already present in the SWRL extension called *SQWRL* [14], whose aim is to extend SWRL with querying mechanism. Fortunately, this built-in can be defined in terms of two built-ins of SQWRL: *hasURI* and *concatString*, therefore we can assume that our rules can be triggered from any SQWRL implementation. We have developed our own SWRL interpreter (equipped with the required built-ins), called *OTL (Ontology based Transformation Language)*, on top of SWI-Prolog in order to test the examples. The interpreter is publicly available from http://indalog.ual.es/mdd.

On the other hand, validation and verification of model transformations is an emerging topic of research (see [3,4,5,6,13,19]). We have found some similarities of our work with the proposed in [4]. The authors work in the context of ATL and OCL, but handle the same kind of properties as our approach (validation of unique names for relations and attributes, together with existence of keys). A more general framework for transformation validation and verification is proposed in [5] including properties about transformation rules. Our approach focused on properties about meta-models, assuming that when some requirement is violated either models or rules are incorrect.

5 Conclusions and Future Work

In this paper we have presented a framework for the specification and validation of model transformations with SWRL/OWL, using the representation of UML models with ODM. We have implemented and tested the approach, including the development of a SWRL interpreter.

Our approach will be extended in the future as follows: (a) We would like to extend the mechanisms for model validation including justifications, diagnosis, reparation, etc. (b) Secondly, we would like to test our approach with other UML diagrams and transformations, and also with bigger examples; (c) Thirdly, we are also interested in the use of our approach for model driven development of user interfaces in the line of our previous works [1,2]; (d) Finally, we believe that our work will lead to the development of an ODM based tool for transformation and validation of models.

References

1. Almendros-Jiménez, J.M., Iribarne, L.: An Extension of UML for the Modeling of WIMP User Interfaces. Journal of Visual Languages and Computing 19, 695–720 (2008)
2. Almendros-Jiménez, J.M., Iribarne, L.: UML Modeling of User and Database Interaction. The Computer Journal 52(3), 348–367 (2009)
3. Blanc, X., Mougenot, A., Mounier, I., Mens, T.: Incremental Detection of Model Inconsistencies Based on Model Operations. In: van Eck, P., Gordijn, J., Wieringa, R. (eds.) CAiSE 2009. LNCS, vol. 5565, pp. 32–46. Springer, Heidelberg (2009)
4. Büttner, F., Cabot, J., Gogolla, M.: On validation of ATL transformation rules by transformation models. In: Proceedings of the 8th International Workshop on Model-Driven Engineering, Verification and Validation, MoDeVVa, pp. 1–8. ACM, New York (2011), http://doi.acm.org/10.1145/2095654.2095666
5. Cabot, J., Clarisó, R., Guerra, E., de Lara, J.: Verification and Validation of Declarative Model-to-Model Transformations. Systems and Software 2(83), 283–302 (2010)
6. Cabot, J., Clarisó, R., Riera, D.: Verification of UML/OCL class diagrams using constraint programming. In: IEEE International Conference on Software Testing Verification and Validation, ICSTW 2008, pp. 73–80. IEEE (2008)
7. Czarnecki, K., Helsen, S.: Feature-based survey of model transformation approaches. IBM Systems Journal 45(3), 621–645 (2006)
8. Hillairet, G.: ATL Use Case - ODM Implementation (Bridging UML and OWL). Tech. rep. (2007), http://www.eclipse.org/m2m/atl/atlTransformations/
9. Horrocks, I., Patel-Schneider, P., Boley, H., Tabet, S., Grosof, B., Dean, M., et al.: SWRL: A semantic web rule language combining OWL and RuleML. W3C Member submission 21, 79 (2004)
10. Jouault, F., Kurtev, I.: On the architectural alignment of ATL and QVT. In: SAC 2006: Proceedings of the 2006 ACM Symposium on Applied Computing, pp. 1188–1195. ACM, New York (2006)
11. Jouault, F., Kurtev, I.: On the interoperability of model-to-model transformation languages. Sci. Comput. Program. 68(3), 114–137 (2007)
12. Knublauch, H., Fergerson, R.W., Noy, N.F., Musen, M.A.: The Protégé OWL Plugin: An Open Development Environment for Semantic Web Applications. In: McIlraith, S.A., Plexousakis, D., van Harmelen, F. (eds.) ISWC 2004. LNCS, vol. 3298, pp. 229–243. Springer, Heidelberg (2004)
13. Le Noir, J., Delande, O., Exertier, D., da Silva, M.A.A., Blanc, X.: Operation Based Model Representation: Experiences on Inconsistency Detection. In: France, R.B., Kuester, J.M., Bordbar, B., Paige, R.F. (eds.) ECMFA 2011. LNCS, vol. 6698, pp. 85–96. Springer, Heidelberg (2011)
14. O'Connor, M.J., Das, A.K.: SQWRL: a query language for OWL. In: Fifth International Workshop on OWL: Experiences and Directions (OWLED) (2009)
15. OMG: MDA Spec. Tech. rep. (2003), http://www.omg.org/mda/specs.htm
16. OMG: MOF 2.0 Query/Views/Transformations RFP. Tech. rep. (2008), http://www.omg.org/docs/ad/05-01-06.pdf
17. OMG: Object Constraint Language (OCL). Tech. rep. (2008), http://www.omg.org/technology/documents/formal/ocl.htm

18. OMG: Ontology Definition Metamodel (ODM). Tech. rep. (2009),
    http://www.omg.org/spec/ODM/1.0/
19. Schätz, B.: Verification of model transformations. Electronic Communications of the
    EASST 29 (2010)
20. TopCased: Topcased: The open-source tool kit for critical systems. Tech. rep. (2010),
    http://www.topcased.org/
21. Tratt, L.: Model transformations and tool integration. Software and System Modeling 4(2),
    112–122 (2005)

Context-Based Query Using Dependency Structures Based on Latent Topic Model

Takashi Yanagisawa and Takao Miura

HOSEI University, Dept.of Elect.& Elect. Engr.
3-7-2 Kajinocho, Koganei, Tokyo, 184–8584 Japan
miurat@hosei.ac.jp

Abstract. To improve and enhance information retrieval techniques, there have been many approaches proposed so far, but few investigation which capture semantic aspects of queries directly. Here we propose a new approach to retrieve contextual dependencies in Japanese based on latent topics. We examine some experimental results to see the effectiveness.

Keywords: Query, Dependency Structure, Latent Dirichlet Allocation.

1 Motivation

Recently there have been several approaches to obtain huge amount of digital text information through internet, and this is why there have been many approaches proposed so far to improve and enhance information retrieval techniques. But because of rapid and tremendous growth of internet world, it is hard to manage all of them easily in a systematically organized and consistent manner. Nowadays there are many discussion about advanced techniques such as ranking, summarizing and authority/hub concepts. Generally, given keywords, information retrieval by queries allows us to find relevant items through inverted index files. By a word *query* we mean a collection of *words* given by users. By putting weights on the words (such as TF*IDF), we may efficiently obtain documents that are strongly connected to weighted words.

On the other hand, there have been many investigations proposed from the view point of context analysis and here we propose how to do that by dependency structure within queries. For example, by applying syntax and dependency analysis of queries, we are able to extract documents correctly that are relevant deeply to queries[4,6]. One important approach comes from *topic model*. In this model each document is assumed to be described by means of random mixture over topics and each topic by probability distribution over words, which means a topic corresponds to latent semantic unit described by a collection of words[1]. Recently more sophisticated retrieval has been proposed based on *Latent Dirichlet Allocation* (LDA) [7]. Unfortunately few approach has been investigated about

---

[1] In other words, a *topic* doesn't mean an explicit subject such as *politics* or *airplane* but a kind of cluster putting together by some probabilistic measure.

A. Abelló, L. Bellatreche, and B. Benatallah (Eds.): MEDI 2012, LNCS 7602, pp. 116–128, 2012.
© Springer-Verlag Berlin Heidelberg 2012

queries containing keywords by which users may give some intention on dependencies among phrases. In this investigation, we propose how to model contextual dependencies in Japanese language based on latent topics.

This work is organized as follows. We describe relevant works mainly in section 2 while LDA is described in section 3. In section 4 we discuss stochastic parsing for queries based on a *dependency structure model*. We examine some experiments in section 5 to see how well our model works. We conclude our work in section 6.

2 Latent Dirichlet Allocation (LDA)

A *topic model* is an assumption that each document can be described as random mixture over topics and each topic as word distribution, while a *document model* is a probabilistic assumption that each document follows a mixed multi-nominal distribution over words.

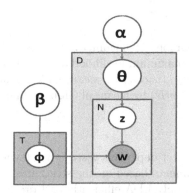
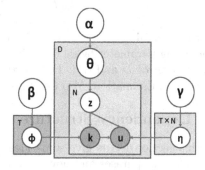

Fig. 1. Graphical Models for LDA

Fig. 2. Graphical Model of Dependency Structure

A topic model is known as an accurate vehicle for document description. One of fundamental approaches is a *probabilistic Latent Semantic Indexing* (pLSI) which is random mixture over topics and each topic is described over word distribution, but the mixture is determined in advance according to training data[3]. LDA [1] is *dynamic* in a sense that mixture is determined in a probabilistic manner, not depending on training data but on Dirichlet probability model. In fact, we estimate the model from *prior probability distribution* of words in training data by means of Gibbs sampling.

In the figure 1, let us illustrate our situation by *graphical model* which contains a latent variable z. A word "*latent*" means it is hard to observe these values explicitly. This is why we like to estimate probability distributions over topics z given observed words w with an assumption of Dirichlet prior distribution of topics. Dirichlet prior distribution $p(\phi)$ over topics is described by a hyper parameter β and Dirichlet prior distribution $p(\theta_d)$ over topics with respect to documents d is described by another hyper parameter α. Then we can show multi-nominal distribution $p(w|z, \phi_z)$ of words w over each topic z represented by ϕ_z with total N words. Also, given a number of topics by T, we may describe multi-nominal distribution $p(z|\theta_d)$ of topics z in a document d represented by θ_d with D documents, $d = 1, .., D$.

In this framework words are generated based on LDA as follows. Given a topic t according to $p(\phi_t)$ drawn from $\phi(\beta)$ and a document d according to $p(\theta_d)$ from $\theta(\alpha)$, we generate a topic z_i from a multi-nominal probability distribution $p(z|\theta_d)$ in a document d at a position i (in a document d) and a word w_i from a distribution $p(w|z, \phi_z)$.

Wei et al.[7] proposes a new framework of information retrieval based on LDA. In fact, LDA plays as an important role as *smoothing* within conventional techniques.

$$P(w|D) = \lambda(\frac{N_d}{N_d + \mu}P_{ML}(w|d) + \frac{\mu}{N_d + \mu}P_{ML}(w|coll)) + (1 - \lambda)P_{lda}(w|d)$$

$$P_{lda}(w|D) = \sum_t P(w|t)P(t|D)$$

In this formulation, we denote the total number of documents by N_d and a smoothing parameter by μ. We estimate the maximum likelihood of a word w in a collection of D and *coll*, $P_{ML}(w|d)$ and $P_{ML}(w|coll)$ by means of Maximum Likelihood Estimation. Also we estimate $P_{lda}(w|D)$ by means of Gibbs sampling.

3 Dependency Structure

In this section let us give some ideas to model dependency structure (syntax structure) of phrases and how to rank documents based on the structures[4,6]. To do that, it is necessary to show how to apply LDA efficiently and precisely to various kinds of dependency structures to capture wide range of intentions among them. In this work, we introduce latent variables in a sense of LDA to capture the dependencies and model our approach of ranking using them.

Let us note that Wei et al. [7] is not suitable for analysis of dependency structure because the approach depends heavily on word frequency and LDA can't be applied directly for smoothing.

3.1 Words and Cases

We know the fact that, in English, a word describes grammatical roles such as *case* and *plurality* by means of word order or inflection. The difference between "John calls Mary" and "Mary calls John" corresponds to the two interpretation of *who calls whom* over John and Mary. Such kind of language is called *inflectional language*. On the other hand, in some languages as Japanese and Chinese, grammatical relationship can be described by means of postpositional particles, and such kind of languages is called *agglutinative language*. For example, let us see the two sentences:

"John ga Mary wo yobu" (*John calls Mary*)
"John wo Mary ga yobu" (*Mary calls John*)

In the two sentences the positions of "John, Mary" and "yobu(*call*)" are exactly same but the difference of postpositional particles("ga,wo"). Because of *cases*, basically we can put any words to any places, as we shown in the above example. One exception is a *predicate* part which appear as the last. In any documents in Japanese, the predicate appears as a *last verb* in each sentence. In our case, we can say:

"Mary wo John ga yobu" (*John calls Mary*)
"Mary ga John wo yobu" (*Mary calls John*)

3.2   Phrases and the Dependencies

First of all let us describe our ideas to model dependency structures (sometimes called *phrase structure*) which capture syntax aspects. By the word *dependency structure*, we mean a binary relationship among phrases, which describes one word/phrase (called a *parent*) attaches to a following word/phrase (a *child* or an *attachment*). A parent can be considered as an adornment of child to make the role of the child more specific. A *phrase* is a semantic unit where any phrase in a sentence constitutes an attachment[5].

Syntactic analysis means we parse sentences and explain their grammatical structures. On the other hand, given a sentence, there may be several interpretation. For example, let us see a sentence in Japanese:

utsukushii (*beautiful*) suishagoya (*miller*) no(-) musume (*daughter*)

This sentence has at least two interpretations, *beautiful miller* and *beautiful daughter*. To identify the interpretation, we should have examine contexts or mental situation. But very often the interpretation is given by means of structure among words:

((beautiful miller) daughter)
(beautiful (miller daughter))

In the former case *beautiful* qualifies *miller* and in the latter *daughter*.

As we said, generally in Japanese, we can move any words to any places because of postpositional particles. But we have some exceptions. One is about predicates. Another exception is that, in any dependency structure, a parent phrase appears first and the child obtains more sharp semantics by the parent. For example, if we examine a dependency between *beautiful* and *daughter*, we mean *(miller (beautiful daughter))* alternatively.

suishagoya (*miller*) no(-) utsukushii (*beautiful*) musume (*daughter*)

But if we like a dependency between *beautiful* and *miller*, we can't move them because *miller* (child word) appears first.

To manage structures of phrase dependencies, it seems possible to analyze wide range of the structures by examining corpus explicitly and putting them into a database. However, it is hard to manage them efficiently because there exist many kinds of the structures. This is why we introduce latent variables to model child phrases to each a parent as well as topics so that we estimate child phrases in a probabilistic manner using topics and parents based on LDA.

3.3   A Generative Model of Dependency

Here we describe a generative model[2] of dependency structure based on LDA. We illustrate our approach in figure 2. In this figure we introduce two distributions over parent and child phrases on LDA instead of word distribution.

Assuming 3 hyper parameters α, β and γ, in the left part of the figure, we show Dirichlet prior distribution $p(\phi)$ over topics z described by β with T topics to describe multi-nominal distribution $p(z|\phi_z)$ over parent phrases. Similarly in the right part of the figure, we give Dirichlet prior distribution $p(\eta)$ over dependencies k described by γ with T topics and N dependencies to describe multi-nominal distribution $p(z|\eta_{z,k})$ over child phrases. Finally we show Dirichlet prior distribution $p(\theta)$ over topics in a document d described by α with D documents to describe multi-nominal distribution $p(z|\theta_d)$ over topics in d.

Let us describe how dependency structure is generated in a probabilistic manner. Assume there exist 3 hyper parameters α, β and γ. Given a topic t according to $p(\phi_t)$ drawn from $\phi(\beta)$ and a parent k according to $p(\eta_{t,k})$ drawn from $\eta(\gamma)$, we assume a document d according to $p(\theta_d)$ drawn from $theta(\alpha)$. At a position i in d, we generate a topic z_i from a multi-nominal probability distribution $p(z|\theta_d)$, and then a parent k_i and its child u_i according to distributions $p(k_i|z, \phi_{z_i})$ and $p(u_i|\eta_{z_i,k_i})$ respectively. Let us note that θ means a probability of a topic j in a document d, ϕ means a probability of a parent $\mathbf{k}$ in a topic j, and that η means a probability of a child $\mathbf{u}$ to a parent $\mathbf{k}$ in a topic j.

Unlike a word generation model, we should have dependency structures from two multi-nominal distributions of parents and children. Our latent topic model, therefore, takes much more time to estimate topics as the next formulation indicates:

$$P(k, u|\alpha, \beta, \gamma) =$$

$$\int \int \int \prod_{z=1}^{T \times N} P(\eta_{z,n}|\gamma) \prod_{z=1}^{T} P(\phi_z|\beta)(P(\theta_d|\alpha)$$

$$(\prod_{n=1}^{N_d} \sum_{z_n}^{T} (P(z_n|\theta)P(k_n|z_n, \phi)P(u_n|z_n, k_n, \eta))))d\theta d\phi d\eta$$

In fact, to estimate unknown parameters in the LDA formula above, we should have apply Gibbs sampling procedure to obtain enough samples according to

---

[2] We mean we may generate dependencies based on this probability distribution.

$P(\mathbf{z}|\mathbf{k}, \mathbf{u})$. Thus we could estimate θ, ϕ and η To do that, we like to obtain conditional probability $P(z_i = j|\backslash i, \mathbf{k}, \mathbf{u})$ as follows.

$$P(z_i = j|\backslash i, \mathbf{k}, \mathbf{u})$$
$$= \frac{(n_{\backslash i,k_i,j}^{(u_i)} + \gamma)(n_{\backslash i,j}^{(k_i)} + \beta)(n_{\backslash i,j}^{(d)} + \alpha)}{(n_{\backslash i,k_i,j}^{(\bullet)} + \gamma)(n_{\backslash i,j}^{(\bullet)} + \beta)}$$

Let us note that n_j^d means a number of topics appeared in a document d, $n_j^{(k_i)}$ a number of parents k_i appeared in a topic j, $n_{k_i,j}^{(u_i)}$ a number of occurrences of children u_i with a parent k_i in a topic j, $n_j^{(\bullet)}$ a total occurrences number of topic j, and $n_{k_i,j}^{(\bullet)}$ a number of occurrences of a parent k_i in a topic j.

4   Queries Using Dependency Structure

Now let us describe how we examine queries using dependency structures in Japanese language. Generally a query means a collection of words by which we give some fragmentary knowledge as a whole. For each word we may assume some intention and a set of answers that satisfy the intention. If we assume any intention can be defined in a constructive manner, all the common answers may satisfy all the intentions, which can be considered as the answers.

In this investigation, we assume dependency structure among query words which share a collection of documents. If we assume any intention can be defined in a constructive manner, all the common answers may satisfy all the intentions, which can be considered as the answers.

For example, we assume 3 words "USA", "JAPAN" and "SUMMIT". We assume these words may appear in several dependency structures and we might think about "USA PREDIDENT", "JAPAN PRIME MINISTER" and "SUMMIT MEETING" by dependency structure. Since each word/phrase appears under some topic distribution in LDA, it is possible to obtain joint probability of the 3 words to each topic. Documents may have the likelihood according to these topics. Then we extract documents as the answers by Maximum Likelihood Estimation. In our case, we may have another kind of topic concerning "USA STUDENT", "JAPAN TRAVEL" and "SUMMIT OF MT FUJI". By estimating LDA models, we get a news article of "Top-level meeting by US and Japan" as more likely answers. Moreover, for each document, we have likelihood values by which we can generate ranking about the documents as answers.

5   Experiments

5.1   Preliminaries

We show how well our approach works. Here we examine Asahi news articles (2009) and extract two collections of the articles. One contains 10,000 articles

122   T. Yanagisawa and T. Miura

(from Jan.01) and another 20,000 (from Jan. 01). We have analyzed all the Japanese sentences in advance by means of Japanese morphological analyzer "JUMAN" and a parser "KNP" [4]. In fact, there are 1,827,545 occurrences of 525,074 dependency structures in 20,000 articles. Also we give several initial parameters by examining preparatory experiments. As input-parameters we give a number of latent topics in test corpus and iteration counts for Gibbs sampling.

First of all, we examine *how well* our approach models News articles. To do that, we introduce a notion of *perplexity* to evaluate probability models. Formally perplexity (PP) of a discrete probability distribution p is defined as:

$$PP = 2^{H(p)}, H(p) = -\frac{\sum_X \log_2 p(X)}{N}$$

Note that $H(p)$ means the average amount of information, i.e., the entropy of p over events X. It is well known that smaller PP means better modeling capability because any random variables $X_1, \cdots, X_N$ have less amount of information.

In our case, given a collection of dependency structures $s = X_1 \cdots X_N$ where each structure X_i in a topic z consists of a parent and a child in the topic z, the perplexity PP means we may expect s be possible structures appeared in a common topic z. Formally we generate $p(X)$ as a probability of each dependency structure X as $p_1(X) \times p_2(X) \times p_3(X)$ where $p_1(X)$ means a topic probability (of some topic z), $p_2(X)$ a word probability of a parent in X in a context of z and $p_3(X)$ a child probability of X in z. Then we obtain all the $p(X)$ in a sentence of N structures in z.

$$P_M(X_1 \cdots X_N) = \Pi_{i=1}^N p(X_i)$$

$$PP(s) = P_M(X_1 \cdots X_N)^{-\frac{1}{N}} = 1/ \sqrt[N]{\Pi_i p(X_1) \cdots p(X_N)}$$

Our second experiment is to show how nice coherence we obtain about classes of documents by our approach, i.e., we obtain similar documents with each other in each class. To examine similarity of documents in a common topic, we should have distribution of documents over a topic in advance. By using (average) cosine similarity with TF*IDF weights, we compare documents in one topic with total documents.

Finally, to evaluate our query approach, we examine query results based on dependency structures.

First we extract 10 articles from 20,000 and analyze each headline part. Then we extract 3 nouns with high TF*IDF to each headline and give them as 10 queries. Table 1 contains the headlines and query words where underline means proper nouns with low frequency. A query with 3 keywords is called "3 words query", and the one with first 2 keywords is called "2 keywords query". We assume that the correct answers are the 10 articles themselves. To evaluate query results, we compare our approach with conventional TF*IDF one[2]. In our approach we expect articles of smaller perplexities with respect to the query words and give the results by ranking.

Table 1. 10 Example Queries

No.	HeadLine	Keywords
1	Ohita Consultant Datsuzei (An consultant in Ohita evades tax): Boryokudan ni 5 Oku yen (5 billion yen to boryokudan)	Ohga (Ohga), Yogi(suspicion), Datsuzei(tax evasion)
2	Kurinton Chokan, Aso to Kaidan : (Clinton, US Secretary meeting Aso:) Domei kyoka de icchi (deepening US-Japan Alliance), Ozawa tomo (also met Mr. Ozawa)	Kaidan (meeting), Kurinton (Clinton), Chokan (US Secretary)
3	Tokyo de Barabara Satsujin (Ripper in Tokyo): Hoshijima Muki (Hoshijima, an accused, life imprisonment), Shikei deha omoi - Chisai (capital punishment too serious - a district court)	Muki (life imprisonment), Shikei (capital punishment), Choeki (penal servitude)
4	NichiRo Shuno kaidan (Russo-Japan Summit Meeting) : Ryodo Mondai (Territorial issue) , - Seiji ga ketsudan (political problem), Shusho shin apurohchi (prime minister taking a new approach)	Shuno(leader), Kaidan (meeting), Rosia(Russia)
5	2009 nen Yosan (2009 budget), Shuin Kuten (the Diet remains idle), Getsunai mo Ki-Shingo (negative outlook in this month), Iradatsu Yoto (Government party irritated)	Yosan(budget), Shingi (discussion), Shuin (the Diet)
6	Zerozero Bukken (zerozero property) : Mimei Tokusoku ni Baisho Shiji (compensation for morning demand), Yachin Hosho Gaisha ni (to rent surety company) - Fukuoka Kosai (Fukuoka high court)	Hosho(surety), Yachin(rent), Zerozero (zerozero)
7	Taigai Jusei (in-vitro fertilization): Juseiran Torichigae (mistaking an egg fertilized in vitro), Ninshin to Chuzetsu (conception/abortion), 20 dai Josei (20's lady) - Kagawa (Kagawa)	Ranshi(ova), Jusei(insemination), Byoin(hospital)
8	Ashita no Joh (Ashita no Joh): Bokushingu Manga (manga in boxing), Fukkoku Rensai (serial publication in reprint)	Fukkoku(reprint), Rensai(serial publication), Ashita(ashita)
9	Juseiran Torichigae (mistaking an egg fertilized in vitro): Waga ko nara (my baby ? can't believed), Shussan Dannen (delivery abandoned)	Ranshi(ova), Jusei(insemination), Fufu(couple)
10	Kan po no Yado (Kan po hotels): 2nen inai no Joto (transfer within 2 years), Keiyaku Tadashi gaki(proviso) - Somusho (minister of internal affairs and communications)	Joto (transfer), Yado (hotel), Kan (kan)

5.2   Results

Let us show the results of the first experiment. Tables 2 and 3 contain perplexities of 10,000 and 20,000 articles respectively with several number T of latent topics and iteration counts for Gibbs sampling.

As shown in these tables, all the values of test-set perplexity become stable eventually after 400 iteration. Thus we examine the perplexity of 1000 iteration and 200 topics in 10,000 articles, and of 1000 iteration and 300 topics in 20,000 articles.

As the 2nd experiment, let us show the similarity results in figure 3. There are 53,388 occurrences of articles spreading over 200 topics with redundancy. Note there are 10,000 articles in total so that each article contains 5.34 topics in average. Each topic contains 266.9 articles in average where the maximum 3,246 articles and the minimum 74. The total similarity is 0.0217, and the average

Table 2. 10000 documents test-set perplexity

T	Iteration				
	200	400	600	800	1000
50	6466.88	6184.02	6110.86	6070.93	6054.05
100	5048.64	4873.80	4791.86	4744.52	4721.45
150	4501.88	4333.43	4281.81	4257.28	4238.26
200	4181.79	4073.29	4033.04	4014.49	3993.93

Table 3. 20000 documents test-set perplexity

T	Iteration				
	200	400	600	800	1000
50	7962.55	7639.58	7509.45	7449.90	7418.68
100	6229.89	6026.60	5963.95	5932.45	5905.87
150	5556.85	5373.78	5309.00	5277.59	5260.03
200	5329.33	5176.40	5138.58	5105.77	5071.59
250	5122.78	4989.31	4950.89	4934.12	4920.05
300	5035.64	4931.95	4889.32	4862.85	4856.43

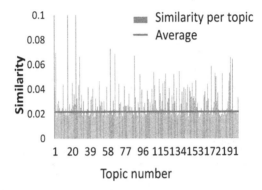

Fig. 3. Average Cosine Similarity in each topic

similarity of articles in each topic is 0.0315 where the maximum similarity 0.1923 (topic 15) and the minimum 0.0174 (topic 158). We get the average similarity 0.0315 in each topic which is better than cosine similarity 0.0217 over 200 topics. Moreover we get higher similarity of 144 topics among 200.

Let us show some examples of top 10 dependency structures about each of 3 topics in table 4. These have been obtained through our LDA approach.

In the table, we see a topic (1) contains mainly words about *TRAIN*, a topic (2) about *JOB OPPRTUNITIES* and a topic (3) about *ARTS* and *THEATRE*.

Finally let us show the results of information queries in table 5 where each entry contains a ranking value in the answers. In the table, we see 5 questions and 6 questions have higher ranking by our LDA approach than TF*IDF approach using 2 words and 3 words respectively. So both approaches seem to work well equally. However, in TF*IDF case, when a query contains "proper nouns" (marked by " *"), the rank goes up. This is because Inverse Document Frequency (IDF) provides us to specify which documents contain the words. On the other hand, in 3 words queries, LDA approach works very well without proper nouns: all of 5 queries are not inferior to TF*IDF. It is worth noting that queries work well with no proper noun.

Table 4. Dependency Structure

Topic (1)		Topic (2)		Topic (3)	
(parent)	(child)	(parent)	(child)	(parent)	(child)
Resha	Tabi	Haken	Kiri	Ai	Gekijo
(train)	(travel)	(temporary employee)	(discharge)	(love)	(theatre)
Eikyo	Deta	Shishoku shita	NominKo	Nezuyoi	Ninki
(effect)	(produce)	(unemployed)	(farmer)	(deep-rooted)	(favor)
Zensen	Miawase	Seishain	Shite	Shio	Moe
(whole line)	(stopped)	(regular member)	(-)	(Shio Asami)	(Moe Midorikawa)
Miawase	Eikyoshita	Koyo	Mamoru	Showa	Nioi
(stopped)	(affected)	(Employment)	(protect)	(Showa)	(smelling)
Baikyaku	Kento taisho	Yatou	Iu	Otoko	Onna
(sale)	(subject)	(engage)	(say)	(man)	(woman)
Unten	Miawase	Rousi	Goi	Ani	Kaeru
(operation)	(stopped)	(capital and labor)	(agreement)	(bother)	(come back)
Teian compe	Jisshi	Tanshuku suru	koto	Ari	Fureta
(competition)	(working)	(shorten)	(-)	(-)	(-)
Shoken shuyou	5sha	Jigyo	Omoni	Haiyu	Kawara Masahiko
(major stock company)	(5 companies)	(business)	(mainly)	(Actor)	san (Mr.Masahiko Kawara)
Tagaku no	Sonshitsu	Mukiai	Tenkai subekida	Sukitoru	Sozai
(heavy)	(loss)	(cope with)	(solve)	(transparent)	(material)
Hantai gawa	Doa	Haken kikan	Jogen	Joen	Naru
(opposite side)	(door)	(temporary labor period)	(limit)	(performance)	(-)

5.3   Discussion

Let us discuss what our results mean. First of all, as shown in our first experiment, all the values of perplexity become stable eventually after 400 iteration which means our language model is suitable for word dependency.

By using LDA approach for dependency structure, document similarities of more than 70 % topics are superior than the whole average, which means articles are well-clustered over topics so that topic distribution works well by LDA learning.

In table 6, we examine some detail. We show word dependencies of the highest 10 probabilities in the highest similarity topic 15 (2284 articles) and the lowest similarity topic 158 (144 articles).

Table 5. Ranking using 2/3 Words

No	2 Words		3 Words	
	TF*IDF	LDA	TF*IDF	LDA
1*	9	6	7	5
2*	2	6	2	5
3	2	4	2	1
4	6	3	6	1
5	12	3	12	1
6*	1	8	1	7
7	3	1	3	1
8*	1	15	1	10
9	1	1	1	1
10*	16	4	16	2

126   T. Yanagisawa and T. Miura

Table 6. Topics in Word Dependencies of Highest/Lowest Similarities

Highest Similarity (parent)	(child)	Lowest Similarity (parent)	(child)
Totsunyu suru *(come out)*	Hyomei *(manifest)*	Kamin chu *(taking a nap)*	Nagasareta *(floating)*
Zenmen Taiketsu Shisei *(general confrontation)*	Totsunyu suru *(come out)*	Datsu kanryo *(post bureaucracy)*	Chiki Shusai *(community organized)*
Tai Kankoku Madoguchi dearu *(contach the South)*	Sokoku Heiwa Toitsu Iinkai *(motherland and peaceful unification committee)*	Saito san *(Mr. Saito)*	chichi *(father)*
Nanboku Shuno Kaidan *(inter-korean summit)*	07 nen *(2007)*	Ani deshi *(senior pupil)*	3 nin *(3 persons)*
Ugoki *(movement)*	Aru *(-)*	Dou Hoan bu *(safety department)*	Yoru *(-)*
Kotei *(agreement)*	Hitei *(disagreement)*	Dai 8 *(No. 8)*	Ki *(-)*
Kaku Hoyukoku *(nuclear power state)*	shite *(-)*	Kaoru *(kaoru)*	Hikoku *(accused person)*
Uchiageru *(launch)*	Koto *(-)*	Shozoga *(portrait)*	Eri *(eri)*
Misairu *(missile)*	Kowai *(scary)*	Oyabun *(boss)*	Kao *(face)*
Muko *(invalid)*	Sengen shita *(state)*	Sumo *(sumo wrestling)*	Tsudukeru *(continue)*

In some words with the highest similarity, we see many dependencies about international politics, and many articles which the words appear. On the other hand, there seems no common aspect in the lowest case, and this is why the articles are not similar with each other. 72 % topics may contain well-structured clusters.

Also let us note that we get to several topics depending on "children" through dependencies. For example, we show dependencies which have "Nihon" (*Japan*) as a parent word with several children words in 2 different topics: Table 7 contains the dependencies with the 4 highest probabilities, and some dependencies of the 5 highest probabilities in table 8. In both tables there seem two kinds of the dependencies in each topic: "AIRPLANE" and "INTERNATIONAL POLITICS" respectively in table 7, and "AIRPLANE" and "THE DISPUTE WITH RUSSIA OVER THE KURILE ISLANDS" in table 8.

Let us discuss query results by LDA approach. Generally queries by 2 words work well with TF*IDF equally but we see more characteristic aspects in queries by 3 words. Our experiment says that TF*IDF works well with proper nouns but not without. On the other hand, LDA approach works well without proper

Table 7. Word Dependencies with "Japan"

Topic (1) (parent)	(child)	Topic (2) (parent)	(child)
Nihon *(Japan)*	Koku Gaisha *(airline)*	Nihon *(japan)*	Shusho *(prime minister)*
Nihon	Kangararreru *(it isi said)*	Nihon	Homon Dan *(delegation)*
Nihon	Shupatsu suru *(depart)*	Nihon	Shien Dan *(support group)*
Nihon	Sora *(sky)*	Nihon	Totte *(-)*

Table 8. Highest Dependencies in 2 Topics

Topic (1) (parent)	(child)	Topic (2) (parent)	(child)
Nihon *(Japan)*	Koku Gaisha *(airline)*	Hoppou *(north)*	4 Tou *(4 islands)*
Hiko Keikaku *(aviation planning)*	Shonin *(approval)*	Shutsunyugoku kahdo *(immigration card)*	Teishutsu *(present)*
Ririku *(departure)*	Hajimeta *(begin)*	Sengo *(after the war)*	Shusho *(prime minister)*
Kanzen ni *(completely)*	Oiharau *(disperse)*	Nihon *(japan)*	Shusho *(prime minister)*
Keganin *(injured person)*	Nakatta *(not found)*	Kizoku Mondai *(identification issue)*	Saishuteki kaiketsu *(final solution)*

nouns because dependency structures can be captured for the purpose of queries. In fact, in 3 words queries, there is no error for ranking. We examine a case "QUERY 4" by 3 words in some more detail in table 1. Here we can get the correct answer as top ranking. Table 9 contains dependencies among the query keywords, and table 10 contains the dependencies of the 5 highest probabilities in a topic which contains all the dependencies appeared in table 9. A topic in table 10 describes "THE DISPUTE WITH RUSSIA OVER THE KURILE ISLANDS", and QUERY4 seems to have a strong relation to the structures in table 9.

Table 9. Dependencies(QUERY 4)

(parent)	(child)
Kobetsu kaidan *(individual meeting)*	Okonau tsumorida *(plan)*
NichiRo Shunou Kaidan Ryodo Mondai *(Russo Japanese relationship - territorial dispute)*	Osaka *(osaka)*
NichiRo soho *(Both Russia and Japan)*	Kanshin Jiko *(concern)*

Table 10. Highest Dependencies (2 Topics)

(parent)	(child)
Hoppou *(north)*	4 tou *(4 islands)*
Shutsuynugoku Kahdo *(immigration card)*	Teishusu *(present)*
Sengo *(after the war)*	Shusho *(prime minister)*
Nihon *(Japan)*	Shusho *(prime minister)*
Kizoku mondai *(identification issue)*	Saishuteki Kaiketsu *(final solution)*

In TF*IDF queries, we got our correct answer as ranking 6 where 3 query keywords "Kaidan"(meeting), "Shunoh(Leader)" and "Rosia"(Russia) have TF*IDF 37.495, 30.3249 and 28.051 respectively. The headline of the top ranked article is "US-Japan Summit Meeting : Closeness Ends in Failure, No Lunch and No Joint Press Meeting " which contains no "Russia". We guess "Kaidan" (meeting) is too specific to give a sort of drifting topics.

In total, our proposed approach provides us to capture structural relationship with articles and to avoid sole effect caused by words. Especially we can avoid characteristic aspect of proper nouns to our queries which cause very often wrong topic drifting in TF*IDF case.

6 Conclusion

In this work, we have proposed a new kind of query processing using dependency structure among words by means of LDA latent topic model. And we have shown better query results that capture semantical aspects very well. By using the approach we have shown that 72 % topics contain better similarity among documents compared to the average.

Acknowledgement. The authors thank the reviewers for their helpful comments.

References

1. Blei, D.M., Ng, A.Y., Jordan, M.I.: Latent Dirichlet Allocation. Journal of Machine Learning Research 3, 993–1022 (2003)
2. Grossman, D.A., Frieder, O.: Information RetrievalAlgorithms and Heuristics, 2nd edn. Springer (2004)
3. Hofmann, T.: Probabilistic Latent Semantic Indexing. In: Proc. of the Twenty-Second Annual International SIGIR Conference on Research and Development in Information Retrieval, SIGIR 1999 (1999)
4. Kurohashi, S., Nagao, M.: KN Parser: Japanese Dependency/Case Structure Analyzer, In: Proc. of the Workshop on Sharable Natural Language Resources (1994)
5. Manning, C.D., Schutze, H.: Foundations of Statistical Natural Language Processing. MIT Press (1999)
6. Shinzato, K., Kurohashi, S.: Exploiting Term Importance Categories and Dependency Relations for Natural Language Search. In: Proc. of the Second Workshop on NLPIX 2010, Beijing, China, pp. 2–11 (2010)
7. Wei, X., Bruce Croft, W.: LDA-Based Document Models for Ad-Hoc Retrieval. In: Proc. of the 29th Annual International ACM SIGIR Conference on Research and Development in Information Retrieval (2006)
8. Yanagisawa, T., Miura, T., Shioya, I.: Sentences Generation by Frequent Parsing Patterns. In: Fyfe, C., Tino, P., Charles, D., Garcia-Osorio, C., Yin, H. (eds.) IDEAL 2010. LNCS, vol. 6283, pp. 53–62. Springer, Heidelberg (2010)
9. Yanagisawa, T., Miura, T.: Sentence Generation for Stream Annoucement. In: IEEE Intn'l Pacific Rim Conference on Communications, Computers and Signal Processing, PACRIM (2009)

Decision Tree Selection in an Industrial Machine Fault Diagnostics

Nour El Islem Karabadji[1], Hassina Seridi[1], Ilyes Khelf[2], and Lakhdar Laouar[2]

[1] Electronic Document Management Laboratory (LabGED), Badji Mokhtar-Annaba University, BP 12 Annaba, Algeria
[2] Laboratoire de Mécanique Industrielle, Badji Mokhtar-Annaba University, Algeria
{Karabadji,Seridi}@labged.net, ilyeskhelf@gmail.com.

Abstract. Decision trees are widely used technique in data mining and classification fields. This method classifies objects following succession tests on their attributes. Its principal disadvantage is the choice of optimal model among the various existing trees types (Chaid, Cart,Id3..). Each tree has its specificities which make the choice justification difficult. In this work, decision tree choice validation is studied and the use of genetic algorithms is proposed. To pull out best tree, all models are generated and their performances measured on distinct training and validation sets. After that, various statistical tests are made. In this paper we propose the diagnosis accomplishment of an industrial ventilator(Fan) based an analysis-decision trees.

Keywords: Genetics algorithm, Decision trees, Evaluation, Datamining.

1 Introduction

Decision tree is one of the most popular data mining techniques, in the classification field, providing explicit classification rules. Decisions trees are in the border between predictive and descriptive techniques, this is downward supervised classification consequence. Decision trees are among the most used classifiers in real application due to the compressibility and interpretability of their results.

The selection of the most robust decision tree for particular application is also an important step, and is confused by the asymmetry of the classes. The most widely used solution, is testing their performances on fixed and predefined training and validation sets, while a robust decision tree for an application must be the most efficient regardless of the couple (Training, Validation sets) choice, another solution is found by the use of cross validation algorithm especially in the cases of low data-set size but this solution is really heavy in term of calculation time. This problem is cited by the research community working on the decisions trees and for which there is no formal justification proven in the choice of the tree model among the various existing(J48, LMT,Id3). Each tree has its specificities making the choice difficult to justify [6].

A. Abelló, L. Bellatreche, and B. Benatallah (Eds.): MEDI 2012, LNCS 7602, pp. 129–140, 2012.
© Springer-Verlag Berlin Heidelberg 2012

To measure the performance of decision trees without falling into combinatorial problems many algorithms have been developed as well as Tabu search, Particle Swarm Optimization or more commonly genetic algorithms could be a solution [7].

In this paper, we investigate these two problems by developing an algorithm for the selection of the best tree by the application of genetic algorithms. The chosen tree must be the most robust regardless the (Training, Validation subsets), in optimized time run. We compared our method with classical validation techniques and cross validation.

2   Related Works

Decision trees are among the most popular methods in supervised learning. They are perfectly mastered and their intensive industrial utilization confirms their robustness. Over the last decades, the decision trees technique was one of the main applied research areas in the field of data mining. Their simplicity, permitted their implementation in other lines of research: the classifiers aggregation [3] and boosting, network intrusion detection[8].

However, there was no improvement on decision trees construction algorithms since the first works [5]. It searches for each node of the tree, the relevant attribute for classes segmentation according to evaluation criterion. The tree is thus constructed recursively from the root to leaves. The most important points are: the choice of segmentation criteria, the determination of the appropriate tree size, and leaves conclusion assignation [3]. Despite much research that followed [5] there were two points on which the tree construction algorithms have changed little in recent years: the ability to predict through the error rate by generalization and speed of construction of the tree.

Generally, the decisions trees algorithms tries to construct a complete tree, Or attempt to heuristics construct of decision tree in order to reduce the complexity of the completely construct. Many and several algorithm have been attempts to generated an optimal decision tree (respect to size only)[9][10][12].

Genetic algorithms (GAs) use an optimization technique inspired on natural evolution. There are many works showing the utilization of Genetic algorithms in order to find optimal decision trees [1][11][12][13], among them: Sung-Hyuk Cha et al. developed a binary tree with an AG, the construction of a tree in multi-values is still open[1]. Jie Chen et al. have developed genetic method for decision trees pruning. A binary coding has been adopted [2]. Ayman Khalafallah et al. developed an algorithm to constructing near optimal binary decision tree classifier using Genetic Algorithm [13].

In this work, our objective is to design an algorithm optimizing the selection of representative tree among the different existent model (id3, j48,...), which is the best classifier for a given knowledge data D. The optimization is in size of the test set. Validation models use a samples set to evaluate performance of the constructed trees. The main challenge in the development of this algorithm is how to groove both choice task and test optimization task. In this paper we show

how this can be done, and we showed application of our algorithm making tree's choice for fault diagnosis in an industrial Fan . We compared our method with the classical and cross validation methods.

3   Methods and Fundamentals Background

3.1   Decision Tree

Decision trees are built recursively, following a top-down approach; they are composed of a root and several nodes, branches and leaves. decision tree technique is based on the detection use of an indicators set, to divide population individuates to n classes. Tree construction can be described as follows. First, it choose the best indicator that ensure better population splitting, the divided population are distributed to nodes. We exercise the same operation for each node (subset population) until no allowed split operation. The terminal nodes are composed of population in the same class (increase proportion in some type of decisions trees). Classification operation is assigning an individual to terminal node by satisfying rules set orienting to this node. The total rules set formed the decision tree.

Splitting Criteria data dividing conditions to n class is related to the splitting indicators set choice, then the constructed tree quality depends on the indicators position in this set. In order to determine indicators separation, and indicators positions, each tree has its own separation criterion (Gini, χ^2, Twoing, Entropy...).

   The separated population subsets number is related to the indicators type, a binary indicator allowing only one split condition, multi-value indicator of n distinct values, allow n-1 split conditions. Construction tree further execution, product Tmax tree with leaves corresponding to perfectly homogeneous classes. In this case, there is a over-fitting learning and there is a risk of underestimating the error probability by the apparent error rate(which is 0). In other case, stopping it too soon causes an overgeneralization. These two problems are considered as the most important disadvantages of decision trees, especially when the number of classes for the endogenous variable is higher.

Stopping Criteria. It depends on the split criteria of setting decisions trees and type. Stopping criteria can be defined as one or combination of fallowing rules:

- Defining a fixed decision tree depth size;
- A fixed classification rules number (terminal nodes number);
- Population node size (individuates number fixed);
- The tree quality is good;
- The decision tree evaluation does not increase because the quality is constant.

3.2 Genetic Algorithms

Combinatorial optimization problems are often easy to define, but they are generally difficult to be solved. Many of these problems are NP-hard problems. These problems resolution can be either by: exact methods (complete) that ensure the completeness of resolution and approximate methods (incomplete) and which loosed completeness for efficiency.

The exact methods have difficulties facing large applications. Approximate methods (metaheuristics, local research, constructive methods) are considered as interesting alternative in treating large size optimization problems previously impossible to treat. We can cite evolutionary algorithms, ant colony algorithms, cross entropy method...

In general, genetic algorithms are reliable methods, they are robust methods, requiring limited information on optimization problem against other cited methods. Genetic algorithm is widely used in optimization because it uses random combination leading in solution. The Genetic algorithm was chosen to avoid falling into combinatorial problems; it is a powerful mix between exploration and exploitation. They are based on natural evolution and selection, and survival of fitness test ideas [14]. Genetic algorithm represents solution to problems as a genome (or chromosome). It then creates a population of possible solutions and applies genetic operators such as mutation and crossover to evolve the fitness test solution.

To be able to use genetic algorithm, the problem must be encoded as a chromosome. A chromosome in Genetic algorithm is an array of bits. The cross over operation can be described as in Figure 1 Cross Over in Genetic algorithm. Here a second genome is chosen (crossover point) and the two chromosomes changed content at this second point.

(a)Chromosome 1 (b)Chromosome 2 (c)Offspring 1 (d)Offspring 2

Fig. 1. Genetic algorithm Cross Over

Another Genetic algorithm operation is mutation where a single genome changes with a very small probability value randomly. Genetic algorithm operation make sure that a new population is being generated from the old one and ensure diversity to without falling into in a local minimum. Genetic algorithm is based on an another important task, it is chromosomes evaluation step, and it is presented as an evaluation function called fitness function. It depends on the kind of optimization problems. It provides a selection chromosomes test value that can be used to select higher one (Chromosomes) to survive to the next population.

4 Selection Algorithm Description

The validation step is the heart of the data mining process; the aim of this step is to test the model validity (built by the training set) on a validation set (different from the training set). Validation allows us to optimize the model parameters, modalities number, decision tree depth or number of leaves, etc.

The validation step is required to avoid overgeneralization and overfetting problem. The proposed approach will be conducted in tree main steps:

1. Indicators extraction (database)
2. Pretreatment phase (trees generation and data set discritization).
3. Optimal tree choice (using genetic algorithm).

Formally, the task t^* representative tree finding can be described as follows. Assume a database D, L and V subsets disjoint of D where L is a learning set and V a test set,a trees models set T, and an objective function F. The problem is the extraction t^* such as $t^* = \{t \in T | max\ F(t)\}$. The objective function is the evaluation of each tree learning with L by V. provided satisfactory results. Figure.2 shows the flow chart of the programmed algorithm.

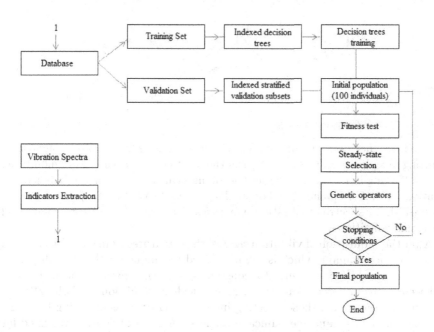

Fig. 2. Adopted Genetic Algorithm flow chart

4.1   Indicators Extraction

The steady is done on an industrial fan, which is considered as one of the most rotating machines used in industry. The fan is diagrammed in Figure 3. The FAN is coupled through a flexible coupling spring to an electric motor, which runs on a rotational speed of 1490 rpm. An accelerometer is used for recording vibration signals and fixed on the bearing housing.

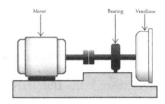

Fig. 3. Dedusting plant
1-Fan 2- Bearing housing
3-Coupling 4-Motor

Fig. 4. Schematization of the plant

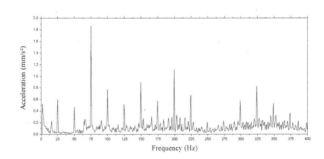

Fig. 5. Frequency spectra with recorded mechanical looses fault

The frequency domain analysis is a reliable technique for the fault diagnosis in rotating machinery. In this work four of the most common faults were monitored those affecting inner and outer races of rolling bearings, the mass unbalance and fixation fault. A frequency band of 400 Hz was used to obtain frequency spectra. Figure 5 shows spectra of vibration signatures recorded in the different monitored operating conditions.

After the acquisition of vibration signals, the signatures were transformed then into frequency domain, which is the most used technique for the fault diagnosis in rotating machinery running at a constant speed. The operating of the fan was followed in five different conditions, first a healthy condition, and the affected by four different fault, those affecting inner and outer races of rolling bearings, the mass unbalance and mechanical looseness . A band of 400 Hz was fixed for the frequency analysis as shown in Fig.3 in the case of inner race fault.

Feature Extraction and Data-Set Post-treatment. Fifteen indicators were extracted for each spectrum. The indicators are: the root mean square , the mean distance between the frequency of the eight greatest peak , Mean Value of all Amplitude Peaks, standard deviation , mode , the amplitude of the lower peak , the amplitude of the greatest peak , variance , median, the average of the two greatest peak, the frequency of the greatest peak , the frequency of the second greatest peak, the frequency of the third greatest peak, the average frequency of greatest three peaks, the amplitude of the second greatest peak.

In each condition 30 signals were recorded to have a total of 150 indicator vectors, divided then in two sets. The first, to training and the second, to the validation. For the data sampling a stratified method was used to take the same rate of data from the different classes, reflecting the variability of the phenomena during trees generalization and validation,in order to prevent falling in over-fitting problems.

4.2   The Pretreatment

After the data extraction step, we separated the dataset in two subsets (training and validation sets), there are several methods (simple, stratified,...) and each method has its specificities. Stratified method was selected in order to take equal rate from the different samples classes and getting a generalization and validation equilibrium of trees. Examples variability of and the rates equality gave equitable opportunities for all trees to be chosen and prevent their specialization.

Trees Training and Indexing. In this step a decision trees set generation is proposed using training samples. We generate twelve trees that are built on the base of numeric attribute DecisionStump, FT, J48, J48graft, LADTree, LMT, NBTree, RandomForest, RandomTree, REPTree, SimpleCart. For each tree a training subset (composed of 100 vectors) is pulled out randomly. The indicators used as nodes are selected using the criterion depending on construction algorithm. In our study, the decision trees implemented on the open source platform Weka have been explored [4].

Validation Sets Sampling. Validation sets sampling: In this step stratified sampling is used in order to divide the validation set to N subsets, where each contains N' vectors. This sampling was performed in order to reduce the validation time and obtain valid decision tree without filling to all validation subsets.

4.3   Genetics Optimization Step

Genetic algorithms optimized finding of best choice representative tree. The decision trees and the test subsets must be encoded so that the genetic operators, can be applied. We encoded the problem into chromosomes composed by two genomes, where the first genome described a decision tree. It is a digit in interval [0,11] described in 4.1 subsection. The second genome designed a test subsets which are a minimum size subsets. The Figure.6 shows the chromosome encoded and a chromosome example encoded J48 tree with the test subset samples indexed by 10.

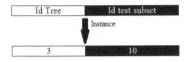

Fig. 6. Chromosome encoded

The Evaluation. This step is the heart of data mining. The performance of a model can be computed from its classification accuracy CA on the validation set. This performance can be converted it into a confusion matrix from which we can derive various statistics on the model performance. The proposed evaluation phase was defined by the following fitness function:

$$F(x) = Mean(CA)$$

It represents the average classification accuracy of the tree with different training sets on the validation set found on the same chromosome. This procedure is to prevent the risk of falling into the cases of random performance on certain validation sets distorting the trees evaluation. This fitness guarantee robustness and reliability of tested selected trees with various training sets.

The Selection. The steady-state selection is used. The genetic algorithm then runs as follows. In every generation few chromosomes are selected (among the fitness test ones) to create children. Subsequently, the worst chromosomes are removed and replaced randomly with new other ones.

Evaluation operators:

Crossover: it applies on two different individuals. As a result it gives a chromosome formed from genes of both parents; two children are generated for the next generation. A percentage of crossovers is set and a cross at a point is applied. This procedure allows changes of two genes on chromosome, as showed in Figure.7.

Mutation: it applies to an individual by modifying one or more genes, chosen randomly from the parents and one new child comes. The mutation percentage in our case is set to 1%. This ratio defines the probability to change an index by another randomly without interaction with other chromosomes.

Stopping Criterion. The algorithm stops at one of the following criteria, the maximum number of iterations be equal to the 100 or 50 % of the population of chromosomes is similar as the first gene.

(a)Chromosome 1 (b)Chromosome 2 (c)Offspring 1 (d)Offspring 2

Fig. 7. Our crossover operator

5 Discussion and Result

Table 1 showed the classification accuracy obtained using classical validation method and we can see the good performances obtained by the BFTree. Those performances were obtained using an unchanging and predefined training and testing subsets.

Table 1. Classification accuracy using classical validation method

Decision Tree	CA
BFTree	90,66
SimpleCart	85,83
REPTree	85,51
RandomTree	85,33
RandomForest	85,11
NBTree	84
LMT	82
LADTree	80,88
J48graft	78,26
J48	75,83
FT	71,77
DecisionStump	65

In the table 2 the ranking trees according to their classification accuracy with the cross validation method is shown. This ranking was obtained after a computation time of 19s.

The table 3 show the occurrence frequency of trees in the genetic algorithm population, a high occurrence frequency means that the tree gave high accuracy with the different testing subsets encountered during the algorithm evolution, and show its robustness against the variability of examples in the data-set. The RandomForest supremacy Tree in term of occurrence frequency during the algorithm progress development, which means that independently of the used training and testing set, this tree provided high performances.

The RandomForest was followed by respectively; Simple Cart, LMT, and RandomTree , Also trees as DecisionStump, FT, LADTree were dropped out from the Genetic algorithm population since the 5th iteration.

Table 2. Classification accuracy using the cross-validation method

Decision Tree	CA
RandomForest	82,11
BFTree	82
SimpleCart	80,50
REPTree	79,81
RandomTree	79,20
NBTree	77,50
LMT	76,85
LADTree	75,66
J48graft	74,40
J48	71
FT	65,33
DecisionStump	61

Table 3. Occurrence frequency of decisions trees in the genetic algorithm population

Id arbre	pop − init	1	2	3	4	5	6	7	8	9	10	11
BFTree	0	9	08	08	10	12	12	12	14	12	14	14	14
DecisionStump	1	9	00	00	00	00	00	00	00	00	00	00	00
FT	2	9	04	04	02	00	00	00	00	00	00	00	00
J48	3	9	10	10	08	08	10	10	12	12	12	10	06
J48graft	4	8	06	06	04	04	06	06	04	04	04	04	04
LADTree	5	8	08	08	06	04	00	00	00	00	00	00	00
LMT	6	8	10	10	06	04	00	00	00	00	00	00	00
NBTree	7	8	14	14	18	04	00	00	00	00	00	00	00
RandomForest	**8**	**8**	**14**	**14**	**18**	**30**	**36**	**36**	**40**	**42**	**44**	**48**	**54**
RandomTree	9	8	08	08	06	06	06	06	04	04	04	02	02
REPTree	10	8	08	08	06	12	12	12	06	08	04	04	04
SimpleCart	11	8	10	10	16	16	18	18	20	18	18	18	16

The table 4 shows the Rank of each indexed tree according to the used selection technique: Classical Validation ClV, Cross Validation CrV, and Genatic
Validation Approach GaV.

The trees rank changed according to the evaluation methods. The BFTree
was ranked 1st with classical validation, 2nd with Cross validation and 3rd with
Genetic validation, which means that it met difficulties facing new validation
subsets encountered with the genetic method. Also we can see trees providing
the high accuracy with classic validation, but limited or nil occurrence frequency
in the final population of Genetic algorithm such as REPTree , Random Tree or
LMT, demonstrating their lack of robustness against new encountered examples
in data . The use of such trees presents a risk of classification instability because
their accuracy ratio changes facing new data.

Table 4. Validations methods results

Decision Tree	Id	arbre pop$_i$nit	ClV	CrV	GaV
BFTree	0	9	1	2	3
DecisionStump	1	9	12	12	7
FT	2	9	11	11	7
J48	3	9	10	10	4
J48graft	4	8	9	9	5
LADTree	5	8	8	8	7
LMT	6	8	7	7	7
NBTree	7	8	6	6	7
RandomForest	8	8	5	1	1
RandomTree	9	8	4	5	6
REPTree	10	8	3	4	5
SimpleCart	11	8	2	3	2
Computing Time			5sec	19sec	8sec

In the other hand RandomForest Tree despite its medium score with classical validations show itself, robust and reliable against the data variability encountered in the two last approaches, The RondomForest Tree is preconized for establishing a diagnostic tool for the studied industrial Fan.

6 Conclusion

Decision tree are commonly used classifiers to the establishment and diagnosis tools in industrial field, and have many algorithms in their construction. For decision trees selection, genetic algorithms were used, to validate their performances on different couples (training, testing sets) to meet the most robustness.

The Proposed algorithm provided robust result as the cross validation in lower computation time. The Random forest decision tree was proposed to fault diagnosis tools construction in the studied case, and demonstrates robustness and good performances.

After locating the difficulties of the classification problem using decisions trees, We identified the processed overfitting and overgeneralization problems directions is our future aim. We seeking an optimal decision tree that generalizes as well the datamining problem.

References

[1]   Cha, S.-H., Tappert, C.: A Genetic Algorithm for Constructing CompactBinary Decision Trees. Journal of Pattern Recognition Research (2009)

[2]   Chen, J., Wang, X., Zhai, J.: Pruning Decision Tree Using Genetic Algorithms. In: International Conference on Artificial Intelligence and Computational Intelligence (2009)

[3]   Breiman, L.: Bagging predictors. Machine Learning 24, 123–140 (1996)

[4]   Hall, M., Frank, E., Holmes, G., Pfahringer, B., Reutemann, P., Witten, I.: The WEKA Data Mining Software: An Update. SIGKDD Explorations, 11 (2009)

[5]   Breslow, L.A., Aha, D.W.: Simplifying decision trees: a survey. Knowledge Engineering Review 12(1), 1–40 (1997)

[6]   Karabadji, N.E.I., Khelf, I., Seridi, H., Laouar, L.: Genetic Optimization of Decision Tree Choice for Fault Diagnosis in an Industrial Ventilator. In: Fakhfakh, T., Bartelmus, W., Chaari, F., Zimroz, R., Haddar, M. (eds.) Condition Monitoring of Machinery in Non-Stationary Operations, vol. 110 Part III, pp. 277–283. Springer, Heidelberg (2012)

[7]   Worden, K., Manson, G., Hilson, G., Pierce, S.: Genetic optimisation of a neural damage locator. Journal of Sound and Vibration 309, 529–544 (2008)

[8]   Stein, G., Chen, B., Wu, A.S., Hua, K.A.: Decision tree classifier for network intrusion detection with GA-based feature selection. In: Proceedings ACM Southeast Regional Conference, Kennesaw, Georgia, USA (2005)

[9]   Zhao, Q., Shirasaka, M.: A Study on Evolutionary Design of Binary Decision Trees. In: Proceedings of the Congress on Evolutionary Computation, vol. 3, pp. 1988–1993. IEEE (1999)

[10] Bennett, K., Blue, J.: Optimal decision trees. Tech. Rpt. No. 214 Department of Mathematical Sciences, Rensselaer Polytechnic Institute, Troy, New York (1996)

[11] Kim, K.M., Park, J.J., Song, M.H., Kim, I.-C., Suen, C.Y.: Binary Decision Tree Using Genetic Algorithm for Recognizing Defect Patterns of Cold Mill Strip. In: Tawfik, A.Y., Goodwin, S.D. (eds.) Canadian AI 2004. LNCS (LNAI), vol. 3060, pp. 461–466. Springer, Heidelberg (2004)

[12] Gehrke, J., Ganti, V., Rama krishnan R., Loh, W.: BOAT- Optimistic Decision Tree Construction. In: Proc. of the ACM SIGMOD Conference on Management of Data, pp. 169–180 (1999)

[13] Khalafallah, A.: Constructing Near Optimal Binary Decision Tree Classifier Using Genetic Algorithm. International Journal of Computer Science and Engineering Technology 1(11), 722–724 (2011)

[14] Goldberg, D.L.: Genetic Algorithms in Search Optimization, and Machine Learning. Addison- Wesley (1989)

Crosscutting Concerns Identification Approach Based on the Sequence Diagram Analysis

Fairouz Dahi[1] and Nora Bounour[2]

LRI Laboratory, Department of Computer Science, Badji Mokhtar – Annaba University
P.O. Box 12, 23000 Annaba, Algeria
{fairouz_dahi,nora_bounour}@yahoo.fr

Abstract. Existence of crosscutting concerns scattered or tangled in the source code complicates the software maintenance, evolution and reuse. To support the improved modularity of software systems, taking advantage of the benefits of aspect-oriented paradigm, several approaches aim to identify the crosscutting concerns, to allow their modeling in aspects. In the absence of early detection of these crosscutting concerns, they tend to be overlooked and become closely linked, not allowing developers to identify optimal design.

We propose in this paper a new approach for identification of crosscutting concerns at the architectural level. The architectural model considered is represented by classes and sequence diagrams. The sequence diagram carries semantic information, which consists in interactions between objects of the software system, and the chronological order of execution of its tasks.

Keywords: Aspect mining, Early aspect, Crosscutting concerns, Message transmissions, Reverse engineering, Software architecture.

1 Introduction

Face to user requirements (change of platforms, new features ...), software systems are unable to respond. Improve performance is, therefore, an imperative, given the many opportunities in various areas. This means rethinking the systems whose size and complexity defy the most current methods of software engineering.

The complexity of understanding the object-oriented code is caused by the dispersion or the duplication of some concerns in different parts of an application. Such concerns are the crosscutting concerns. In general, these crosscutting concerns can be characterized by the tangling or the scattering. Scattering occurs when the same functionality is distributed across the system (at the implementation level, similar code is distributed across multiple program modules). While the tangling is, when two or more concerns are merged with each other (at the implementation level, two or more concerns are implemented in the same body of module code, making it harder to understand) [11].

These concerns cannot benefit of a proper encapsulation in oriented object paradigm. Aspect oriented paradigm has emerged in order to support improved modularity

A. Abelló, L. Bellatreche, and B. Benatallah (Eds.): MEDI 2012, LNCS 7602, pp. 141–152, 2012.
© Springer-Verlag Berlin Heidelberg 2012

of software systems. The concept of aspect is a new unit which modularizes crosscutting concerns.

To benefit from the aspect-oriented paradigm, it is necessary to develop approaches and tools that identify and separate the crosscutting concerns. The identification of crosscutting concerns at the implementation level has certain limits [1, 8]. The source code is linked to a specific platform. In addition, his understanding is difficult, because of its complexity and large size.

Approaches of early identification of crosscutting concerns, at requirements or design level, aim to allow an aspect-oriented development [1, 9] and an early management of crosscutting concerns, and they benefit, therefore, from the application of aspect oriented techniques in the early stages of software development cycle. In the absence of early detection of crosscutting concerns, these concerns tend to be overlooked and become closely linked, not allowing developers to identify optimal architectural design. The architect will be able to design a system that better satisfies user requirements through early identification of the crosscutting concerns, instead of focusing only on functional concerns. Aspect identification approaches in early phases suffer from certain weaknesses:

- Approaches that are based on interviews with stakeholders are often imprecise, full of contradictions and lack of essential information.
- Lack of the use of the semantic information about the software system.
- Lack to rigorous and precise definition of the aspect or crosscutting concern that makes the candidates aspects identified in the early cycle of software development cannot all be refactored (encapsulated) in aspects.
- Lack to take into account simultaneously the two symptoms of crosscutting: scattering and tangling.
- The crosscutting concerns detected early in the development cycle can be changed in later phases: disappear or emerge.
- During the crosscutting concerns identification, conflicts can emerge. It is necessary to resolve these conflicts

In this paper, we aim to exceed the limits of existing approaches for early aspects identification. We propose a new approach for identifying crosscutting concerns from the architectural model, by detecting the two symptoms of crosscutting. The system architecture is a more abstract level, independent of implementation technology. We materialize it by the UML class and sequence diagram [3]. The class diagram is a structural description of the software system. So it allows us to identify all methods that exist in the system, while the sequence diagram carries semantic information: call relations between system objects and the chronological order of execution of its tasks, which help us to detect the crosscutting concerns. Thus, the sequence diagram is a version close to the final version that represents the full tasks of the system. In other words, objects and messages of the system sequence diagram reflect, respectively, objects and methods of the implementation of this system.

Section 2 presents sequence and class diagrams. Our proposed approach of crosscutting concerns detection will be the subject of Section 3. A case study is presented in Section 4. Section 5 describes related works and a conclusion will allow us, finally, to create opportunities for future development.

2   Sequence and Class Diagrams

Software architecture is a global view of the internal organization and software structure. The software architecture diagrams describe the nature of the different modules of software, responsibilities and functions of each module. They also describe the nature of relationships between modules. In our approach, we consider the software architecture that described via UML class and sequence diagrams. UML has become an important reference in the software engineering domain. Its richness and power of expression also make it eligible for the modeling [7].

The class diagram is a very important element of structural modeling. It defines the components of the final system. This diagram can also structure the development work very effectively, by identifying the class structure of a software system, including properties and methods of each class.

Sequence diagrams are used to describe the communication between different parts of a system (e.g. between various components or objects), or between a system and its users. Sequence diagrams are used within a broad range of application domains, and for different methodological purposes, including requirements analysis, test case specification and user documentation. Sequence diagram focuses on the chronological order which affect the message transmission between objects. In most cases, the reception of a message is followed by the execution of a method of a class. This method can receive arguments, and the syntax of messages is used to transmit these arguments. To facilitate the notation, we use in this paper the notation $O.m$ to denote the message transmitted by object O that invokes the method m.

Combined fragment is an interaction fragment which defines a combination (expression) of interaction fragments. A combined fragment is defined by an interaction operator and corresponding interaction operands. Through the use of combined fragments the user will be able to describe a number of traces in a compact and concise manner. Combined fragment may have interaction constraints also called **guards**. Interaction operators that have impact on crosscutting are following:

alt: alternative multiple fragments (equivalent to *if .. then .. else*).
opt: optional fragment;
par: parallel fragment (competitive treatments).
loop: the fragment is executed repeatedly.
critical: critical region (only one thread at a time).

We use the class diagram to capture all the methods that exist in the system, and to see if the context of transmission is dispersed. We use the sequence diagram to detect crosscutting concerns, because this diagram provides semantic information on the call relationships between system's objects, and the chronological order of its task's execution.

3   Our Approach

Most interactions (messages transmissions) between the different objects in sequence diagram reflect the method invocations of the system (these methods exist in the UML class diagram) and the chronological order of message transmissions reflects the execution order of the system tasks.

In our approach, we consider only the messages transmissions of sequence diagram that invoke methods. We use repetitive transmissions of these messages to detect the scattered concerns, and we analyze the transmission order to detect the tangling ones. A sequence diagram describes the behavior of a single use case scenario. For this reason, we will consider all the sequence diagrams of the system.

3.1   A System's Abstract Model via Messages Transmissions

A software system is modeled by several sequence diagrams. Each diagram represents a set of objects that transmit messages. These objects are instances of classes in the class diagram. We offer in figure 1 an abstract model of a software system through message transmissions.

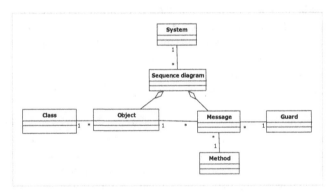

Fig. 1. The system's abstract model via messages transmissions

3.2   Crosscutting Definition

From the model previously proposed, we propose the following definitions for tangling, scattering and crosscutting.

Definition 1 (Tangling):
We consider that a recurrent call model consists in two successive message transmissions that invoke two different methods, and which are repeated a number of times greater than a certain threshold for the same methods in different contexts (by objects belonging to different classes). We define tangling as the fact of the occurrence of a recurrent call model. The recurrent model is one of the following types:

- **Before Type:** If, in sequence diagrams, the message which calls method A is always transmitted before one which calls the method B, then there will be a before type aspect, where method A is its code advice, and method B represents its pointcut .
- **After Type:** If the message which calls method A is always transmitted after one which calls the method B, then there will be an after type aspect, where method A is its code advice, and method B represents its pointcut.
- **Symmetric Type:** If the message which calls method A is always transmitted before the one which calls the method B, and the message which calls method B is always transmitted after the one which calls the method A, then the before type aspect where method A is its code advice and method B represents its pointcut, and the type after aspect where method B is its code advice and method A represents its pointcut, are two symmetrical aspects.
- If the message which calls method A is always transmitted before one which calls the method B and/or one which calls the method C, then there will be a before type aspect, where method A is its code advice, and methods B and C represent its pointcuts.

From the system's abstract model presented previously (figure 1), we derive in figure 2 the model of tangling.

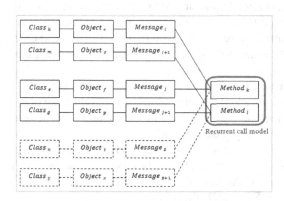

Fig. 2. The tangling model

Definition 2 (Scattering):
The scattering occurs when a method is invoked at least twice by messages that are transmitted by different objects. These objects must belong to different classes.

Although, the refactoring to aspect of a method called only once does not improve the system structure (The modification of the manner of its invocation is not expensive). For the same reason, a method which its transmissions are not dispersed (transmitted by the same object or object that contains the method transmitted) is not taken into account.

From the system's abstract model presented previously (figure 1), we derive in figure 3 the model of scattering.

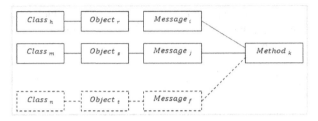

Fig. 3. The scattering model

Definition 3 (Crosscutting) :
Crosscutting = Tangling ∨ Scattering.

3.3   Crosscutting Analysis

Sometimes, the detection of a crosscutting concern also removes the presence of crosscutting of a different other concern. So, the crosscutting concerns with a lower degree of crosscutting do not need to be detected as aspect, and we must start by identification of concern which has the higher degree ofcrosscutting.

To compute the degree of crosscutting, from the system's abstract model presented previously (figure 1), we build our matrix of crosscutting called *Matrix of Message Transmission Order* (MMTO), by exploiting all transmitted messages that invoke methods. This matrix is binary and square ($n \times n$). Its rows and columns represent the methods invoked during message transmissions. Initially, the entire matrix is initialized to zero.

The binary relation between the rows and columns is the order of message transmission (method invocation). In other terms, if method i is invoked just after method j, then we increment the cell $[i, j]$, else we do nothing. The value of each cell in the matrix will be used to detect the tangling.

We add to the matrix a row called "after" and a column called "before". These last two are then used to detect the scattering in message transmission. The value of each cell in the row "after" is the sum of all cells values of the same line:
$$MMTO[n + 1, j] = \sum_{i=1}^{n} MMTO[i, j].$$
The value of each cell in the column "before" is the sum of all cells values of the same column:
$$MMTO[i, n + 1] = \sum_{j=1}^{n} MMTO[i, j].$$
To resolve the conflict, the matrix MMTO should be modified, and we must firstly identify tangling then scattering, respecting tangled aspects already obtained. Let M the matrix MMTO, and L_i the method which is located in the row i of the matrix M, and C_j the method that is located in column j.

3.3.1 Tangling Detection
From the matrix MMTO, the tangling is identified from cells (except the row *after* and the column *before*) who their value is higher than 1, as following

(M is the matrix MMTO, and L_i the method which is located in the row i of the matrix M, and C_j the method that is located in column j):

1. We search the highest value in the matrix M (the aspect of the highest weight), if there are several equal, we choose one among them, let $M[i, j]$;
2. For all cells in row i (except the cell $M[i,j]$), we calculate the number of cells (nbi) that have the value different than zero;
3. For all cells in column j (except the cell $M[i,j]$), we calculate the number of cells (nbj) that have the value different than zero;
4. If $nbi=nbj$ then :
   - Pointcut $=C_j$;
   - Code advice $=L_i$;
   - Type = *symmetric*;
   - We put $M[i,n+1]= M[n+1,j]=M[n+1,i]= M[j,n+1]=0$, because the aspect that are detected as tangled should not be detected again as scattered;
5. Else if $nbi \geq nbj$ then :
   - Pointcuts are all C_k where $M[i, k] \geq 1$, ($k=1..n$);
   - Code advice = L_i;
   - Type = *before*;
   - We put $M[i,n+1]= M[n+1,j]=M[n+1,i]= M[j,n+1]=0$, because the aspect that are detected as tangled should not be detected again as scattered;
6. Else if $nb1<nb2$ then :
   - Pointcuts are all L_k where $M[k, j] \geq 1$, ($k=1..n$);
   - Code advice = C_j;
   - Type = *after*;
   - We put $M[i,n+1]= M[n+1,j]=M[n+1,i]= M[j,n+1]=0$, because the aspect that are detected as tangled should not be detected again as scattered;

We repeat steps 1 to 6, and each time we decrement the high value, until to be equal to 1.

3.3.2   Scattering Detection

From the matrix MMTO, the scattering is identified through the row $n+1$ (row *after*) and the column $n+1$ (column *before*). The row *after* indicates a transmission that is repeated after others transmissions, while the column before indicates a transmission that repeats after other transmissions.

For each cell of row *after*, if $M[n+1, j] \geq 2$ then :

   - Pointcuts are all L_k where $M[k, j] = 1$, ($k=1..n$);
   - Code advice = C_j;
   - Type = *after*;

For each cell of column *before*, if $M[i, n+1] \geq 2$ then

- Pointcuts are all C_k where $M[i, k] = 1$, $(k=1..n)$;
- Code advice $= L_i$;
- Type $= before$;

3.3.3   Additional Aspects with Guards

Candidate Aspects obtained must be completed by taking into account the guards of sequence diagrams (except guards **critical** and **par** that must be taken into account respectively before and during filling the matrix MMTO). If message transmission is preceded by a guard:

- **alt:** if the execution condition is valid then we add it to the pointcut list of the candidate aspect obtained, else we add the condition equivalent to the operator **else**.
- **opt:** if the execution condition is valid then we add it to the pointcut list of the candidate aspect obtained.
- **par:** during filling of the matrix MMTO, we must respect this guard. In other words, if for example we have:

  ....

  par
     O.a
     <u>*P.b*</u>
     Q.c
     R.d

  ....

  We don't say in this case that the method c is invoked just after method b, because the two fragments separated by a line passing in parallel. We say rather that the method b is invoked just after the method a and the method d is invoked just after the method c.
- **loop:** Here, the same fragment is repeated. If the transmission of a message is made n times, it does not refer to the existence of a candidate aspect, because the context of this transmission doesn't change.
- **critical:** Here, the interactions described in this guard cannot be interrupted by other interactions of the diagram. The methods invoked inside the guard means the existence of a tangled aspect. Its pointcut is the method invoked just before the guard **critical**, and the code advice will be all the methods invoked within the fragment of this guard.

4   Case Study

In order to assess and validate our proposed approach, we have developed a tool and we have applied it to a case study. The case study that we have chosen is an online library system. There are two operations (use cases) to be performed: borrow and restore. The class diagram is shown in figure 4. Figure 5 presents all methods of online library system. Figures 6 and 7 show the sequence diagrams of borrow and restore use cases, respectively. The matrix MMTO of this model is presented in figure 8. The candidate aspects found by our tool are presented in figure 9. To facilitate the implementation, we exploit the message transmissions of the sequence diagram in the form of XML file.

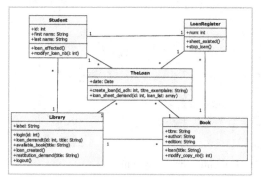

Fig. 4. The class diagram of online library system

Fig. 5. The methods of online library system

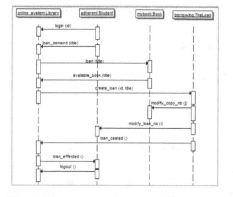

Fig. 6. The sequence diagram of *Borrow* use case

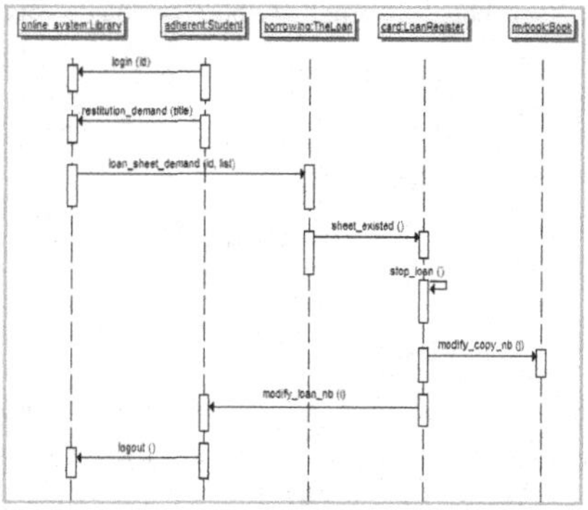

Fig. 7. The sequence diagram of *Restore* use case

From the matrix of figure 8, we find in figure 9 that there is one tangled concern in online library system where: *Code advice:* m14 (modify_copy_nb), *Pointcut:* m2 (modify_loan_nb) and *Type:* symmetric. The concern of update is a tangled concern, and it must be refactored in an aspect, because it includes two tasks that are strongly linked: changing the number of borrowing of a book and changing the number of its available copies

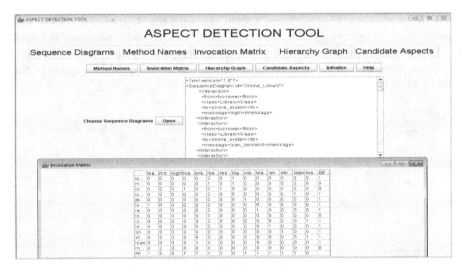

Fig. 8. Matrix MMOT of online library system

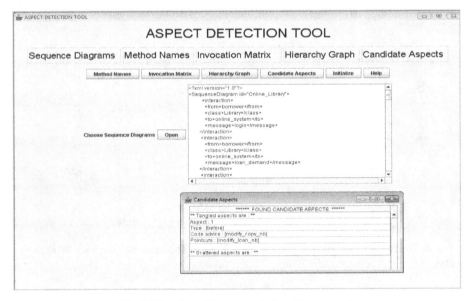

Fig. 9. List of candidate aspects found by our tool

Furthermore, the method m2 (modify_loan_nb) is identified as the pointcut of tangled aspect, so it won't be considered as scattered aspect. Same for the method m14 that is identified as code advice. Then, we see that the methods m3 (login) and m8 (logout) are invoked by messages transmitted by objects of the same class (student). Therefore, they are not detected as scattered.

5   Related Works and Conclusion

Method invocations have been exploited at the source code to detect the crosscutting. In our previous work, we used Formal Concept Analysis (FCA) to group the methods according to their calls. The method that contains calls belonging to different classes is seen as a candidate aspect. This approach detects only the symptom of the scattering [2].

Another approach which exploits the calls between the methods was represented in [10]. The author has defined two types of crosscutting. The static one is due to the (scattered and tangled) declarations of substitutable methods and types that are generated by means of static relationships (inheritance, implementation or containment). With this static crosscutting, the author defines the concerns of the system. The dynamic crosscutting is introduced by means of scattered and tangled method invocations. Indeed, an invocation to a method alters the run-time control flow by adding the behavior of the called method to the calling one. Thus, when a method of an identified concern is invoked by several other methods belonging to different other concerns, the behavior of the invoked concern is dynamically scattered (at run-time) within the concerns associated to the callers. Similarly, when a method makes calls to other methods belonging to different Concerns, the behavior of such Concerns is tangled together within the calling method. This approach is not complete because crosscutting concerns that have not also a static structure (in terms of system modules) are not considered.

The identification of aspects from UML diagrams for reverse-engineering perspective has been discussed in [3]. The author proposes to understand, identify and re-modularize the extracted aspects from the existing legacy object oriented source codes. In sequence diagram, the concerns that cross the sequences of messages are crosscutting. To detect these crosscutting concerns, recurring execution patterns generated from the execution traces of object-oriented program will be considered as aspects, because they describe the features duplicated in the program. To incorporate the aspect in the sequence diagram, the aspect (recurring pattern) must be modularized using the composite structure of the UML (collaboration), and the stereotypes <<aspect>>, <<advice>>, <<call>> and <<crosscut>> [3]. The crosscutting concerns of activity diagram are those that cross multiple procedures or threads [3]. The most important crosscutting concerns can be synchronization or mutual exclusion operations. Then, through the fusion and the addition of nodes in the activity diagram, it will be aspect oriented. However, the only detected symptom of crosscutting is the tangling.

In our paper, we propose definition of crosscutting, and detection of the two crosscutting symptoms at architectural level. Based on sequence diagrams, we exploit, on one hand the call relationship, and on the other hand the chronological order of system task executions. It was possible for us to overcome the limitations of existing approaches.

Our approach can be used from two perspectives. The first is the aspect-oriented development, and the crosscutting concerns will be identified at the original sequence diagrams (conceptual level), allowing the developer to separate the concerns at this level, benefit from early aspect-oriented development, and exceeds the limits of approaches that are based on interviews with stakeholders, because these interviews are often imprecise, full of contradictions and they lack essential information. The second perspective is reverse engineering. In this case, the sequence and classes diagrams can be easily and automatically generated from the legacy system source code [4, 5, 6].

Our proposed approach gives a precise identification of concerns and facilitates the aspect-oriented refactoring of the candidate aspects obtained, by specifying the pointcuts of the aspect and its code advice, and the type of the latter.

The opened perspective of our work is to validate our tool with large systems, and to compare its results with those of other existing tools.

References

1. Dahi, F., Bounour, N.: Etude critique des approches de découverte d'aspect à travers le cycle du développement de logiciels. In: The Second International Conference on Complex Systems, CISC 2011, Algeria, Jijel University (2011)
2. Dahi, F., Bounour, N.: Identification d'aspects par l'analyse des concepts formels. In: 1st International Conference on Information Systems and Technologies, ICIST 2011, Algeria, Tebessa University (2011)
3. Su, Y., Li, F., Hu, S., Chen, P.: Aspect-oriented software reverse engineering. Journal of Shanghai University 10(5) (2006)
4. Automated Drawing of UML Diagrams, http://www.umlgraph.org/ver.html
5. Bouml, http://bouml.free.fr/screenshots.html
6. Staruml, http://staruml.sourceforge.net/en/
7. Siau, K., Cao, Q.: Unified Modeling Language: A Complexity Analysis. Journal of Database Management 12 (2001)
8. Mens, K., Kellens, A., Krinke, J.: Pitfalls in Aspect mining. In: Proceeding WCRE 2008 Proceedings of the15th Working Conference on Reverse Engineering (2008)
9. Moreira, A., Araújo, J.: The Need for Early Aspects. In: Fernandes, J.M., Lämmel, R., Visser, J., Saraiva, J. (eds.) GTTSE 2011. LNCS, vol. 6491, pp. 386–407. Springer, Heidelberg (2011)
10. Bernardi, M.L., Di Lucca, G.A.: Identifying the Crosscutting among Concerns by Methods' Calls Analysis. In: Kim, T.-h., Adeli, H., Kim, H.-k., Kang, H.-j., Kim, K.J., Kiumi, A., Kang, B.-H. (eds.) ASEA 2011. CCIS, vol. 257, pp. 147–158. Springer, Heidelberg (2011)
11. Aspectj, http://www.eclipse.org/aspectj/doc/released/faq.html

Inductive UML

Franck Barbier and Eric Cariou

University of Pau, BP 1155, Avenue de l'université,
64013 Pau CEDEX, France
{franck.barbier,eric.cariou}@univ-pau.fr

Abstract. The increasing importance of metamodeling calls for metamodels that are free of ambiguities, contradictions and redundancies. This is specifically the case for the core of UML (Infrastructure). This paper proposes to rewrite a part of this core, the *Class* and *Property* metaclasses especially. To avoid infinite regression, the notion of meta-circularity is used. This rewriting is done by means of inductive types in constructive logic. The proposed specification is proven correct using the Coq automated prover. Proven lemmas and theorems about a "metaness" relationship are proposed.

Keywords: Unified Modeling Language, Metamodeling, Constructive logic.

1   Introduction

The *Unified Modeling Language* (UML) [1] is historically based on metamodeling [2-4]. Because models are "instances of" or "conform to" metamodels, they are tinged with errors when metamodels they come from have anomalies. This phenomenon is even more important when metamodels are implemented in operational environments like the *Eclipse Modeling Framework* (EMF) [5]. Model transformations occur at design time or there is a possibility of having executable models at runtime. In the latter case, persistent metamodels act as a reflection mechanism (metadata) and Java may act as an action language to manage models at runtime.

UML has chosen a four-layer metamodel hierarchy with an upper level named M3. This level is a set of booting notions called "Infrastructure" [6] that reuses elements from the *InfrastructureLibrary* and the *Meta Object Facility* (MOF) [7]. UML promotes the "anything must be an instance of something" adage. In this scope, the key *Class* and *Property* metaclasses at M3 (Fig. 1) must then be instances of something at M4. However, introducing a M4 layer leads to the introduction of a M5 layer that leads to... Avoiding such an infinite regression requires an appropriate specification named meta-circularity [8]; the *Class* and *Property* metaclasses must then be formally specified such that:

– They are instances of something without the need of extra metamodeling layers. This in particular supposes a clear (explicit) characterization of *Instantiation*;
– They are generative. All of the other highly useful core metaclasses like *Object*, *Type*, *Association*, *Generalization*... even some missing like the *Composition*

A. Abelló, L. Bellatreche, and B. Benatallah (Eds.): MEDI 2012, LNCS 7602, pp. 153–161, 2012.
© Springer-Verlag Berlin Heidelberg 2012

metaclass (black diamond in the UML notation)[1], may be defined through appropriate instantiation protocols. This approach called "inductive UML" is such that UML can be recursively defined.

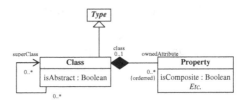

Fig. 1. The "very core" of UML with *Class* and *Property* as booting notions

Numerous research works [8-12] (see also *Related works* section) are attempts to better clarify the semantics of metamodels in the UML universe: MOF, Infrastructure, Superstructure and any possible extension. Out of these, metamodel re-formalizations often rely on "theories" (*e.g.*, non-classical logics) beyond the set theory.

In this paper, metaclasses are rewritten in the form of inductive types coming from the constructive logic supported by the Coq automated prover [13] as follows:

```
Inductive X : Type := (* Type is a predefined Coq sort
among Type, Set and Prop *)
| God (* First constructor *)
| cons : X -> X. (* Second constructor *)
```

God and *cons* are the names of the two chosen constructors for the *X* type along with their signatures. Common functions may be defined as follows:

```
Definition father(x : X) : X := match x with
| cons source => source (* father x is equal to source
when x has been constructed by means of the 2nd
constructor, i.e., cons source *)
| _ => God (* Result is God for the remaining
constructor(s); underscore sign means "any" in Coq *)
end.
```

Proofs are based on "tactics" to converge towards a given goal from initial and intermediately computed hypotheses.

So, in this paper, we specify and prove the correctness of a metamodeling framework based on Coq. For that, Kühne's metamodeling framework [2-3] is the main stream of inspiration. In his categorization, Kühne proposes in [3, pp. 377-378] a general-purpose mathematical relationship called "metaness" having the following characteristics: acyclicity, antitransitivity and level-respecting.

To make explicit a proven metamodeling framework, we structure this paper as follows: Section 2 is a reminder about the current UML design principles and

---

[1] This kind of relationship is intensively used at the M3 level without any formal semantics (see for instance Fig. 1).

organization. We specify *Class* and *Property* in Coq and how to use them by introducing metanavigations and by showing how to instantiate any other metaclass. Accordingly, the *Instantiation* relationship is formalized. Section 3 is the specification of Kühne's metaness along with short proofs. Section 4 is about related work while Section 5 draws some conclusions and evokes some perspectives.

2   UML Core Organization as Dependent Inductive Types

The model in Fig. 1 means:

- A *Class* instance is composed (black diamond) of either zero or many *Property* instances (*ownedAttribute* role). A given *Property* instance belongs (or not) to at most one *Class* instance (*class* role); unsharing applies, *i.e.*, a given *Property* object cannot belong to distinct *Class* objects;
- A *Class* instance is linked to either zero or many *Class* instances having the *superClass* role[2]. The reverse navigation means that a given *Class* has (or not) direct descendant classes; this metarelationship embodies *Generalization* links at the immediately lower metamodeling level;
- *Class* inherits from *Type*;
- Classes are either abstract (in italics) or they are not. For instance, the *Type* metaclass is abstract. Moreover, the *Class* metaclass has a Boolean attribute named *isAbstract*. This means that any instance of *Class* owns this attribute with a value among *true* or *false*. So, *Type* is an instance of *Class*[3] with value *true* for this attribute. In terms of instantiation, one thus cannot construct a new metaclass[4] as direct instance of *Type*.

For conciseness, other key metaclasses (*e.g.*, *NamedElement*), metaattributes (*e.g.*, the *name* attribute inherited by *Class* from *NamedElement*) are ignored. Moreover, "hidden" features of the model in Fig. 1 are:

- *Class* is an instance of itself. In the four-layer metamodel hierarchy of UML (M3 to M0), a *Class* element at the M2 level is an instance of a *Class* element at the M3 level. There are no reasons to distinguish between *M2::Class* and *M3::Class*. Conceptually, they are the same (same set of features especially). Accordingly, we consider the existence of an *Instantiation* link from *Class* to itself.
- The *Type* and *Property* elements are instances of *Class*;
- *isAbstract* in *Class* at M3 is an instance of *Property* at the immediately upper level with *isComposite* = *true*. So, *isAbstract* is semantically equivalent to a composition

---

[2] This association materializes direct inheritance, *i.e.*, it does not represent all of the super classes of a class (transitive closure).

[3] This *Instantiation* link does not appear in Fig. 1. In common practice, links that cross metamodeling layers are omitted.

[4] While *Type* belongs to the M3 level, such a hypothetical metaclass would belong to the M2 level.

relationship from *Class* to *Boolean* with the *1..1* cardinality and the *isAbstract* role both being next to Boolean.

- *isComposite* in *Property* is an instance of *Property* with *isComposite* = *true*;
- The *Composition* link from *Class* to *Property* is an instance of *Property* with *isComposite* = *true* (for brevity, some original attributes of *Property* are omitted);
- The *Association* link from *Class* to *Class* (*superClass* role) is an instance of *Property* with *isComposite* = *false*;
- Finally, the *Generalization* link (*i.e.*, inheritance) from *Class* to *Type* is an instance of the *Association* link from *Class* to *Class*.

2.1   Inductive Definition of *Class* and *Property*

In this section, *Class* and *Property* are introduced as Coq types while *BBoolean*, *CClass*, *PProperty* and *TType* are UML concepts (*i.e.*, Coq constants). It is also shown that *Class*, *Property* and *NonAbstractClass*[5] are mutually dependent types.

```
Inductive Class : Type :=
    BBoolean | (* UML Boolean type *)
    CClass |
    PProperty |
    instantiate : NonAbstractClass -> Property ->
Property -> Class |
    inheritsFrom : Property -> Property -> Property ->
Class
with Property : Type :=
    Null | (* Null is introduced in [7, p. 11] *)
    set_isAbstract : Property |
    set_isComposite : Property |
    set_ownedAttribute : string -> Class -> nat -> nat
-> Property -> Property | (* Expected order: attribute
name, attribute type, lower bound, upper bound,
isComposite or not *)
    set_superClass : Class -> Property (* Inheritance
*)
with NonAbstractClass : Type :=
    instantiate' : Class -> NonAbstractClass.
```

2.2   Metanavigations

The definition of metanavigations is straightforward. For example, *ownedAttribute* in Fig. 1 is specified as an ordered list of *Property* objects:

---

[5] This type is introduced for preventing abstract classes are to be instantiated.

```
Definition ownedAttribute(c : Class) : list Property :=
match c with
 | CClass => cons (set_ownedAttribute isAbstract_label
BBoolean 1 1 set_isComposite) nil
 | PProperty => cons (set_ownedAttribute
isComposite_label BBoolean 1 1 set_isComposite) nil
 ... (* other constructors here*)
 | _ => nil (* remaining cases *)
end.
```

So, by construction, computing the expression *ownedAttribute CClass* leads to a one-element list: its *isAbstract* attribute (see Fig. 1).

2.3   Constructing New Metaclasses

The generative nature of the above specification allows the creation of other core concepts through different protocols. For example, instantiating a Coq *Class* object (that is equivalent to a UML *CClass* object):

```
Definition Object : Class := instantiate (instantiate'
CClass) Null Null. (* [7, p. 15] *)
```

Here, the first *Null* occurrence means that *Object* coming from the UML kernel is not abstract while the second means that it has no "owned attribute" (note that simplified *instantiate* methods may be easily provided to avoid using *Null*).

2.4   A Formal Version of the UML «*instanceOf*» Relationship

To solve the problem of assigning a mother class to *CClass* (meta-circularity), we specify the recursive *class* function over the *Class* inductive type:

```
Fixpoint class(c : Class) : Class := match c with
 | instantiate (instantiate' c') _ _ => c'
 | inheritsFrom (set_superClass super) _ _  => class
super
 | _ => CClass (* BBoolean => CClass | CClass => CClass
 | PProperty => CClass *)
end.
```

Consequently, the UML «*instanceOf*» relationship can be easily derived from the *class* above function as follows:

```
Inductive instanceOf(c' : Class) : Class -> Prop := (*
e.g., instanceOf CClass Object *)
def : forall c, c' = class c -> instanceOf c' c.
```

In Coq, predicates using recursive constructions (*def* constructor above) may also be inductively defined.

3   Proven Metamodel Infrastructure for UML

3.1   Metaness

Kühne lays down the principle of composition of the *class* function for expressing metaness. Metaness is viewed "as a two-level detachment of the original".

In Coq, we pose the possibility of recursively computing the $meta_i class$ of any UML element e for any natural number i with $meta_0 class\ e = e$ and $meta_1 class\ e = class\ e$. The i index materializes levels in metamodeling.

```
Fixpoint metaness(n : nat) (c : Class) : Class := match
n with
| 0 => c
| S m => class (metaness m c) (* S m is the successor
of m for natural numbers in Coq *)
end.
```

So, *metaness 0 c* is the *c* entity itself while *metaness 1 c* is the direct class *c*. *metaness 2 c* is the class of the class of *c*, namely the metaclass of *c*, etc. An interesting lemma to be proven is, when *n* is not equal to *0*, *c = metaness n c* is only possible when *c = CClass*:

Lemma Metaness_majorant : forall c : Class, forall n : nat, n <> 0 -> c = metaness n c -> c = CClass.

3.2   Metaness Acyclicity, Antitransivity and Level-Respecting

The proof of metaness acyclicity is based on the following Coq theorem:

Theorem Metaness_acyclicity : forall c c' : Class, forall n : nat, c <> CClass -> c' = metaness n c -> c <> class c'.

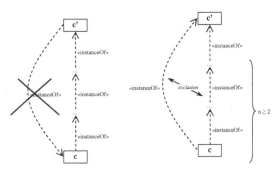

Fig. 2. Metaness acyclicity (left hand side) and antitransitivity (right hand side)

This rule is illustrated through Fig. 2. A proof by contradiction is necessary to justify this theorem (for conciseness, we hide Coq tactics). We imagine the absurd consequence that $c = class\ c'$. If so, from the initial assumption $c' = metaness\ n\ c$ (c <> CClass), we are able to write:

```
class c' = class (metaness n c)
c = metaness (S n) c (* absurd hypothesis is used *)
```

From the inductive specification of the *nat* type in Coq, we know that $S\ n$ <> 0. From the *Metaness_majorant* lemma, we conclude that $c = CClass$. This result is in contradiction with our initial hypothesis part: c <> $CClass$. So, $c = class\ c'$ is absurd.

The final conclusion is therefore: c <> $class\ c'$. In other words, this paper's specification of metaness is acyclic as advocated by Kühne in [3].

The proof of metaness antitransitivity (Fig. 2) is based on the following Coq theorem:

```
Theorem Metaness_anti_transitivity : forall c c' :
Class, forall n : nat, c <> CClass /\ n >= 2 -> c' =
metaness n c -> c' = class c -> c' = CClass.
```

The proof of level-respecting is based on the following Coq theorem:

```
Theorem Level_respecting : forall n m : nat, (exists c
: Class, exists c' : Class, c <> CClass /\ c' =
metaness n c /\ c' = metaness m c) -> n = m.
```

4   Related Work

There are two general-purpose categories of research works that stress the weakness of UML. In [9] for instance, the authors use conceptual graphs to re-formalize the *Class* (renamed *Node* in the proposed formalization), *Association* (renamed *Link*) and *Specialize*[6] (renamed *super*) metaelements. An interesting point in this contribution is the introduction in the foreground of the *Instantiation* relationship through a *meta* predicate. The paper offers conceptual graphs as a set of first order predicates including the specification of meta-circularity as follows:

```
[NODE:NODE]->(meta)->[NODE:NODE] (* [t:i] means i of
type t *)
```

This pioneering work also introduces the *sem* predicate (*instanceOf* inductive predicate above) as the counterpart of the *meta* predicate. However, no proofs are offered to show that these two constructions are mutually consistent, even though it is written: "The *sem* relation is derived from the *meta* relation." The *Instantiation* relationship is recursively defined without termination capabilities:

---

[6] This metaclass has been removed from the last versions of MOF and UML.

```
[LINK:meta]->(meta)->[NODE:LINK]
```

One observes that this specification is not generative in the sense that there is no bootstrapping: *meta* is an instance of *Association* which is an instance of *Node*. Another paper inspired by a graph theory is [10]. Authors propose the introduction of a formal semantics that in particular crosses over all diagram types. More ambitious works [8] [11-12] consider the pure invention of a metamodeling framework (even theory) and/or a dedicated language (*e.g.*, MML in [8]). For example, Paige *et al.* in [12] benefit from using another automated prover (PVS). They demonstrate how models may be accordingly checked in an Eiffel-like fashion: invariants, pre-conditions and post-conditions are kept in PVS to limit Eiffel as a formal language only.

5 Conclusions and Perspectives

From version 1.1 in 1997, the overall UML metamodel has undergone many changes. However, the current formalization (metamodels expressed in the Entity/Relationship paradigm along with OCL constraints, *i.e.*, well-formed rules) has not gone beyond the set theory. Based on this style, precise metamodeling does not preclude from having rules that contradict each other, that create overlapping or that are silent on hot topics. The latter issue may be illustrated by the absence of a formal semantics of the *Composition* relationship in UML.

This paper's research seeks to be faithful to the original UML spirit. As much as possible, we intend to avoid any restructuring of the existing dependencies between metaconcepts. However, as shown in Section 4, new constructs seem useful to move from precise metamodeling to formal metamodeling. In this scope, constructive logic and Coq are powerful helpers.

References

1. OMG Unified Modeling Language^{TM}, Superstructure, Version 2.3 (May 2010)
2. Atkinson, C., Kühne, T.: Model-Driven Development: A Metamodeling Foundation. IEEE Software 20(5), 5–22 (2002)
3. Kühne, T.: Matters of (Meta-) modeling. Software and Systems Modeling 5(4), 369–385 (2006)
4. France, R., Rumpe, B.: Model-driven Development of Complex Software: A Research Roadmap. In: The ICSE 2007 Future of Software Engineering Workshop, Minneapolis, USA (2007)
5. Steinberg, D., Budinsky, F., Paternostro, M., Merks, E.: EMF - Eclipse Modeling Framework, 2nd edn. Addison-Wesley (2008)
6. OMG Unified Modeling Language^{TM}, Infrastructure, Version 2.3 (May 2010)
7. Meta Object Facility (MOF) Core Specification, Version 2.0 (January 2006)
8. Clark, T., Evans, A., Kent, S.: The Meta-Modeling Language Calculus: Foundation Semantics for UML. In: The 4th International Conference on Fundamental Approaches to Software Engineering, Genova, Italy, pp. 17–31 (2001)

9. Bézivin, J., Gerbé, O.: Towards a Precise Definition of the OMG/MDA Framework. In: Automated Software Engineering, San Diego, USA, pp. 273–280 (2001)
10. Kuske, S., Gogolla, M., Kreowski, H.-J., Ziemann, P.: Towards an integrated graph-based semantics for UML. Software and Systems Modeling 8(3), 403–422 (2009)
11. Jackson, E., Sztipanovits, J.: Formalizing the structural semantics of domain-specific modeling languages. Software and Systems Modeling 8(4), 451–478 (2009)
12. Paige, R., Brooke, P., Ostroff, J.: Metamodel-based model conformance and multiview consistency checking. ACM Transactions on Software Engineering and Methodology 16(3) (2007)
13. Bertot, Y., Castéran, P.: Interactive Theorem Proving and Program Development Coq'Art: The Calculus of Inductive Constructions. Springer (2004)

Formal Software Verification at Model and at Source Code Levels

Anthony Fernandes Pires[1,2], Thomas Polacsek[1], and Stéphane Duprat[2]

[1] ONERA, 2 avenue Edouard Belin,
31055 Toulouse, France
[2] Atos Intégration SAS, 6 impasse Alice Guy, B.P. 43045,
31024 Toulouse cedex 03, France
{anthony.fernandespires,stephane.duprat}@atos.net,
{thomas.polacsek}@onera.fr

Abstract. In a software development cycle, it is often more than half of the development time that is dedicated to verification activities. Formal methods offer new possibilities for verification. In the specification phase, simulation or model-checking allow users to detect errors in models. In the implementation phase, analysis techniques, like static analysis, make the verification tasks more exhaustive and more automatic. In that context, we propose to take advantage of these methods to improve embedded software development processes based on the V-model.

Keywords: Verification, formal methods, development process, Model Based Engineering.

1 Introduction

In software development, verification activities are significant costs. In the seventies, [8] was reporting that over half the software development time was devoted to tests. Today, in critical embedded software projects at Atos, we notice that the cost of verification activities can sometimes reach 60% of the total workload. In the DO-178b certification standard[1] verification means are reviews, analysis and tests, but the new version includes a specific text on the use of formal methods (DO-333). Formal methods are mathematically-based techniques, for instance, formal logic, model checking or discrete mathematics. Although not all errors can be found with tests, most of them could be detected by the addition of formal methods in the early stages of development. It enables more effective identification of software defects and allows to reduce verification costs.

We propose to extend the embedded software development process based on V-model by introducing formal methods at the earliest stages of the life cycle and to use it to perform verification tasks. In this paper, our main contribution is to introduce links between model, formal verification and source code formal verification in an industrial context. Indeed, a lot of works focus on model verification and, more particularly, on OCL checking like we can see in [12] or [2].

---

[1] DO-178b *Software considerations in airborne systems and equipment certification.*

A. Abelló, L. Bellatreche, and B. Benatallah (Eds.): MEDI 2012, LNCS 7602, pp. 162–169, 2012.
© Springer-Verlag Berlin Heidelberg 2012

Moreover, source code verification is successfully used now in industrial projects like [13]. But, all these works use verifications only in one step of the development cycle. Furthermore, because of our industrial context, it is necessary to consider the formalisms and the practices used by development teams. It is impossible to introduce a disruptive innovation. Consequently, we limit our work to OMG standards UML[2] and SysML[3] adapted to embedded software domain for the design stages and to Frama-C[4] for code analysis implementation stages.

In section 2, we introduce the addition of formal methods at the different phases of the left branch of the V-model. In sections 3, 4 and 5, we give a quick view of existing methods which can be used in the phases of our process, we describe what we do in our approach and we illustrate its use on a simple example. In section 6, we conclude the paper and give perspectives for our work.

2   The Global Picture

The V-model is the most widely development process used for embedded software. Even if it is often replaced, in other industrial domains, by other practices, it is not the case in our context. The V-model has two main streams: the development stream, the left side of the "V", represents the program refinement from requirements to code; the testing stream, the right side of the "V", represents integration of parts and their validation. In this paper, we propose to extend the left side of the "V" by adding earlier verification steps (figure 1).

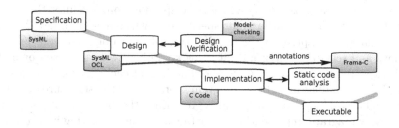

Fig. 1. Left side of our V-model with verification tasks

In order to illustrate our approach, this paper uses a simple example of software development. We will represent the controller of a component in charge of the verification of the power. The controller is driven by a clock. At each clock tick, the controller does a task. During verification performed by the controller, if a problem is detected, the controlled component jumps to a maintenance status. While this maintenance status is maintained, no verifications are done by the controller. When the component status becomes normal, verifications start again.

---

[2] http://www.uml.org/
[3] http://www.sysml.org/
[4] http://frama-c.com/

3   Specification

3.1   Modeling Languages

There are many ways to specify software. The common one is to use natural language to write specifications, but it often leads to ambiguities and misunderstandings like explained in [9]. Modeling languages offer ways to produce formal specifications, which are better understandable, make communication easier between users and allow code and documents generation activities.

Our scope is UML/SysML standards. Some works adapt these modeling languages to the embedded domain. The UML profile MARTE [7] is an OMG standard for the modeling of embedded and real-time systems. It defines concepts in order to take into account the notions of time, concurrency, software and hardware platform, resources and characteristics like execution time. It is also possible to annotate models to perform analysis.

The SysML profile AVATAR [10] is dedicated to the modeling and the formal verification of real-time embedded software. The language is a specialization of SysML which focuses on activities realized in upper-stream of the development cycle. It offers solutions for: requirements engineering, system analysis, system modeling and safety and security properties modeling.

3.2   Our Approach

We choose to use a subset of SysML for the specification. We limit the scope of elements and we define patterns for specific use, without adding new concepts. Our language is adapted to the specification of embedded software in a synchronous and scheduled environment. This kind of software is driven by a clock so it is expected to do a certain number of actions at each clock tick. Our subset is based on three diagrams: block diagram representing the structure of software components, state machine diagram representing the behavior of components and activity diagram, representing the detailed actions occurring in a state. The functioning is the following: for state machines, we constrain the triggers of all the major transitions with a unique event named "NextStep" in our case. At each clock tick, which corresponds to one cycle, this event occurs. It allows the firing of a transition of the state machine. In this way, we control the evolution in a synchronous way. For more information and industrial use, see [6].

3.3   Application on the Example

The behavior specification of the controller using the modeling language described above is given Figure 2. The controller starts by a state of verification of the component status (*check_status*). If it is normal, the controller goes to a state of power verification (*check_power*). If not, it repeats and waits for the next cycle to check the status again. Once in state *check_power*, the verification is proceeded. At the next cycle, if the verification is correct or if the component

status is maintenance, the controller goes to *check_status* and repeats the behavior. If the verification is not correct and the component status is normal, the
controller goes to a state of maintenance (*maintenance*) and the component status changes from normal to maintenance. The controller has to wait the end of
the maintenance, which can last some cycles, before going to *check_power* again.

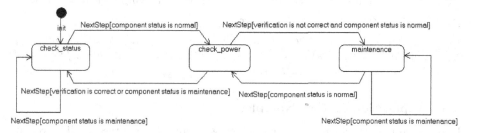

Fig. 2. The controller specification

4 Design and Verification

4.1 Formal Models Analysis

Model notations like those introduced in section 3, even though really efficient at
conveying intelligible visual clues to the designers, lack the expressiveness needed
to capture the finer details of a complete specification. For instance, expressing
transition condition in natural language is a source of many ambiguities. To
address this, formal constraints specification languages were introduced. The
major interest of a fully formalized specification is the ability to perform analysis
tasks in early phases of the development process.

Analysis tasks can be performed with model checking. Model checking, introduced in [11], allows users to verify if a system model respects a set of
requirements expressed as properties. For example, in the embedded domain,
UPPAAL [1] provides an environment for the modeling, simulation and verification of real-time embedded systems. The model checker can verify properties
expressed in temporal logic Timed CTL, for which model checking is decidable.
A gateway exists between UPPAAL and SysML. TTool [5] gives the possibility to
check safety properties on AVATAR models with the UPPAAL model-checker.

4.2 Our Approach

Here, we want to refine the specification model to meet a complete formalization
of our specification. We translate guards in state machine diagrams from natural
language to Object Constraint Language (OCL). OCL has been designed to be

---

[5] http://ttool.telecom-paristech.fr/index.html

easy to read, to write and to understand. We can also detail for each state the set of actions that must be done in a cycle thanks activity diagram.

In addition, we want to use the formal specification of transition guards to check some simple properties. Our goal is to make the verification completely transparent to the user and to propose a set of properties to automatically verify thanks model checking. An example of property is the deadlock freeness of each state of the state machine. It is expressed with the following logical formula.

Definition 1 (Deadlock freeness of a state).
Let s a state of a state machine and $G(s)$ the set of guards of all outgoing transitions of s where $G(s) = \{g_0, g_1, \ldots, g_n\}$. The state s is deadlock free if and only if $Dfree(s)$ is valid, with $Dfree(s) \equiv \bigvee_{0 \leq i \leq n} g_i$

4.3   Application on the Example

In our example, we formalized each guard with an OCL expression. The result of the controller verification became a variable named *check_result* defined as enum type *checking_result* whose possible values are OK or KO. The component status became a global variable named *status*. This variable is of enum type *component_status* whose possible values are NORMAL or MAINTENANCE.

Today, we are not able to show the verification step, our work has just begun and the choice of the tool has not been yet decided. But these formalizations are sufficient to obtain code from the state machine and to conduct code analysis.

5   Implementation and Static Code Analysis

5.1   Formal Analysis of Code

Static code analysis allows users to detect runtime errors or check properties on the source code without execution. The framework Frama-C is an open-source modular environment dedicated to the static analysis of C programs. The framework uses ACSL [6] specification language to specify properties and contracts on functions. Frama-C relies on different static analysis techniques available through plugins and linked solvers.

The value analysis technique, based on the abstract interpretation [3], can be used to ensure the absence of run-time errors in a program. This method is available with the Frama-C Value Analysis plugin [7]. It is based on the computation of variation domains for the variables of a program. The plugin gives warnings if it detects possible runtime errors, for instance access to invalid pointer.

Another method is the verification by proof obligations derived from the weakest precondition calculus introduced by [4]. It is a deductive method for proving properties. This kind of analysis is managed by Frama-C WP plugin [8] or Jessie plugin [9].

---

[6] ANSI/ISO C Specification Language, http://frama-c.com/acsl.html
[7] http://frama-c.com/value.html
[8] http://frama-c.com/wp.html
[9] http://krakatoa.lri.fr/jessie.html

5.2   Our Approach

In this step, our main goal is to ensure that source code conforms to the speci-fication. In the same vein as [5], we want to derive ACSL annotations from the design model (here in SysML) to the code and check them with static analysis.

In our approach, the behavior of the software is represented by state machines. Each state machine is implemented by two C functions, a transition function dedicated to the choice of the triggered transition, the other for the behavior of each state. Each function is constructed as a *switch/case* structure. At each cycle, the two functions are called in sequence, in order to determine which transition is triggered and what will be the actions done in the cycle.

To verify the global behavior, we add a function contract for the C transition function. This contract is composed of one ACSL behavior for each state of the state machine. One behavior is composed of two types of clause. *Assumes* clause which specifies the property that must be true for the behavior to apply. In our context, it is the current state at the call of the function. Then, *ensures* clause which specifies the property that must be true at the end of the behavior. In our context, there is one *ensures* clause for each possible outgoing transition of the state. Each *ensures* clause is an implication defining that if the condition of the transition is true, it implies that the new state of the state machine is the targeted state of the transition.

In addition, we translate into ACSL the property expressed in design phase. We want to verify that a state, expressed in the model, is deadlock freeness using the enum types of the code. In that way, we use Frama-C to verify a property of the specification. For that we add annotations for each state in the C function. *Requires* clause will concern the range of the possible values of all variables used in the guards of all outgoing transitions of the state. The behavior, composed of one *assumes* clause will represent an implication defining that if we are in the current state, it implies our property (the translation of the logical expression defined in definition 1 to ASCL). Then, we will use a little trick. We will use the *complete behaviors* annotation, originally used to check the completeness of behaviors with Frama-C. In our case, this annotation will allow us to verify that the *requires* clause implies the *assumes* clause and so to prove our property.

5.3   Application on the Example

The C code of the transition function of the example (see figure 2) is given below:

```
power_ctrl_state Power_Controller_T(power_ctrl_state state){
  power_ctrl_state o_state;
  switch(state) {
    case init :
      o_state=check_status;
      break;
    case check_status :
      if (status==NORMAL) o_state=check_power;
```

```
      if (status==MAINTENANCE) o_state=check_status;
      break;
    case check_power :
      if(check_result==KO && status==NORMAL) o_state=maintenance;
      if(check_result==OK || status==MAINTENANCE)
        o_state=check_status;
      break;
    case maintenance :
      if (status==NORMAL) o_state=check_power;
      if (status==MAINTENANCE) o_state=maintenance;
      break;
    }
  return o_state;
}
```

An example of ACSL behaviors is given below. This function contract checks the outgoing transitions of the state *check_power*.

```
/*@behavior state_check_power :
    assumes state==check_power;
    ensures (status==NORMAL && check_result==KO)
            ==> \result==maintenance;
    ensures (status==MAINTENANCE || check_result==OK)
            ==> \result==check_status;*/
```

The behavior representing the deadlock freeness for this state is given below.

```
/*@requires status==NORMAL || status==MAINTENANCE;
  requires check_result==OK || check_result==KO;
  behavior dfree_check_power :
  assumes state==check_power
          ==> ((check_result==KO && status==NORMAL)
          || (check_result==OK || status==MAINTENANCE));

  complete behaviors dfree_check_power;*/
```

Static analysis is performed with the WP plugin version 0.4 of the Frama-C Nitrogen version. For our example, all the proof obligations are verified which means our transition function is compliant with our specification and the deadlock freeness is verified for each state of the state machine.

6   Conclusion

There are many formal methods for verification tasks and all of them can be incorporated in the different steps of the V-model. In this paper, we have presented how to use some of them throughout the development cycle to gain confidence on the specification, design and implementation, and to detect errors in early stage of the development cycle. In addition, we have begun to discuss how to link design and design verification with source code verification. Furthermore, we have presented a way to verify a model property using code analysis tool. This work is a first proposal. We still need to work on generation of ACSL annotations from SysML models. Today annotations are manually created from state machine models. We need to work on the consideration of activity behaviors and the automatic generation. We should also propose OCL patterns for properties and gateways to model checkers for the design verification step.

References

1. Behrmann, G., David, A., Larsen, K.G.: A Tutorial on UPPAAL. In: Bernardo, M., Corradini, F. (eds.) SFM-RT 2004. LNCS, vol. 3185, pp. 33–35. Springer, Heidelberg (2004)
2. Cabot, J., Clariso, R., Riera, D.: Verification of uml/ocl class diagrams using constraint programming. In: Proceedings of the 2008 IEEE International Conference on Software Testing Verification and Validation Workshop, ICSTW 2008, pp. 73–80. IEEE Computer Society, Washington, DC (2008)
3. Cousot, P.: Abstract interpretation. ACM Comput. Surv. 28(2), 324–328 (1996)
4. Dijkstra, E.W.: A constructive approach to the problem of program correctness. BIT Numerical Mathematics 8, 174–186 (1968)
5. Duprat, S., Gaufillet, P., Moya Lamiel, V., Passarello, F.: Formal verification of sam state machine implementation. In: ERTS, France (2010)
6. Fernandes Pires, A., Duprat, S., Faure, T., Besseyre, C., Beringuier, J., Rolland, J.F.: Use of modelling methods and tools in an industrial embedded system project: works and feedback. In: ERTS, France (2012)
7. Gérard, S., Espinoza, H., Terrier, F., Selic, B.: 6 Modeling Languages for Real-Time and Embedded Systems. In: Giese, H., Karsai, G., Lee, E., Rumpe, B., Schätz, B. (eds.) Model-Based Engineering of Embedded Real-Time Systems. LNCS, vol. 6100, pp. 129–154. Springer, Heidelberg (2011)
8. Hoare, C.A.R.: An axiomatic basis for computer programming. Commun. ACM 12(10), 576–580 (1969)
9. Meyer, B.: On formalism in specifications. IEEE Software 2(1), 6–26 (1985)
10. Pedroza, G., Apvrille, L., Knorreck, D.: Avatar: A sysml environment for the formal verification of safety and security properties. In: 11th Annual International Conference on New Technologies of Distributed Systems (NOTERE), pp. 1–10 (2011)
11. Queille, J., Sifakis, J.: Specification and Verification of Concurrent Systems in Cesar. In: Dezani-Ciancaglini, M., Montanari, U. (eds.) International Symposium on Programming. LNCS, vol. 137, pp. 337–351. Springer, Heidelberg (1982)
12. Soeken, M., Wille, R., Kuhlmann, M., Gogolla, M., Drechsler, R.: Verifying uml/ocl models using boolean satisfiability. In: Proceedings of the Conference on Design, Automation and Test in Europe, DATE 2010, European Design and Automation Association, 3001, Leuven, Belgium, pp. 1341–1344 (2010)
13. Souyris, J., Wiels, V., Delmas, D., Delseny, H.: Formal Verification of Avionics Software Products. In: Cavalcanti, A., Dams, D.R. (eds.) FM 2009. LNCS, vol. 5850, pp. 532–546. Springer, Heidelberg (2009)

Enterprise Ontology Learning for Heterogeneous Graphs Extraction

Rania Soussi and Marie-Aude Aufaure

Ecole Centrale Paris, Grande Voie des Vignes
92 295 Chatenay-Malabry Cedex, France
{rania.soussi,Marie-Aude Aufaure}@ecp.fr

Abstract. In the enterprise context, people need to visualize different types of interactions between heterogeneous objects in order to make the right decision. Therefore, we have proposed, in previous works, an approach of enterprise object graphs extraction which describes these interactions. One of the steps involved in this approach consists in identifying automatically the enterprise objects. Since the enterprise ontology has been used for describing enterprise objects and processes, we propose to integrate it in this process. The main contribution of this work is to propose an approach for enterprise ontology learning coping with both generic and specific aspects of enterprise information. It is three-folded: First, general enterprise ontology is semi-automatically built in order to represent general aspects. Second, ontology learning method is applied to enrich and populate this latter with specific aspects. Finally, the resulting ontology is used to identify objects in the graph extraction process.

Keywords: enterprise ontology, ontology learning, graph matching.

1 Introduction

In the enterprise context, people need to visualize different types of interactions between heterogeneous objects, e.g. customers and products and etc, in order to make the right decision. Graphs are a structure relevant to analyze these interactions and facilitate their querying. Nevertheless, in a business context, important expertise information is stored in files, databases and especially relational databases (RD). Many types of data, from e-mails and contact information to financial data, are stored in RD. This data source is a rich one to extract objects interaction. We have proposed a method for extracting a graph of heterogeneous objects from a RD. The latter one is first transformed into a graph model. Then, the heterogeneous graph which describes the interaction between objects is extracted from this model. Then, we provide a set of patterns for reorganizing the graph – nodes and relationships – according to the objects selected by a user. The automatic identification of entities is the process used to identify graph nodes containing the elements of interest for the user (for example Project or Customer). This problem is not a simple one as many problems may occur. For instance, an object can be described by the means of different tables in the RD, and then many nodes can represent the same object. Since enterprise ontology (EO) has been used for describing enterprise objects

A. Abelló, L. Bellatreche, and B. Benatallah (Eds.): MEDI 2012, LNCS 7602, pp. 170–177, 2012.

and processes in order to represent a common semantic layer of enterprise resources, we integrate such ontology to enhance the object identification process. The proposed approaches of EO building are too generic or too specific. Moreover, in the EO we need to have the two types of concepts in order to have all the available information about enterprise objects. In this paper, we define an approach for EO learning coping with both generic and specific aspects of enterprise information. It contains the following steps: (1) a general EO is manually built in order to represent general aspects (core ontology), and (2) ontology learning method is applied to enrich and populate this latter with specific aspects. Finally, the resulting ontology is used to identify objects in the graph extraction process. The main contribution of this work is to propose a learning approach adapted to the enterprise context and which can be adapted for specific enterprise and integrated in their application. This paper is organized as follows: we start by presenting the previous works on EO building. The general architecture of the EO learning approach is presented in Section 3. Section 4 details how we build the general part of this ontology. Section 5 describes the enrichment and population of the ontology. Then, we present the object identification process in section 6. The section 7 presents the evaluation of the approach.

2   Enterprise Ontology

EO has been used to describe the domain, or parts of the domain of an enterprise [4]. It was defined in [1] as a top level ontology containing basic concepts, that concern enterprises and their activities, such as Project and People. More formally the EO is defined by: $\mathcal{O} := \{C, H^c, OP, DP, A\}$ where:

-C is the set of concepts

-H^c is the set of directed relations $H^c \subseteq C \times C$ which is called concept hierarchy.

- OP is the set of object properties $op \in OP$ with $op := <n, c_1, c_2>$ where n is the name of the object property, c_1, $c_2 \in C$ with c_1 is the range of op and $c2$ is the domain of op

-DP is the set of datatype properties $dp \in DP$ then $dp := <n, c_1, t>$ where n is the name of the property, $c_1 \in C$ with c_1 is the range of op and t is the type of the relation.

-A is the set of axioms.

In the literature, some enterprise ontologies have been proposed. The Enterprise Ontology [1], the TOVE ontology [2] and Uschold's work [3] have designed methods for manually build such ontologies. Uschold *et al.* [3] have developed a top-level EO which does not contain information about the specific terminology of the domain of the enterprise, and contains only general concepts of products, services and processes. In the SEMCO Project [4], a semi-automatically method was proposed for building EO using ontology design patterns in order to create enterprise ontologies for small-scale application contexts. The resulting ontology was an EO for a specific enterprise and a specific application. Our objective is to build an ontology containing the general concepts of the business domain but also the specific one related to a specific enterprise. This ontology will be a reference of the objects and their characteristics in an enterprise. In the next section, we present our approach.

3   Enterprise Ontology Learning Approach

As we already stated, in the enterprise context, the most important data are stored in RD. A heterogeneous object graph, which describes the interactions between different objects like social network graph products and costumers graph, project and employee, will facilitate analyzing the interactions and will help making better decisions. We have proposed an approach of heterogeneous graph extraction from RD [9]. A RD is first transformed according to a graph model. An heterogeneous graph is extracted from this model according to the user interest. This last step leads to cope with two main problems: objects of interest identification and relations extraction.

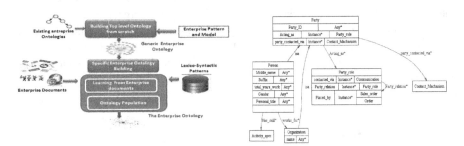

Fig. 1. The proposed approach   **Fig. 2.** The Person concept in the generic EO

We propose an EO learning approach which designs a general ontology that can be adapted to specific enterprises needs and which is based on two phases (see Fig.1):

1. Building the generic ontology manually using existing resources.
2. Building the specific part of the ontology by enriching the generic EO.

In the next sections we will describe the different steps of the proposed approach.

4   The Generic Enterprise Ontology Design

The generic part of the EO aims to outline the common processes and elements that enterprises share. For this step we have used the following resources:

(1)   Existing ontologies. Several EO have been designed in the literature. In our work, we have used the ontology proposed in [3].

(2)   Patterns from other domains. Knowledge already accumulated in other areas can act as inspiration or may even be directly transformed into concepts and relations useful for EO construction. Database schemas are modeled to describe a domain, with the intent of storing data efficiently, but schemas share many properties with ontologies. Such schemas may be particularly suitable when, as in our case, the ontologies in focus are ontologies describing information within enterprises. Based on this reasoning, we have used the data model pattern proposed by [6]. In order to build our generic EO from scratch, we have used a methodology similar to the one

proposed by [5]. To begin with, the common concepts from the different resources have been regrouped. Secondly, the relations between the concepts were defined. In this last step, the hierarchical relation was defined: Defining the synonyms, the super and sub classes. Moreover, resolving contradictory relations, the other existing relations were sorted to avoid cycles and multiple inheritances. The third step consisted of specifying the concept properties by merging existing ones and adding new ones. An expert of the resulting ontology is depicted in Fig.2. The resulting ontology contains 90 concepts about the enterprise actors (Person, Team and etc), their role (Employee, Customer and etc), the production   (Product, Order, Price, etc), the communication and the work effort.

5   Learning and Populating EO Using the Unstructured Data

In order to collect the local concepts used in an enterprise, we have used a learning process to add this specific part in the generic ontology using the enterprise documents such as web sites, wikis and e-mails. The learning process is followed by a population process using the same document in order to add new instances to the ontology. In what follow, we detail these steps to create the specific EO.

5.1   Learning Process

Document Treatment. we start by processing the documents   using linguistic method. Linguistic preprocessing starts by tokenization (divides the text into tokens) and sentence splitting (divides the text into sentences). The resulting annotation set serves as an input for a Part-of- speech (POS) tagger which, in the following, assigns appropriate syntactic categories to all tokens. Then, lemmatizing or stemming is done by a morphological analyzer or a stemmer respectively. After that, the sentences are divided into noun phrase chunks using a noun phrase NP chunker. After this preprocessing, the generic ontology concepts are searched on the annotated documents. Each detected concept is annotated by a specific tag. We add other annotation by the use of the named entity recognition which can detect certain types of named entities (Person, Location, Organization).

New Concepts and Relations Identification. This step uses the documents processed and a set of lexico-syntaxic patterns in order to identify new elements to be added to the ontology, and to extract new patterns to enrich the set of patterns.

Candidate Concepts, Attributes and Relations Detection. We have identified different sets of patterns to identify candidate elements. These patterns are grouped using the type of relation or elements which can be identified by it. In the next patterns, *NPC* designs the noun phrase containing a concept from the initial ontology and *NP* is another noun phrase which contains a candidate element.

Pattern for Taxonomic Relations. These patterns are used to extract new concepts which share a hyponymy or a meronymy relation with an existing concept. They include the Hearst patterns and the Lexico-Syntactic Patterns corresponding to

Ontology Design Patterns. For instance, in the sentence "Other *forms of* **company**, **such as** *the cooperative*", the Hearst pattern *"NPC such as {NP,}* {and | or} NP"* can detect that "cooperative" is a sub-concept of the concept "company".

Pattern for Non Hierarchical Relation. The verbal phrases can reveal semantic relations between two terms. The two verbal patterns can be summarized by: *[P] V (NPC,NP)* and *[P] V(NP,NPC)*, where *P* represents a proposition.

Indeed, in the phrase "**Organization** provides services", if "Organization" is a concept in the EO using the verbal pattern we can detect the relation: *Provide (Organization, service)*. Then "service" is a candidate concept to be added in the ontology with the relation Provide

Pattern for Attributes. Attributes are defined as relations with a datatype as range. Typical attributes are, for example, name or color with a *string* as range, date with a *date* as range or size with an *integer* or *real* as range.

Candidate Elements Processing. The previous patterns allow the identification of candidate relations to add to the EO. Each candidate relation has the form *CR:=<r,tc,c>* where:

- *r*: the type of the relation which can be an object property or a data property.
- *tc*: the candidate element, a new data property where r is a data property or a new concept where r is a new object property.
- *c*: the existing concept on the ontology (obtained from the NPC)

For each candidate relation, we compute the similarity *sim(tc,c)* between the concept *c* and the candidate element t_c. If *sim(tc,c)>α* (where α is a threshold value) then *tc* and *r* are added to the ontology. For the similarity, we have used the WebOverlap measure [7] which is based on the web co-occurrence. This measure exploits page counts returned by a Web search engine to measure the semantic similarity between words. WebOverlap is defined by: $WebOverlap\ (c,t_c) = \dfrac{hits\ (c\ and\ t_c)}{hits\ (c) \times hits\ (t_c)}$ where the

notation *hits(P)* denotes the page counts for the query *P* in a search engine.

5.2   Population Process

In order to build rich EO dedicated to a particular enterprise and useful in its local application, we add to the learned concepts from the enterprise document instances using an ontology population process. Populating ontologies means finding instances of the conceptualization [8]. The documents are annotated with the previous annotations techniques and with gazetteers. The gazetteers used at this step can identify cities, organizations, person's names, enterprise names and software products names. This preprocessing allows us to identify more named entities and to facilitate the instance detection. In order to identify the concept instances, we use the set of patterns and the ontology relations. We first apply patterns for taxonomic relations to identify its instances. If the identified pattern contains an existing concept, and the hypernyms are a proper noun, these hypernyms will be added as instances.

6 Integration of the Ontology in an Object Identification Process

6.1 The Application Context

We have proposed in [9] an approach that extracts from relational database the interactions between heterogeneous objects based on two steps: (1) Transformation of the relational model into a graph model in order to extract all the existing objects and the relations between them; (2) Extraction of the graph of interactions between particular objects chosen by the user. The first step produces a heterogeneous graph (example in Fig.5) defined by: $G := (\mathcal{N}, \mathcal{E})$ where:

- $\mathcal{N}$ is a set of nodes N (which represents the existing objects in the RD) where

  $N := (n, A_n)$; n is s the name of N and A_n is set of attributes $A_n := \{ \ a_n \big| a_n := \langle n_{a_n}, t \rangle \ \}$

  where n is the attribute name, t is the node type.
- $\mathcal{E}$ is a set of labeled edges where $\mathcal{E} \subseteq \mathcal{N} \times \mathcal{N}$

This graph contains two levels: a schema level which describes the whole structure and an instance level which instantiates the schema level. The second step is composed of two sub-steps. The first one deals with the detection of the objects of interest. In this level the EO can be integrated to detect the chosen objects from the input graph. The second sub-step is dedicated to extract the corresponding relations to the identified objects of interest. The graph containing the objects of interest is defined by: $GO = (O_I, R_O)$ where: O_I is a finite set of object such $O_I := \{ o_I \big| o_I \in \mathcal{N} \}$ and R_O is a finite set of relations between objects such $R_O :=$ $\{ \ r \big| r := \langle l, o_{I_1}, o_{I_2} \rangle, o_{I_1}, o_{I_2} \in O_I \}$ where l is the relation name.

In what follow, we will describe the object identification process.

6.2 Object Identification Using the Enterprise Ontology

Object identification is the process used to identify the nodes of graph extracted from the RD that contain the elements of interest of the user based on the EO concepts. Indeed, the user chooses the enterprise concepts for which he wants to see the interactions and relations. Then, the similar nodes to the concepts will be added to the graph. The identification can be seen as a schema and string matching problem. In this step, we will try to find the corresponding nodes (in the schema level) of a designed concept by adopting some schema matching techniques. The proposed algorithm takes as input the set of concepts which a user wants to visualize on the graph and the first graph extracted from the RD. The first step consists in finding the most similar nodes regarding the input concepts using names matching. Then, we extract a set of nodes which are candidates to represent these concepts. Finally, each candidate node is analyzed using its attributes to calculate the similarity with the input concepts. This algorithm is based on the following steps:

Step 1.Names treatment. Each node N name and concept $c \in C$ are transformed to a set of tokens $T_N := \{t_i |\ t_i \subseteq n\ \}$ and $T_c := \{t_{ci} |\ t_{ci} \subseteq c\ \}$, respectively.

Step 2. String Matching between the Nodes Name and the Concept Label. In order to compare the nodes names and the label of a concept, each T_N is compared with T_c. This comparison is summarized by the following cases:

(1) If the T_N elements are equal, sub-concepts or synonyms of c then, the node is added to the graph of chosen objects.

(2) If one of T_N elements contains one of the T_c elements then N is a candidate. If one of T_N element is a suffix of one of T_c elements then N is candidate.

(3) In the other case we calculate the similarity between T_c and T_N using the name similarity measure proposed in [10]:

$$Sim(T_c, T_N) = \frac{\sum_{t_1 \in T_c}\left[\max_{t_2 \in T_N} sim\ (t_1, t_2)\right] + \sum_{t_2 \in T_N}\left[\max_{t_1 \in T_c} sim\ (t_1, t_2)\right]}{|T_c| + |T_N|}, \quad \text{where} \quad sim(t_1, t_2) \quad \text{is}$$

calculated using the Jiang and Conrath measure [11] using WordNet as reference. The node N is added as a candidate object if $Sim(T_c, T_N) > \alpha$.

Step 3. Candidate objects treatment. The candidate objects are analyzed by using their attributes. For each chosen concept C, we will compare its datatype attributes (DP) with each candidate nodes attributes by calculating the similarity:

$$Simatt\ (C, N) := \frac{\sum_{n_c \in DP} \sum_{n_{n_h} \in N_h} sim\ (n_c, n_{a_n})}{|DP| + |A_n|}, \quad \text{where } n_c \text{ is the name of a } DP \text{ of } C \text{ and } n_{a_n} \text{ is}$$

the name of attribute. If $Simatt(C, N) > \beta$ then N is added to the object set.

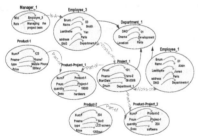

Fig. 3. The resulting graph

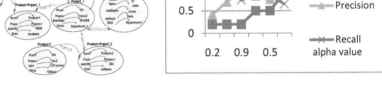

Fig. 4. Excerpt of the instance level graph

7   Evaluation

In order to evaluate our approach of ontology learning, we have implemented a java application. This application is charged to build the EO by taking as input a generic EO, which is built manually using Protégé 3.7.4, and the enterprise unstructured data (websites and wiki). It uses the Protégé JAVA API to load, edit and save ontologies and GATE (http://gate.ac.uk/) component to treat the documents. After having built the EO, we have used it to identify objects. We have tested our work on a graph containing 90 heterogeneous objects in the schema level. We have remarked that the precision and the recall of the approach depend on α value and β value. These value variations are represented by the schema in Fig.6 using the recall and the precision measures.

Precision= (number of identified objects correctly)/(total of identified objects).
Recall=(number of identified objects correctly)/(total of objects to identify).

8   Conclusion

In this work, we have presented an approach for learning EO from enterprise documents. The proposed approach allowed obtaining an ontology containing general concepts of the business domain and specific ones for a particular enterprise. We have used the resulting ontology in an approach of interacting objects graph extraction. The ontology is used to identify the objects of interest from a user's point of view, by filtering the schema of an input graph. As a future step of our work, we will use the value of the existing instances to improve the matching between the ontology concepts and the graph nodes. We will also use the ontology relations to enhance the extracted graph.

References

1. Uschold, M., King, M.: Towards a Methodology for Building Ontologies. In: Workshop on Basic Ontological Issues in Knowledge Sharing. International Joint Conference on Artificial Intelligence (1995)
2. Grüninger, M., Fox, M.: Methodology for the Design and Evaluation of Ontologies. In: Proc. of IJCAI 1995's Workshop (1995)
3. Uschold, M., et al.: The Enterprise Ontology. The Knowledge Engineering Review 13(1) (1998)
4. Blomqvist, E., Ohgren, A.: Constructing an enterprise ontology for an automotive supplier. Engineering Applications of Artificial Intelligence 21(3), 386–397 (2008)
5. Noy, N., McGuinness, L.: Ontology Development 101: A Guide to Creating Your First Ontology. Stanford Knowledge Systems Laboratory Technical Report KSL-01-05 and Stanford Medical Informatics Technical Report SMI-2001-0880 (2001)
6. Silverston, L.: The Data Model Resource Book - A Library of Universal Data Models for All Enterprises, 1st edn. John Wiley & Sons (2001)
7. Sahami, M., Heilman, T.D.: A web-based kernel function for measuring the similarity of short text snippets. In: WWW 2006, pp. 377–386 (2006)
8. Cimiano, P.: Ontology Learning and Population from Text: Algorithms, Evaluation and Applications. Springer-Verlag New York, Inc., Secaucus (2006)
9. Soussi, R., Aufaure, M.A., Baazaoui, H.: Graph Database For collaborative Communities. In: Community-Built Databases: Research and Development (2011)
10. Madhavan, J., Bernstein, P.A., Rahm, E.: Generic schema matching with Cupid. VLDB Journal, 49–58 (2001)
11. Jiang, J.J., Conrath, D.W.: Semantic Similarity Based on Corpus Statistics and Lexical Taxonomy. In: Proceedings of International Conference Research on Computational Linguistics (ROCLING X), Taiwan (1997)

Toward Propagating the Evolution of Data Warehouse on Data Marts

Saïd Taktak and Jamel Feki

University of Sfax, FSEGS Faculty, P.O.Box 1088
Miracl Laboratory, Sfax, Tunisia
{said.taktak,jamel.feki}@fsegs.rnu.tn

Abstract. Modern Decision Support Systems (DSS) are composed of a Data Warehouse (DW) which stores all data necessary for decisional purposes, and a several Data Marts (DMs). A DM is a subject oriented extract of the DW data; it facilitates evaluating the performances of a business process. However, in practice, business processes may evolve as well as new ones may be created, consequently the DW model evolves in order to capture the changes. The maintenance of DMs due to the evolution of their DW is time-consuming, expensive and error-prone process. This paper studies the evolution of DM schemas in the case of a new table is added to the DW.

Keywords: Evolution operation, Data warehouse, Data mart.

1 Introduction

There is a strong dependency of DMs from their filler DW. This dependency raises a new evolution problem which is the impact of the DW schema evolution on its DMs. This resembles to the transactional information systems (IS) evolution problem which was treated by several researches and according to many viewpoints [1-2]; but it has its specificities: distinct models for the DW and its DMs. Few recent works have been interested with the evolution in the DW domain. We can classify these works into *Schema Evolution* [3-4], *Schema Versioning* [5], and *View Maintenance* [6].

We can claim that all evolution strategies proposed in the literature situates at a single modeling level. Indeed, schemas before and after changes are expressed conforming to the same meta-model. To our knowledge, in the DW domain schema evolution problems impacting dependent schemas compliant to different models have not yet received their full part of investigation. Typically, the DW is often structured as a conventional database whereas the DMs are expressed into a different model: the multidimensional model.

Our objective is to study the impact of the DW schema changes on its DMs. Due to space limitation, we restrict ourselves to the operation of creating a new DW table.

This paper is organized as follows. In section 2 we give an overview of the DW evolution. Section 3 discusses the related works. Section 4 outlines our approach for DSS evolution. In section 5 we define a set of transformation rules. Finally, section 6 concludes the paper.

A. Abell\'{o}, L. Bellatreche, and B. Benatallah (Eds.): MEDI 2012, LNCS 7602, pp. 178–185, 2012.
© Springer-Verlag Berlin Heidelberg 2012

2   Related Works

Hurtado et al. [3] treated the problem of evolution mainly in the multidimensional model (fact and dimension tables) for the star or snowflake schemas. The authors proposed an abstract model and a set of evolution operators to define the alterations applicable to dimensional structures and their instances. These operators modify a multidimensional schema by allowing the addition or removal of hierarchical levels. In addition, the authors studied the effect of these modifications on the materialized views and, proposed certain adaptations and an algorithm for view maintenance. Note that this approach is purely theoretical. Moreover, to our knowledge, no prototype has been developed to validate the approach.

Blaschka, et al. [4] proposed the FIESTA tool for the DW modeling; they also suggested evolution operations for dimensions and facts. These evolution operations are expressed by means of a conceptual graph called ME/R (Multidimensional Entity-Relationship model) to be later propagated to the relational or multidimensional model. Blaschka et al. study the evolution of dimensions and hierarchies as in [3]; in addition, they treat the changes affecting the fact table and adding of a new hierarchical level without positional constraint. The developed software tool supports a methodology for the evolution of multidimensional schemas allowing the passage from the conceptual to logic level. However, these operations are dedicated to the star schema.

Benitez-Guerrero et al. [7] proposed a prototype WHES ("Warehouse Evolution System") for the creation and the evolution of DWs. The authors defined an *evolution model* and the *MDL* (Multidimensional Data Language). Their model includes a set of primitives for multidimensional schema evolution. These primitives are inspired from those in [3-4]. However, to ensure the consistency of the modified schema resulting from successive changes, the authors developed a set of complementary primitives "High level" qualified

Favre et al. [8] based the DW evolution on the evolution of the analytical requirements. Their user-driven evolution model consists in collecting the user's knowledge and integrating them into the DW in order to create new hierarchies. They define transformation rules of type "If-Then" to update the dimension hierarchies by inserting a level of granularity which provides users with new analytical alternatives.

Papastefanatos et al. [9] tackles the inconsistencies that may appear in ETL (Extract-Transform-Load) processes after data source evolution. They proposed the "HECATAEUS" tool which offers to the designer a mechanism for adapting ETL activities to the changes happening in the data source schema. Their approach is based on a technical representation that maps all the essential components of the ETL process and produces a graph evolution. However, this approach is limited to the ETL process; it neglects the impact of the IS evolution on the schemas of the DW/DMs.

3   Discussion

These previous works were interested with different components of the DW as the dimensions, facts, hierarchy levels... We note that these operations are based on the evolution of decision makers' analyses or even on structural changes in the DW. In addition, some authors studied the effect of these evolution operations on the DW data instances and on the materialized views [3] or on data cubes [7].

In order to ensure the genericity of their approaches, few authors proposed the use of meta-models [4], [8] for the representation of an evolutionary DW.

Practically, the alteration of the DW schema and its dependent DMs is manual; therefore the data migration from the old to the new schema is also a manual task and often requires writing the migration code. This requires good knowledge of the operated evolution as good skills in order to perform a safe migration of the data, that means, without loose of information. To the best of our knowledge, we can claim that the problem of data source evolution was discussed at a single level where the study of its impact on the DW was limited to the loading ETL process [9].

4   Proposal Approach for Propagating DW Evolution

We focus on studying the impact of each change operation that can undergo the DW schema on its DMs. In fact, the DW data are dynamic since they are periodically loaded; in addition, the DW schema may change over time. Kimball claims that it is difficult to definitively determine the schema of a DW during the design phase. Consequently, it is necessary to modify this schema after its implementation. These changes can have multiple reasons, for example, i) evolving needs of decision makers, leading to the enrichment of the DW with new topics or axes of analyses, ii) the incompleteness of needs initially captured during the design phase of the DW (case of Top down approaches): decision makers can express their needs precisely and completely only when they start operating the warehouse iii) changes in organization business processes over time, this evolution affects the working procedures and even the data models of their operational system.

In all these situations, this evolution merit to be propagated on the DMs. In order to consider the evolution of the DW and to automate its propagation onto the DSS components, we propose the overall architecture described in Figure 1. It is based on two evolution models.

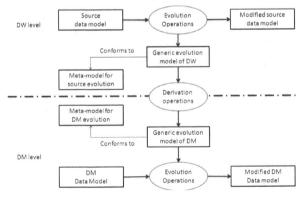

Fig. 1. Architecture of the proposed approach for propagating DW evolutions towards the DMs

The first model concerns the DW schema evolution operations. In fact, these modifications are captured in order to identify the DM to be affected. The second evolution model treats evolution operations of DM schemas. These operations must be derivable from the previous model and should represent the different alterations applicable on each multidimensional schema such as adding or modifying a fact, a dimension, a hierarchy level, etc.

Our approach studies the impact of the DW evolution on its dependent DMs. To do so, we define a set of transformation rules.

5   Transformation Rules

5.1   Formalization

Generally the DW is a normalized database, each DM is a star schema (i.e., a single fact table F linked to a non empty set of d dimensions D_1, D_2, ..., D_d) structured according to the (DFM). We adopt the following notation:

− S: a normalized relational DW,
− T_i : a relational table belonging to S,
− DM_i : a data mart loadable from S,
− $DM_i.D_j$: a dimension D_j belonging to DM_i,
− F_i : the fact table F of DM_i,
− ΩT_i : the set of attributes A_1, A_2, ..., A_n of T_i,
− $T_i.Pk$: the set of primary key attributes of table T_i ($T_i.Pk \subseteq \Omega T_i$),
− $T_i.Fk$: the set of foreign key attributes of table T_i ($T_i.Fk \subseteq \Omega T_i$),
− εD: a set of dimensions D_1, D_2..., D_d linked to fact F.
− C : constraint specification
− A: Attribute
− A_{spec} : Attribute specification

DW Evolution Operations. The evolution operations discussed in this section affect the schema of the DW. We classify them into two categories: *basic operations* and *composite operations.*

− Basic operations are among the DBMS data definition language commands. Mainly, they are addition, deletion and modification of attributes and tables.
− Composite operations are composition of basic operations; the split of table T into tables T_1 and T_2 requires the following basic operations: create two tables T_1 and T_2 each composed of a subset of columns from T ($\Omega T_1 \cup \Omega T_2 = \Omega T$ and $\Omega T_1 \cap \Omega T_2 \neq \varnothing$), then drop table T, and finally modify referential constraints.

In the next that follows, we restrict ourselves to study the basic evolution operations. Table 1 shows the set of operations supported by our proposed DW evolution model; they address the adding, deletion and modification of table attributes and constraints.

Table 1. Basic DW evolution operations

Basic operation	Attribute	Table	Constraint
Add	AlterT_Add_Att (T$_i$, A, A$_{Spec}$)	CreateT(T,ΩT,T.Pk)	AlterT_Add_Cnstr(T$_i$,C)
Delete	AlterT_Drop_Att (T$_i$, A)	DropT (T)	AlterT_Drop_Cnstr(T$_i$,C)
Modify	AlterT_Mod_Att (T$_i$, A, A$_{Spec}$)	(Non Basic)	(Non Basic)

DW-DM Mapping Functions. Mapping functions establish the correspondences between each component of the DW schema (table, attribute ...) and those of each DM (dimension, fact ...). For example, *Country_Name* (cf., Figure 2) supplies the parameter *Country_Name* (cf. Figure 3).

The definition of these functions requires an access to the mapping metamodel used by the ETL process for loading DMs from the DW. In order to propagate the evolution performed on the DW towards DMs, it is essential to find the correspondences between the modified element and its dependent multidimensional elements. To find out these mappings, we define the following four functions:

— *Fact (T$_i$):* returns a set {F$_1$, F$_2$ .., F$_m$ } of facts loadable from the DW table T$_i$
— *Dim (T$_i$):* returns a superset {DM$_1$.εD, DM$_2$.εD ..., DM$_m$.εD} of dimensions loadable from T$_i$. Each DM$_k$.εD ($1 \leq k \leq m$) denotes the set of all dimensions of DM$_k$.
— *Referred_Tab (T):* returns a set {T$_1$, T$_2$ ..., T$_t$} of tables linked to T via a foreign key constraint from T$_i$ to T.
— *Referenced_Tab (T):* returns a set {T$_1$, T$_2$ ..., T$_t$} of tables linked to T via a foreign key constraint from T to T$_i$.

DM Evolution Operations. The execution of each basic evolution operation on the DW schema must generate a set of evolution operations to be applied on each affected DM in order to achieve the propagation of the initial change. These operations will be identified referring to the initial operation and to the mapping functions defined above; they represent the output of the evolution model of the DW. Currently, we describe each propagation operation by a generic function among the four following:

— *Add_Dim (Dname, F$_i$, T):* Adds a new dimension called *Dname* to the fact of data mart *i*. The attributes of the created dimension are the primary key T.Pk and the subset of textual attributes of T.
— *Append_Lev (DM$_j$.D, T, T$_i$.Pk):* Adds the primary key of T as a terminal parameter, located after the highest level parameter T$_i$.Pk, to all hierarchies of dimension D of DMj. The weak attributes for the added parameter are textual attributes of T. T$_i$ is the table that references T.
— *Insert_Lev (DM$_j$.D, T, Pprev, Pnext):* Inserts the primary key of T as a parameter between parameters *Pprev* and *Pnext* of dimension D *belonging to DM$_j$*. The weak attributes of the added parameter are the subset of textual attributes of T.
— *Add_Fact (Fname, T, εD):* Adds a new fact called *Fname* with dimensions εD. The fact measures are numeric attributes issued from T.

5.2   Rules Definition

We define textually and algebraically rules for identifying operations to be applied to DM schemas and we illustrate them on the DW of Figure 2 and DM of Figure 3.

```
CUSTOMER (Id_Cust, First_Name, Last_Name, #Id_City ...)
CITY     (Id_City, City_Name ...,#Id_Cntry)
COUNTRY  (Id_Cntry, Country_Name...)
SALE     (Id_Sale, Date, #Id_Cust, Sale_Amount)
SALE_ITEM (Id_Sale, #Id_Prod, Sold_Qtity)
PRODUCT  (Id_Prod, PName, Unit_Price, #Id_Categ)
CATEGORIE (Id_Categ, CName)
```

Fig. 2. Relational DW schema

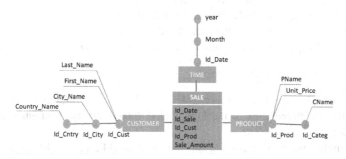

Fig. 3. DM Star schema *SALE*   built on the DW schema of Figure 2

Add Table: *CreateT (T, ΩT, T.Pk)*. A table T added to the DW can play different roles: it can be used to define new contexts of analyses within existing DM, or to create a new subject of analyses. We distinguish several cases according to whether table T is referenced, or T references other tables. In the following, we describe four significant cases.

- Case 1. *T creates a new dimension*

   If the table T added to the DW is referenced by one table T^F (of the DW) that feeds a fact F, then T may feed a new dimension denoted D_T for F. The attributes of D_T are all the attributes issued from T.

   For example, the creation of the table *RETAIL_OUTLET* referenced by the table *SALE* which feeds the fact $DM_{Sale}.SALE$, leads to the creation of a new dimension called *D_RETAIL_OUTLET* linked to the *SALE* fact.

   The following sequence of operators transforms *RETAIL_OUTLET* table into a dimension called *D_ RETAIL_OUTLET*:

```
CreateT ('RETAIL_OUTLET', {Id_Ro, RoName, zone}, Id_Ro)
Referred_Tab (RETAIL_OUTLET) returns {SALE}
Fact (SALE) returns {DMSale.SALE}
Add_dim ('D_RETAIL_OUTLET', DMSale.Sale, RETAIL_OUTLET)
```

- Case 2. *T appends a terminal level to an existing hierarchy*

If a DW table T i) is referenced by n $(n{\geq}1)$ DW tables $T_1^{D'}$ ... $T_n^{D''}$ those feed dimensions with data, and *ii)* T does not refer to any table, then T can feed a new level of hierarchy in each of these dimensions. The identifier of T will be a terminal parameter in multiple hierarchies. Textual attributes of T become weak attributes for the added level.

For instance, when $n=1$, creating *CONTINENT* table referenced by table *COUNTRY* which feeds the dimension $DM_{Sale}.CUSTOMER$ leads to the creation of a new terminal level of hierarchy within the *CUSTOMER* dimension. The following sequence of operators appends the identifier *Id_Cont* of *CONTINENT* as a terminal parameter in dimension *CUSTOMER*:

```
CreateT(CONTINENT, {Id_Cont , CoName }, Id_Cont)
Referred_Tab (CONTINENT) returns {CUSTOMER}
Dim(CUSTOMER) returns {DM_Sale.CUSTOMER}
Append_Lev(DM_Sale.CUSTOMER, CONTINENT, Id_Cntry)
```

- Case 3. *T* creates a new fact table

If table T is not referenced by any table of the DW and T references several tables loading different dimensions of the DM, and if T has numeric attributes then T is a plausible fact.

For example, the creation of the SCORE_PROD (#Id_Prod, #Id_Cust, Score,...) table referencing *PRODUCT* and *CUSTOMER* tables that respectively feed the two dimensions $DM_{Sale}.PRODUCT$ and $DM_{Sale}.CUSTOMER$ may result in the creation of a new fact *'F_SCORE_PROD'* related to both dimensions *CUSTOMER* and *PRODUCT*. The new fact will have numeric attributes of *SCORE_PROD* as its plausible measures. The following sequence transforms *SCORE_PROD* table into a fact.

```
CreateT('SCORE_PROD',{Id_Prod,Id_Cust,Score},{Id_Prod, Id_Cust})
Referenced_Tab(Score_Prod)gives{PRODUCT,CUSTUMER}
Dim(CUSTOMER) returns {DM_Sale.CUSTOMER}
Dim(PRODUCT) returns {DM_Sale.PRODUCT}
Add_Fact (F_SCORE_PROD, SCORE_PROD, {PRODUCT, CUSTOMER)}
```

- Case 4. *T inserts a new hierarchy level in the middle*

If table T i) is referenced by a DW table T_1^D loading a dimension D, and *ii)* if T references a table T_2^D which loads the same dimension D, then T can feed a new hierarchy level in D. The identifier of T becomes a parameter inserted between parameters $T_1^D.Pk$ and $T_2^D.Pk$ of D; textual attributes of T are candidate weak attributes for the added level.

For example, creating the table *REGION (Id_Region, RName, #Id_Cntry)* referenced by the table *CITY and* referencing the *COUNTRY* table, leads to the insertion of a new parameter located between *Id_City* and *Id_Cntry* parameters. The sequence of operators below uses the *REGION* table to insert the new level into the *CUSTOMER* dimension.

```
Createt(REGION , { Id_Region, Rname, Id_Cntry}, Id_Region)
Referred_Tab (REGION) gives {CITY}
Referenced_Tab (REGION) gives {COUNTRY}
Dim(CITY) returns {DM_Sale.CUSTOMER}
Dim(COUNTRY) returns {DM_Sale.CUSTOMER}
Insert_Lev (DMSale.CUSTOMER, REGION, Id_City, Id_Cntry)
```

6   Conclusion

In this paper, we studied the impact of the DW schema evolution on DM schemas and classified evolution operations into: *basic operations* and *composite* ones. As a basic operation, we studied the creation of a new table in the relational DW and then, in order to propagate its impact on the DMs, we defined a set of rules and operators. The rules serve to identify multidimensional components which will be affected while the operators allow defining the operations of evolution required for the alteration schema of the concerned DMs. Currently, we are studying the remaining evolution operations on the DW and their effects on DMs. We are also developing a software prototype to apply these transformation rules in the context of MDA paradigm.

References

1. Banerjee, J., Kim, W., Kim, H.J., Korth, H.: Semantics and implementation of schema evolution in object-oriented databases. In: ACM SIGMOD International Conference on Management of Data (SIGMOD), pp. 311–322. ACM, NewYork (1987)
2. Aboulsamh, M.A., Davies, J.: Specification and Verification of Model-Driven Data Migration. In: Bellatreche, L., Mota Pinto, F. (eds.) MEDI 2011. LNCS, vol. 6918, pp. 214–225. Springer, Heidelberg (2011)
3. Hurtado, C.A., Mendelzon, A.O., Vaisman, A.A.: Maintaining Data Cubes underDimension Updates. In: XVth International Conference on Data Engineering (ICDE 1999), pp. 346–355. IEEE Computer Society, Sydney (1999)
4. Blaschka, M., Sapia, C., Höfling, G.: On Schema Evolution in Multidimensional Databases. In: Mohania, M., Tjoa, A.M. (eds.) DaWaK 1999. LNCS, vol. 1676, pp. 153–164. Springer, Heidelberg (1999)
5. Golfarelli, M., Lechtenborger, J., Rizzi, S., Vossen, G.: Schema versioning in datawarehouses: enabling cross-version querying via schema augmentation. Data and Knowledge Engineering 59(2), 435–459 (2006)
6. Bellahsene, Z.: Schema Evolution in Data Warehouses. Knowledge and Information Systems 4(3), 283–304 (2002)
7. Benitez-Guerrero, E.I., Collet, C., Adiba, M.: The Whes Approach To Data Warehouse Evolution.e-Gnosis (online), 2, Art. 11 (2004)
8. Favre, C., Bentayeb, F., Boussaïd, O.: Dimension Hierarchies Updates in Data Warehouses: a User-driven Approach. In: IXth International Conference on Enterprise Information Systems (ICEIS 2007), Funchal, Madeira, Portugal (2007)
9. Papastefanatos, G., Vassiliadis, P., Simitsis, A., Sellis, T., Vassiliou, Y.: Rulebased Management of Schema Changes at ETL Sources. In: The International Workshop on Managing Evolution of Data Warehouses (MEDWa 2009), Riga, Latvia (2009)

Author Index